PARENTING

Guide to
Your Toddler

PARENTING

Guide to Your Toddler

by Paula Spencer
with the editors of
PARENTING magazine

BALLANTINE BOOKS
NEW YORK

A Ballantine Book
Published by The Ballantine Publishing Group

www.randomhouse.com

Library of Congress Card Number: 00-190361

ISBN 0-345-41181-1

Text design by Michaelis/Carpelis Design Associates, Inc.
Cover photo © K. Coppieters/Superstock

Manufactured in the United States of America

First Edition: April 2000

10 9 8 7 6 5 4 3 2 1

For my parents, Eleanore and Sylvester Patyk, who raised five toddlers of their own and always encouraged the middle one's love of scribbling and felt certain she'd someday write a book (though I'm sure they never dreamed it would be about anything domestic).

Contents

Contents

Contents

Contents

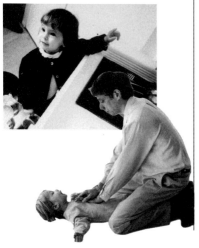

Contents

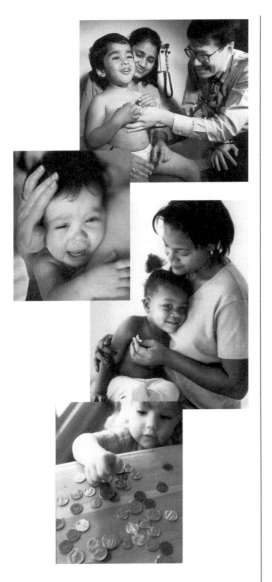

Foreword

From PARENTING's Editor in Chief

During the crucial first year, your baby relies on you for every basic need, from feeding and transportation to warmth and comfort. But as soon as she literally takes those tentative first steps into toddlerhood, rapid-fire changes begin. Your toddler is still your "baby," but she's definitely on the thrilling threshold of independence.

It's exciting to share your 18-month-old's glee when she zooms down the slide all by herself. Or to watch your 24-month-old—who just weeks, or days, before seemed to rely on grunts, groans, and finger-pointing to express himself—suddenly tell you not only *what* he wants but *why*.

This period of nonstop growth comes with many challenges—for both you and your toddler. As your child masters new skills, from buttoning her own coat to singing a new song (over and over again!), she'll bring to the party a love of the word "no," insatiable curiosity, unexpected meltdowns, and boundless energy and affection.

To help you weather the storms *and* cherish the triumphs: PARENTING *Guide to the Toddler Years*. Like PARENTING magazine, it offers reality-tested advice from experts as well as moms and dads around the country. We walk you through all the changes—big and little—that you and your child will experience during this exciting time. Here's to the wonders of toddlerhood!

Janet Chan
Editor in Chief
PARENTING

Acknowledgments

Sending a book into the world feels a bit like leaving your toddler at nursery school for the first time. You're anxious on the little guy's behalf, slightly mournful, and also a bit relieved to finally have a few free minutes to yourself. Both children and books require collaboration. I'd like to thank the following individuals at PARENTING magazine for their confidence and support: Bruce Raskin, franchise development editor, and Janet Chan, editor in chief, as well as Lisa Bain and Maura Rhodes.

Heidi Kotansky wrote all of the parent profiles and provided primary research assistance. Valerie Fahey provided fact-checking research. Lisa Hilgers and Gabrielle Revere served as photo editors. The UCLA-based medical advisory board reviewed the entire manuscript and provided useful feedback. My gratitude to all.

I'd also like to thank all the experts and parents whom I've interviewed on related subjects over the years for my magazine articles. That includes all my friends whom I've endlessly grilled for their opinions, solutions, anecdotes, and networking leads. My special appreciation to toddler experts Leigh Wahl, Dian Taylor, Laura Patyk, and Patricia Anderson for reviewing the manuscript in progress, and to Dr. Donald Larmee, Bertha Madden, and Becca Curry.

Finally, anyone who knows me knows I couldn't have written a sensible word for this book without the unfailing help of my husband, George, or the experience of raising our four amazing children, Henry Hartsfield, Eleanor Louie, Margaret Meriwether, and Page Jubilee.

THE MEDICAL ADVISORY BOARD FOR

PARENTING
Guide to Your Toddler

Paula Spencer and the editors of PARENTING wish to thank the
UCLA Center for Healthier Children, Families, and Communities and its
affiliated faculty for carefully reviewing the manuscript of this book.

NEAL HALFON, MD, MPH, Professor in Pediatrics and Public Health,
University of California at Los Angeles School of Medicine; Codirector,
UCLA Center for Healthier Children, Families, and Communities

NEAL KAUFMANN, MD, MPH, Director, Division of Academic Primary Care,
Pediatrics, Cedars-Sinai Medical Center

CLAIRE KOOP, PhD, Professor in Psychology and Applied Developmental
Psychology, Claremont Graduate University

MICHAEL REGALADO, MD, Director of Developmental and Behavioral
Pediatrics, Children's Hospital, Los Angeles

WENDY SLUSSER, MD, MS, Assistant Clinical Professor, Department of
Pediatrics, University of California at Los Angeles; Director, UCLA
Breast-feeding Program

Introduction

- An excited 14-month-old wobbles pell-mell down the sidewalk, swaying like a grown-up trying out in-line skates for the first time. "Birr! Birr!" she exclaims, pointing a pudgy finger across the lawn toward a robin.
- Wearing her favorite flowered hat and a pair of ballet slippers, struggling to zip up a dress, a busy 23-month-old sits in a heap of clothes that she's been putting on and pulling off all morning. "My dress!" she insists, spurning all offers of assistance. "Do it all by self."
- An enthusiastic 30-month-old, in brimmed cap and worn sneakers, swaggers about the yard, swinging a plastic baseball bat. At the top of his lungs, he belts out a medley of "Take Me Out to the Ball Game" (at least, as many words as he can remember), "Heigh-Ho, Heigh-Ho" (from *Snow White*), and "Oh, a Pirate's Life for Me" (from *Peter Pan*). When he accidentally conks himself on the head, the refrains dissolve into sobs. He reaches for his faithful companion, a frayed yellow blankie.

*T*hose snapshots are of three of my own children as toddlers. The first one described is Margaret, brand-new walker, brand-new talker, who entered toddlerhood as I wrote this book. Eleanor, now 5, had just left it, her characteristic self-sufficiency and fashion sense still very much intact. The third description is of my oldest, Henry. Now 7, his race through the hectic but delicious years of toddlerdom is already a blurry memory (although he still has a soft spot for the yellow blankie).

How dramatically a baby changes between the ages of one and three—and how quickly. Toddlerhood flies by, even though it may not seem that way on any given day. Between getting a small child dressed in the morning and ready for bed at night, the hours sometimes would drag like an eternity for me. A single tantrum could also stop time, especially when it occurred right in the middle of the grocery store. Even though I was sleeping through the night once again by the time my children were toddlers, somehow I felt more wiped out by 8 P.M. than I had during their first year. Toddlers move faster than babies, for one thing. And they nap less.

Yet all the wilder aspects of toddlerhood are nicely balanced by heaps of bliss. For one thing, it's when my children began to talk, which, aside from making life easier was also frequently hilarious. Count on a toddler to say and do the unexpected. Kids this age also make so many momentous (albeit ordinary) discoveries—how a light switch works, what sound a cow makes. A toddler still fits cozily in your lap, if not quite so easily on your hip. A toddler is never stingy with hugs and kisses. Best of all, my kids' personalities began to clearly reveal themselves during these magical years.

With all these new experiences came new questions. Was it okay if my son ate nothing but cottage cheese for lunch and dinner for weeks on end? How should I prepare a 2-year-old for a new baby brother or sister? Why did my youngest have a vocabulary I could count on one hand, when at the same age her older sister was beginning to use sentences? What could we do on a rainy day? When would all these baby teeth come in, anyway? My appetite for information grew right along with my children.

This book offers answers. They're not always absolutes. Families—and individual children—are too different for a one-size-fits-all approach to child rearing. Rather, as in PARENTING magazine, the idea here is to share the insights and opinions distilled from a wide range of experts: child-development specialists, pediatricians, psychologists, and, of course, fellow parents. You'll find the latest thinking on classic issues such as raising a good eater and handling sleep problems. And I've also made a point of including such twenty-first-century topics as computers, play dates, preschools, co-sleeping, and more.

But the most important advice I hope you'll glean about these delicious, topsy-turvy years is this: Enjoy every minute (okay, maybe not the tantrums). Because these years will be mere snapshot memories before you know it.

Paula Spencer

PARENTING

Guide to
Your Toddler

CHAPTER ONE

Your Growing Toddler

Toddlerhood is the brief whirlwind from about 12 months to 36 months. By your child's first birthday, he or she may still look babyish, follow his or her babyhood schedule, and do many babylike things—but your little one is tottering on the brink of big changes.

Friends and relatives may smile knowingly and warn you of the "terrible twos" ahead. The *two* is used variously to refer both to the second year of life and to the next year, when the child is age 2—making the phrase synonymous with all of toddlerhood. Some upbeat child-rearing experts have spin-doctored the period as the "terrific twos." In reality, however, *terrible* and *terrific* are both euphemisms, neither one totally accurate. On the other hand, *fun, funny, exhausting, exasperating, eye-opening, magical*—now those descriptions are a lot more like it.

This chapter maps out the way your child blossoms—physically, emotionally, mentally, and in language skills—during the short, terribly terrific span between baby and preschooler.

Physical Development

From Baby to Toddler

Once your baby learns to pull up and walk (or "toddle"), the world will never look the same to her. Nor will she look the same to you.

The snapshot you take on her first birthday will show a round-cheeked plumpkin whose rubbery legs dangle from the high chair while she mashes cake with her hands. She is transfixed by the candle, though you have to help her blow it out. She likes the singing, loves the crackling colorful wrapping paper. Despite the celebration, to her the day is like any other, although the grown-ups might seem especially cheerful. Maybe she can say a few words: "Mama! Daddy! More!" Maybe she likes to practice standing, or has already taken her first tentative steps along the sofa or across the floor.

A year later, the photo album will show a giddy 2-year-old dazed by the sight of a cake, candles, and presents. She'll look enormous in the old high chair, the safety belt pulled out to its largest size, her long legs perhaps reaching the footrest. Her still-chubby face is smeared with icing, although she managed to get most of the birthday cake into her mouth with her own spoon. She can sing "Happy Birthday," or at least a recognizable rendition, right along with you, and after she blows out both candles she applauds and commands, "Do it again!"

Another year later, a lean, leggy 3-year-old grins back at the camera. She has picked the cake decor, the ice cream flavor, and the party theme. She's dressed herself in her favorite outfit because she knows it's her special day. She'll be the center of attention! She's been counting down the days all week. Since sunrise, she's been asking how long until dinnertime, so she could get at those coveted presents. By her third birthday, she's become a bona fide preschooler, a toddler no more.

By now, you've probably compared enough notes with other parents to know that there's a huge range

---

WHAT IF...

My 15-month-old isn't walking yet?

Nine months to 18 months is the general window considered normal for a child's first steps. A 1½-year-old who has yet to take his first solo steps may a contented whiz-bang crawler or have a generally tentative, low-key personality. Heavy children tend to be slower walkers because they require stronger muscles to support their weight. Late walking does not mean your child will be athletically inept or otherwise slow. Some children skip crawling and simply stand up one day and take off.

Give your child plenty of opportunities to move around freely, and help him to stand or practice walking holding your hands. There's some evidence that overreliance on stationary walkers (more than one or two hours a day) holds kids back. Wean your child off this device by early toddlerhood. *Never use a mobile walker, which have been condemned by pediatric experts because of their high association with accidents.*

HOT TOPIC

ADHD

By the mid-1990s, attention deficit/hyperactivity disorder (ADHD) had become a wildly popular and controversial pediatric diagnosis. ADHD is not a disease but a syndrome of related symptoms, including hyperactivity, impulsiveness, forgetfulness, and an inability to pay attention or concentrate. The cause is uncertain, possibly a combination of biological and environmental factors. No one knows how many children actually have it, but two-thirds of those diagnosed are boys. If your toddler is especially boisterous, active, and nonstop, you may wonder if ADHD is the reason.

It's not. Toddlerhood is too early to diagnose hyperactivity. All 1- and 2-year-olds are extremely active, and all of them have short attention spans. In fact, many cases of ADHD are believed to be mislabeled. Some children are simply more restless, impulsive, and wiggly than others—a result of their natural temperament rather than a function of their brains. Despite the fact that hundreds of millions of dollars are spent on medication (particularly Ritalin) for ADHD each year in the United States, it remains a questionable diagnosis. Some experts believe it is a legitimate syndrome but is grossly overdiagnosed in a country that wants a quick fix rather than being willing to invest the time and attention many high-need children warrant. Diagnosis requires a battery of evaluations and tests by physicians, psychologists, and educational specialists. But, again, toddlerhood is too early to worry.

of what's considered normal in terms of children's growth and development. What was true of infants is also true of toddlers. Be careful to resist the temptation to measure your child's size or skills against those of his companions at the sandbox. An 18-month-old who seems too chubby is probably just fine, for example, and his weight will naturally fall into proportion with his height by his third birthday. Or you may notice a neighbor's 30-month-old hopping on one foot, something your child has never even tried. Make note of your child's overall progress to reassure yourself that he's reasonably on track, but don't obsess about it. Physical development *isn't* rigidly predictable. Every child is different.

Here's an overview of the physical changes that occur during toddlerhood:

Growth. The fantastic rate at which your baby grew from birth to 12 months slows in the second year. You won't be replacing shirts and pants quite as often as you did in infancy, but it's unlikely that a 1-year-old will still be wearing the same clothes six or twelve months later. Between 1 and

WHEN DO BABY TEETH APPEAR?

From start to finish, it takes two to three years for all twenty baby teeth to appear.

TYPES OF TEETH	HOW MANY	WHEN THEY TYPICALLY ARRIVE
Second molars	four	20-33 months
First molars	four	13-19 months
Canine teeth	four	16-23 months
Lateral incisors	four	9-16 months
Central incisors	four	6-16 months

From start to finish, it takes two to three years for all the baby teeth to appear.

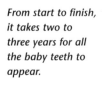

second molars
first molars
canine teeth
lateral incisors
central incisors

2, the typical toddler grows five inches and gains four to five pounds. Between 2 and 3, she'll sprout up an additional two to three inches and add up to five pounds.

A child may measure in the 75th percentile in height or weight at one checkup, but in the median range a year later. That's normal. Your child's doctor will be looking for progressive growth from checkup to checkup. He or she will also look for a reasonable balance between height and weight.

Overall build. Your child will begin to elongate and thin out. Until sometime in the third year, he'll still have a pot belly, swayed back, and wide-legged gait. His head will continue to appear slightly large atop his pudgy body. But gradually the head and body fall into better proportion, the torso slims, and the arms and legs lengthen. By age 3, he looks lanky, clearly older than he did at 2. Also by the third birthday, those chubby cheeks and button noses tend to take on a more sculpted, childlike appearance, too.

Teeth. More baby teeth (called primary teeth) come in during toddlerhood than infancy. Your child will collect his full mouthful of twenty choppers sometime between the second and third birthdays. The rate at which they arrive varies from child to child, though the sequence is generally the same. Before the first birthday, a child will usually have cut the two lower central incisors (also called the cutting teeth), followed a month or two later by the two upper central incisors and the four lateral incisors. The four first molars appear shortly after the first birthday. Then come the pointed canines and the second baby molars. Note that it's also normal for a child not to cut a first tooth until 18 to 24 months. (Baby teeth usually don't start to fall out until age 6 or 7.)

Teething pain is also very individual. Some kids never feel any discomfort, while others may suffer tender gums or low-grade fever, and generally act fussier than normal. The molars, especially, may cause pain since they are larger than the incisors. Indulge your child's need to chew during teething. You can buy special plastic toys for teething or just let your child mouth any safe toy. Many toddlers resort to gnawing on their own fingers to comfort themselves. This is perfectly fine; there's no need to force your child's thumb or fingers away from his mouth during this tender time. Consult your doctor about the advisability of an over-the-counter anesthetic for gums. Some parents swear by them, but many medical professionals believe they're unnecessary because saliva quickly rinses them away. Teething pain shouldn't last longer than a day or two per tooth. (For information on caring for baby teeth, see "Grooming and Dressing," page 90.)

Most children enter toddlerhood flashing as many as eight baby teeth.

Getting around. Gross motor skills are the activities that involve the large muscle groups —crawling, standing, sitting, and, of course, walking. Your child has been practicing for the big first step for months, by crawling and pulling up. As the legs become more muscular and strong, most 12-month-olds can briefly stand alone without holding on to anything. You might first see this while your child is in the crib, where she

WHAT IF...

I want my child to be right-handed but she seems to be a lefty?

Most toddlers are ambidextrous, switching between hands easily until somewhere between 3 and 5. If your child seems to have a clear preference already, there's little you can, or should, do to change it. Handedness is thought to be inherited. Trying to rewire your child's natural preference may only slow down the process of learning to use a fork, throw a ball, and write—skills that take time for both righties and lefties to master.

NOT TO WORRY

"Carry Me!" Toddlers

Chances are good that a tot who begs for a lift after you've gone just a few paces is seeking security more than rest. Wanting to be carried is an expression of the ambivalence toddlers feel about getting bigger. They want to grow up and do new things (such as walking in the park or visiting the zoo) but sometimes feel a little overwhelmed or fearful. It's reassuring to touch base with Mom or Dad. A child begging to be carried may simply not be able to keep pace with you, and falling behind is scary, too.

That said, you needn't break your back. Make life easier on yourself by bringing along the stroller on long outings after your child is walking well on his own. Help your child feel connected by holding hands or patting your child's head as you walk. Give in briefly in the guise of a game: "Here we go, up, up—and now down, down." Or agree to hold your child "until we get to that sign" or "for one more block." When "Carry me!" becomes a habit, negotiate. Say, "If you're too tired to walk and don't want to ride in the stroller, I think we'd better stop." With a lot of love and a little patience, the problem usually disappears by mid-toddlerhood.

can use the railings to help hoist herself upright. *Be sure to lower the mattress to its lowest position once your child can stand in the crib;* otherwise she could lean over and fall out.

PARENT TIP

See How They Grow!

Now that your child can stand straight (if he'll also stand *still* for a few seconds), it's fun to begin tracking his height with dated pencil marks on a wall or removable growth chart. You'll all be amazed at how he shoots up over time.

Typically, "cruising"—walking while holding on to sofas and chairs—begins around the first birthday. Some infants cruise as early as seven months, though this does not mean they will be early solo walkers. Some children skip the crawling stage altogether, progressing directly from pulling up to cruising. This is perfectly normal. A few kids never cruise at all, preferring to boldly strike out on their own. Whenever your child pulls up to walk, make the feat easier by pushing together furniture, so she can navigate from handhold to handhold. Clear the floors of throw rugs that could slip or cause trips. Once your child is a confident cruiser, try setting up little gaps in the furniture along her favorite pathways; this will require her to take a short step or two before she can reach the next chair or table. Or, stand a short distance from your child and encourage her, with your arms outstretched, to "Come to Mommy."

The first solo steps, usually wobbly and tentative, follow soon after. Every child has a comical variation: the Frankenstein's Monster, with outstretched arms; the Charlie Chaplin duck waddle; the staggering Drunken Sailor; the Magnet, who needs the psychological connection of your fingertips. Generally, a cruiser or a beginning walker clings to some of the placid cuddliness of babyhood. He's still content to be held or carried as well as to take

---

MILESTONE

FIRST SHOES (12 months)

Shoes protect a beginning walker's feet when it's not possible to go barefooted. So choose your child's first pair soon after the first steps. The most important feature is flexibility, to allow normal foot motion. Quick test: Try to bend a shoe in the middle—it should fold easily. Canvas or buttery leather are good choices, as they are both soft and porous, minimizing rashes. Look for shapes that are boxy, like a toddler's foot, not pointy. Choose soles with just a bit of traction; smooth or soft leather bottoms are too slippery, and gym shoes with an exaggerated tread will hinder his gait.

Baby's first shoes serve a purpose: They protect the feet and steady a beginning walker.

It doesn't matter so much whether they're high-tops or low, so long as they stay on. For that reason, select Velcro straps or lace-ups. (Thread shoelaces through lace keepers, available in dime stores, so they can't be untied by chubby fingers, or double-tie them.)

Cheap brands that meet the above criteria are just as good as pricier models. Exception: Avoid well-worn hand-me-downs, which have already been molded to the shape of another child's foot and won't give the proper support. Loaners that have been barely used (such as dress shoes) are fine, though.

It helps to have your child's foot professionally measured at a shoe store the first time. Err on the side of a little too big rather than too tight. But don't buy more than a size too large, expecting her to "grow into them." Recheck the fit every three or four months. All that said, going barefoot is the best way to practice muscle control and surefootedness. It's perfectly fine for a walker to go shoeless indoors.

PHYSICAL MILESTONES

12 months	Crawls well or stands without support; may cruise furniture or walk.
14 months	Uses gestures, such as an index finger to point.
15 months	Scribbles, feeds self with hands.
17 months	Walks well unsupported; climbs; can roll or throw a ball.
18 months	Stacks blocks; uses a shape sorter, holds a cup and drinks without spilling.
20 months	Throws a ball overhand; climbs well; may kick a ball accurately.
24 months	Pushes a wheeled toy; runs without falling; strings beads; can copy a circle.
30 months	Balances on one foot briefly; builds a five-block tower; begins working simple puzzles well.
36 months	Navigates stairs; pedals a tricycle; helps put thing away.

some steps. He may fall back on crawling when he wants to get somewhere in a hurry. But soon after those first steps, things change quickly.

Eager to practice, your child will want to walk all day long. And if he's sitting, he'll get up to walk the moment you sit down. Once his gait becomes more confident, around 15 to 18 months, the rambunctious "into everything" stage begins. Your toddler will be able to squat down to inspect something, or pick up an object and carry it off while walking. Twirling, climbing, and walking backward follow. The ability to get around where he desires dovetails with an increased curiosity about everything he sees. By 18 to 24 months, he's on the run, although still a bit shaky when it comes to stops and turns. After 2, a toddler's random meandering begins to become a bit more orderly. He still loves to run around, but he can also sit and look at a book or play with a toy for short spells. Again, realize that walking is a skill with a huge range of normal. Your 15-month-old may be a runner or may not yet have taken his first steps.

After the second birthday, coordination steadily improves. Now a toddler can jump, dance, go up stairs with one foot on each step, and run faster than ever, and with better control over direction. In fact, toddlers' nonstop squirming and general inability to sit still very long are normal. They help your child's muscles to learn and practice overall coordination.

By the third birthday, a child moves assuredly. She can probably skip, gallop, stand on one foot, hop, throw a ball somewhat accurately, and change directions and stop confidently.

Fine motor skills. Between 12 and 15 months, your child will be able to make her first marks on paper. Until around 30 months, these "drawings" will be mostly random lines and scribbles. Eventually your toddler may be able to draw a recognizable circle, rainbow, or simple stick figure. At first she will use her whole fist to grip the crayon. Around 2½, she may begin holding it between her thumb and fingers. Hand-eye coordination doesn't really take off until the third year of life. Everyday activities help a child practice dexterity and coordination. Examples: picking up food for self-feeding, turning doorknobs, zipping zippers, buttoning clothes, manipulating simple puzzles, turning the pages of board books.

WHAT IF...

My toddler is bowlegged or flat-footed?

A crook-legged cowboy stance is natural until around 18 to 24 months. If the legs don't appear to be straightening by 2 or 2½, ask your pediatrician. Bowlegs rarely indicate a physical problem. As for flat feet, that too is absolutely normal until age 2 or 3.

WHAT IF...

My child still sucks her thumb (or a pacifier)?

Relax. Few pediatricians or dentists worry about thumb sucking until age 5, if then. There's little evidence it can ruin teeth before the permanent pearlies appear. Usually the behavior persists into toddlerhood either out of habit or because it provides comfort. If there is a fear or stress triggering the habit, show your child other ways to confront it. But if the thumb sucking is an old habit and not constant, the best approach is to ignore it. Don't nag.

Opinions are divided on pacifiers. Though not harmful, they're associated with a higher incidence of ear infections, can hinder speech, and cause night waking if the tot can't locate one in the middle of the night. Some doctors believe that a child who relies on a pacifier is less likely to mouth objects, an important way babies explore their world. Most children give them up by the third year. But if they make you uncomfortable, gradually restrict their use, first to home, then to bedtime.

HOT TOPIC

Budding Sexuality

Nose, eyes, ears, belly button—toddlers love to learn the names of things. So expect your child to ask what her genitals are called. Out of surprise or embarrassment, parents often are tempted to use made-up names or to ignore the subject altogether. Most experts advise seizing the opportunity to instill a healthy attitude toward sexuality: Use the real names—*vagina, vulva, penis*—just as you do for all the other body parts.

By age 2, children gain an awareness that girls and boys are different, and they're clear to which group they belong. Exploration is part of this gender discovery, especially after toilet training begins. Your child may play with his penis, try to insert objects into her vagina, ask about your genitals or breasts, play in the potty, smear feces on a wall, or otherwise experiment. And all toddlers revel in running around naked. Take these very normal activities in stride. Making a fuss only injects unwarranted overtones of shame or embarrassment. If a child is exploring himself in a circumstance that makes you uncomfortable, you can introduce the notion of appropriate places for touching oneself. Say something like, "I know it's interesting [or feels good] to touch your penis. You can do that later at home, when you're in private. Right now, let's go see that fish pond." Distraction works wonders.

What You Can Do

Frisky toddlers need their exercise several times a day. Of course that doesn't mean putting them through a pint-sized video workout. It simply means that you should provide regular opportunities for physical play every day, to release pent-up energy and help your child flex her growing muscles. One- and 2-year-olds are proud of all the new things they can do. Beware, however, that younger toddlers, especially, have little common sense about what's safe, foolish, or impossible. Fearlessness and exuberance can be a dangerous combination. That's why it's now more important than ever to make sure your child's play area is free of obvious dangers, and to keep an eye on his play.

Some ways you can promote motor skills safely and channel energy:

Head outside. Properly dressed, a young child can play outdoors in almost any weather. Plan the day to include two or three outings.

Provide active toys. Give your child toys that involve running, moving, and throwing. Examples: balls, punching bags, plastic sports equipment (such as

True Toddler Tales

"My Toddler Gets into Everything!"

Call him "Joe On-the-Go." From morning to night (luckily punctuated by a few all-important naps), Joseph Arthur Anderson keeps his parents, Patricia and Larry, on the alert. "He's always been curious, but once he started walking at 13 months, his explorations increased exponentially," says Patti, who lives in Cincinnati, Ohio.

Their basic strategy is to let him go full tilt within a structured routine. "His routine is, wake up, eat, play and explore, get difficult and cranky, go to bed [for a nap or for the night]," Patricia says. "Anticipating his schedule helps make the full-steam-ahead parts of the day easier on both of us."

The couple have childproofed but give Joe a pretty wide roaming range. "You don't want to make everything off-limits," Patricia says. She allows him to rummage through the cupboards filled with baking tins, measuring cups, and pots and pans, and some of the food-storage areas. "I've found macaroni and cheese boxes in some interesting places," she says with a laugh, "and I spend a lot of time cleaning up after him."

When he gets into something he shouldn't, such as the china cabinet, she says firmly and in a disapproving tone, "That's not for Joe," and leads him away. Sometimes she has to do this over and over to make the point. "It took time, but it really works. He's trained himself not to go there," she says.

The Andersons' tips for living with a high-energy toddler:

- **Have a flexible routine.** "Having a routine is a good way to predict my son's behavior—when he gets cranky, I can tell he's just too wound up and it's time for a nap. A more-or-less predictable order to the day helps me pace his high-energy times with slower activities, too."
- **Do basic childproofing.** "I read everything I could in order to pick up tips or ideas, from magazine articles to childproofing kits to the backs of bottles and boxes."
- **Teach—and have patience.** "You can't expect a little child to know what's good or safe. If you tell and show him over and over, he'll begin to learn, but that takes time. Meanwhile, redirect him."
- **Be proactive.** "If there's something around that you don't want your child to get into, put it away."
- **Take breaks.** "It really helps when my husband spells me for a while. If you don't have a spouse, it's worth it to hire a baby-sitter so you can get time for yourself to recharge."

WHAT IF...

I have trouble keeping up with my child in public? Are "kids leashes" a good idea?

Toddler tethers—usually a rein held by the parent attached to the child's harness vest or wrist—are a modern invention, born of urban streets, shopping malls, and fears of abduction. Many parents abhor them because of their canine connotations. Others find them a legitimate means of keeping a child safe in a crowd. But to prevent strangulation, you must always use them properly. Never leave your child unattended or secure him to a fixed object. If used only sporadically during early toddlerhood, it's unlikely a child will have any recollections of being tethered. But to keep your toddler safest, nothing beats holding hands or using a stroller in a crowd.

golf clubs, bowling pins, a low basketball hoop), push toys (such as play lawn mowers, grocery carts, buggies, slides and swings, tricycles). Don't overlook less obvious outlets: a toy tool bench or clay for pounding, small pools for splashing, instruments for making music, rocking horses to ride. Create an indoor obstacle course of boxes, pillows, and books to practice coordination.

Provide alternatives for dangerous behavior. If your child wants to jump on the bed, try placing a mattress on the floor instead. If there's no room for running inside, organize races in the backyard. When you can't keep a little climber off the kitchen table, it may be time for a visit to a jungle gym or a toddler gymnastics class.

Enroll in an exercise class. At this age, your child doesn't need a formal activity. But it can be a fun alternative for thirty or sixty minutes a week. Physically exerting options include tumbling, music, and creative-movement dance classes. Look for classes targeted to the high energy, coordination, and attention span of toddlers. Make sure the schedule suits your toddler's, at a time when she is rested and fed. A good program emphasizes parental participation—1- and 2-year-olds are too young to be dropped off and left. Be prepared for the possibility that a young toddler may not do well in such a class.

Provide quiet time, too. It's easy to get the misconception that all your busy child wants is constant activity. Periods of calm, however, help balance a physical day. Incorporate into your day such soothing activities as listening to stories, scribbling, working puzzles, sandbox play, and using play dough.

Be vigilant about safety. With advanced motor skills come increased odds of running into danger. Toddlers who can climb and reach can pull pots or glasses down from tables. Speedy runners can crash into glass doors or cut themselves on sharp-cornered tables. Agile-fingered experimenters figure out how to twist open medicine containers. Be sure your childproofing efforts progress along with your child.

Developmental Concerns

Nagging doubts about your child's progress can lead you to worry even when everything is, in fact, all right. Maybe he seems far behind on developmental milestones that you've read on charts. Perhaps some habits or behaviors give you pause, or he seems shorter or thinner than his peers. Your pediatrician or family doctor assesses your child's growth and general progress at regular checkups. Sometimes, however, a problem can slip by a primary health care provider. For example, it can be hard to assess certain developmental delays in a relatively brief well-child checkup, particularly if they are mild.

> ## WHAT IF...
>
> ### My child is very pudgy? How fat is too fat?
>
>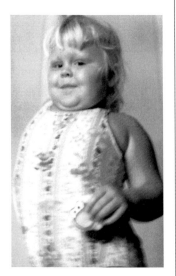
>
> **U**sually toddlerhood is too early to be worried about fat. As toddlers grow and become more active, they'll gradually shed their chubby baby bodies. This natural, short-lived stage doesn't destine your child to be a fat adult. The doctor monitors height and weight to see if they are in reasonable proportion to each other. It's possible for a toddler to be overweight, sometimes because of constant access to a bottle of milk. But the circumstances under which a toddler's diet should be restricted in order to reduce weight are rare and should be done only under a doctor's instruction and supervision.

It's true that constantly comparing your child to those of a similar age is a frustrating no-win exercise. You'll always find kids who seem more advanced in one area or another than your own. But it's also true that no one knows your child as well as you do, and if you feel uncomfortable about his progress, it's well worth exploring further. That's why it's vital to trust your instincts. If you suspect that something is "not right" about your child, be insistent. Don't let naysaying relatives or dismissive doctors dissuade you. Observe your child over a period of time and take notes about what troubles you. If you don't feel satisfied by your primary-care provider's assessment, it can't hurt to seek a second opinion or ask for a referral to a specialist.

Emotional Development

The Quest for Independence

A toddler's mind and heart are growing as rapidly as his body. He's intoxicated with the world around him. So much to see, do, explore, and enjoy! As he walks away from babyhood, a toddler also begins to understand that he's a separate person from his mother, an individual with his own feelings, ideas, wants, needs, and will. These newfound powers are heady. He feels unstoppable.

Unfortunately, he's limited in all sorts of ways. He wants to dress himself but can't manipulate the buttons. He's discovered candy and balloons in the checkout lane, but you won't let him have any. He knows who sat in which chair yesterday, but now Grandpa is occupying Daddy's seat. So he howls, cries, tussles, gets mad, and falls apart—often. Or at least until the next alluring thing comes along to distract him. A toddler has yet to learn how to control his impulses and desires, his temper, or even his bodily functions. This emerging individuality has another downside for the child, too. Although giddy about his increasing self-awareness, the prospect is also a little unnerving. After all, he's depended on you for everything—food, sleep, comforting, entertainment—for his whole life. Even as he moves away, your toddler needs to frequently reconnect with you for reassurance. You are the secure base from which all his explorations can flow.

By remaining calm, you can sometimes circumvent a test of wills.

This ambivalence over becoming his own little person—equal parts thrill and uncertainty—is the central push-pull of toddlerhood. And parents can't help but feel a tad trampled in the process. In order to figure out who he is, your child must do things his own way, at his own pace. Unfortunately, the child's ways don't always jive with yours, or your schedule. There are ample opportunities for wills to clash. But if the "terrible twos" is what you expect, then terrible is what you may get. On the other hand, if you understand where your child is coming from and are willing to open your own heart to the adventure at hand, you're more apt to

True Toddler Tales

"My Shy Guy"

*E*ver since Andrew Coughlin was an infant, he had stranger anxiety. Faced with an unfamiliar person, he'd run away, cling to his mom, Carol, or stand behind her. "It takes a while for him to warm up to people," explains Carol, who lives in Leicester, Massachusetts. "He'll come out when he feels comfortable, but he needs to be sure of what's going on."

At preschool, Andrew was easily overwhelmed by the idea of twenty-one people doing different things in different places. He often shut down, refusing to participate. Sometimes he'd ask the other children to be quiet. His shyness extends to home, too. Carol works at home, and Andrew dislikes when her clients or his older sisters' friends come to visit, often telling them to leave. Carol doesn't make excuses for him, instead explaining to visitors that he will warm up to them gradually. "I'm patient and don't try to force any situation, because it only makes it worse," Carol says.

"I honor his requests to do things like hold my hand even when I feel it's unwarranted," she explains. "I know he won't want to hold my hand when he's a teenager. They're little for such a short time."

Carol's tips for living with a reserved toddler:

- **Respect his personality.** "Don't try to change him into an outgoing person or try to draw him out. Look at his way of dealing with things and let him be himself."
- **Find the positive aspects of his temperament.** "Being shy isn't all bad or all good. Andrew is very observant and doesn't miss a thing. He also has a wonderful imagination."
- **Give reassurance.** "I let my son know that I'll be there. Or if he needs to go into another room and back away from everything, I'll go with him."
- **Go easy.** "Encourage your child to try new things, but don't push."
- **Don't label.** "Try not to describe your child to others as shy. It puts a label on him."

think of these brief years in the sunshiny light they deserve. Sure, you'll still have frustrating moments and some really long, tiring days. But toddler emotions tend to pass quickly, with as many rainbows as thunderstorms. Everything is interesting to a young child. The whir of clothes in the dryer, a new book, splashing water in the tub, and the ants at a picnic hold equal fascination. Curiosity and enthusiasm are infectious. A toddler's capacity for love is limitless.

You'll also have an easier time of it if you gently provide an atmosphere in which your toddler's whims and wonderings can flourish. In fact, research shows that the way parents manage children between 1 and 3 years makes a difference in how easy or difficult they are to handle later on. The trick is to encourage his budding individuality while minimizing his inevitable frustrations. How is that done?

Respect the fact that your baby is an emerging little person. Your toddler has a will and desires and needs all her own. Sure, you're the person in charge. But you can no longer expect to zip your child into a coat without a protest or pick her up and buckle her into the car seat just like that when you need to run an errand.

Provide a safe place to explore. Toddler learning requires constant trial and error. "What will happen if I pull on this tablecloth? Can I reach that

GOOD ADVICE
Overcoming Fears

"Sarah Willow, 16 months, asks to be picked up when she's near a dog. We talk about the puppy across the street and approach it as close as we can. Little by little she has become less fearful. She will even pat the puppy's ears if someone's holding it. I think the more control she has over the situation, the better it goes."

—*Tonia Saxon, Trumansburg, New York*

"Malcolm holds his ears, screams and cries, and runs into his closet when he hears the hair dryer, the mower, or loud cars on the freeway. When we put on something noisy that scares him, like the hair dryer, we tell him beforehand. We also talk about what frightens him about the noise and praise him when he doesn't run away."

—*Anne Bean, Flint, Michigan*

shelf? How does this box open?" Constantly hovering behind your child and saying "Don't touch that!" or "Be careful!" is no fun for either of you. Minimize meltdowns and boost confidence by creating a safe environment for your child, rather than a space full of no-nos. (See "Toddler-proofing," page 224.)

Give him chances. "Me do it!" is the toddler mantra. And he's bound and determined to try, even when he can't possibly push the grocery cart or pour milk out of a full gallon container. It's not always safe or suitable for a toddler to do things his way, and those are the times when you must intervene and weather the tantrum that follows. But in a given day there are plenty of opportunities to let your child try. Pour the milk into a smaller pitcher and let him pour it into his cup, for example. Let him struggle with getting his toes into his socks and then casually pull them up and turn the heel into the right place while you're assisting with the shoes. The extra effort or patience you give it will pay off in the long run.

Build in successes. It's easy for your child to become frustrated when he's unable to master a task that is beyond him. And his day is filled with challenges that may seem insurmountable, from putting on his own shoes to turning on the water faucet. Be sure that his day is filled with doable activities. Little triumphs—completing a puzzle, filling the dog's dish—help your child grow just as much as the big milestones like learning to run.

Let him win a few. This bolsters confidence while circumventing power struggles. Does it really matter if he brings one stuffed animal to the doctor's office or three? If he makes a mess trying to feed himself? That's not to say you should give in to every whim. But do accede to some of your child's demands or requests when they are reasonable or don't cause any real harm. Such opportunities help your child feel a sense of control over his day.

PARENT TIP

Does Your Child Prefer One Parent?

Try not to take it personally when only Mommy will do at bathtime or Daddy's hand is the only one your child wants at the mall. It's not unusual for children to bounce from one parent to the other as their emphatic favorite, even to the point of snubbing the other. There may be no apparent trigger. Playing favorites can be inspired by pure whim. Or the favoritism may begin after a more obvious incident, such as a business trip or a hospital stay which separated parent and child. In that case, preferring one parent over another may be your child's way of saying, "I missed you, I didn't like it, and I'm afraid you're going to do it to me again." The parent on the outs should try to spend as much time as possible with the child upon returning. Don't force it, though, and don't relax your typical standards of behavior as a way to make up for your absence. Your child doesn't really want special treats or treatment—she just wants you, even if she acts like she doesn't.

Provide limited choices. This is an easy way to give your child some authority. Asking if she wants to wear the blue jacket or the bunny sweater empowers your child, within reason. (If you ask open-endedly, "What coat do you want to wear?" your child may not pick something appropriate to the weather.) Take care not to go overboard, though, in involving your child in every decision-making process. Many kids don't care which color socks they're wearing or whether they drink apple, grape, or orange juice. Too many choices can be stressful and overwhelming.

Don't push. Every parent feels proud when their child masters a new skill. Likewise, it's common to fret when your child seems to fall behind his peers. But don't let your child in on your angst. Children develop at an enormously individual pace. Rest assured that your child will master all the basics in good time. Resist the temptation to make your child practice a skill over and over. Probably the most helpful advice regarding child development you'll ever hear is, "They'll do it when they're ready."

Relax your standards. You can't expect a toddler to shake hands with strangers and say, "How do you do?" Don't insist all the pieces of one toy be picked up and put in their proper places before your child moves on to the next activity. Nor is it wise to feel mortified in the face of an all-out public tantrum; a toddler won't understand why you're upset, and is likely to sense only your disapproval and feel he's let you down somehow. Rather than expecting perfect behavior of your child, be a model for him. Demonstrate civility and calm through your actions. Remember—he's only a toddler.

Common—and Frustrating—Behaviors

A toddler's headlong quest for independence is charming, entertaining, and often hilarious. Alas, it's not all fun and games. Other aspects of a toddler's behavior try even the most easygoing parent. Try to remind yourself that

NOT TO WORRY

Blankies and Bears

Linus has his blanket. Christopher Robin has Pooh. A dragged-everywhere soft toy or other favorite object provides a toddler with a measure of security. Called "transitional comfort objects," these special, cuddly teddies and blankies serve as portable substitute mommies. They make a child feel safe in times of worry, such as during separations from you (at day care or at bedtime) or when he's facing new experiences, from an illness to angry feelings. Not all children have these "loveys," though they are common. Sometimes they are used only to fall asleep. There may be a single favorite or an assortment of different stuffed toys or blankets used in this way. Take seriously the object's significance to your child. Pack it when you go on trips; let him bring it to the grocery store or the doctor's office. A good child care center shouldn't frown on a single security toy at this age, especially for naptime.

Fuzzy animals and favorite dolls provide much-needed security.

Transitional objects are usually chosen around 12 months. Devotion peaks between 18 and 30 months. You can't force such an attachment, although you can encourage it by having her hold a particular object while you're reading to your child or putting her to bed at night. Nor should you force a child to give up such attachments. They tend to be gradually outgrown between 3 and 5 years. In the meantime, yes, the chosen objects get dirty, but there's no need to be zealous about cleanings. In fact, it's the very scent of the object that's often as comforting as its texture and appearance. Once the child's preference for a given object becomes clear, some parents buy a duplicate so that the object can be washed from time to time or in case it gets lost.

these behaviors are developmentally inspired and will, for the most part, be outgrown. Among toddlerhood's hallmark quirks:

Mood swings. One minute your cherub has all the charm of a prince and the patient wonder of an explorer. Then *bang!*—in the nanosecond it takes you to say something as innocuous as "Here's your juice," he reverts to the angry inflexibility of a dictator. A toddler's emotions are like the weather—if

WHAT IF...

We've lost our son's beloved blankie?

Chances are you feel nearly as awful as your child. Recognize that, to your child, such a loss is traumatic. Give extra cuddles and consolation. Think about what was most appealing about the old blanket: the satin binding, the fuzzy texture, the color scheme? Sometimes you can replace a lost love object by buying either an exact replica or a similar one. If the substitute is rejected, you need to let your child know that the old favorite probably won't be coming back. Encourage him to pick out something new. Then leave the rest up to him.

you don't like it, just wait. It will change. That's because to the toddler, there is only the here and now. The block tower that crashed so distressingly five minutes ago may seem like last year to him; he's moved on to the delightful sight of a cement mixer outside the living room window, or the discomfort of a dirty diaper, or the frightening sound of an airplane flying low overhead. Don't let his whims trip you up. The more benevolently flexible you can be, the better you'll be able to withstand these personality morphs.

Negativism. *No* is a powerful word. "No, we can't stay at the park any longer." "No, don't touch." "No more cookies." "No biting." Little wonder that a toddler loves to use the word herself. What's so alluring? The word is emphatic. It clearly means something. It bears the indelible stamp of one's personal opinion. And it implies control, a precious resource to a toddler.

Many toddlers use *no* indiscriminately, even when they mean yes. They may just like the sound of the word. Sometimes, in the frustration of being misunderstood, "No! No!" is the only thing that comes to mind while a child is struggling to get his desires across. To reduce hearing it echoed back from your child more often than you'd like, it helps to avoid saying the word yourself. Reserve it for really terrible dangers—grabbing hot pots on the stove, picking up knives, that sort of thing. If you use it for every little infraction, you dilute its significance.

Clinginess. All parents find a toddler firmly attached to one of their legs at some point. It's both endearing and frustrating. Clingy spells are common for 1-year-olds. They're a physical demonstration of anxiety. Clinginess can be situational—usually a new or stressful event, such as a party or a new child care arrangement. Or, for some reserved, slow-to-warm-up children, it can be an ongoing pattern. Working parents, especially, may find such exaggerated shows of affection wearying at the end of a long day. Indulge them. They're the child's way of reconnecting.

Your role is to provide the reassurance your toddler craves while not babying her to her own detriment. After all, a child can't do much playing and exploring while attached, koala-style, to your knees. Make sure your child has plenty of opportunities for your love and attention. When you have to leave her for a moment, say "I'll be right back," and don't be long. Even when you need to get something done that requires more time, like cooking dinner, reassure her with your voice. Caress her head as you pass by. Or let her follow you around. Find simple ways she can help, which will distract her from her need to physically hold you. If she keeps hanging on, use a reasonable, matter-of-fact voice: "I have to fold this laundry now. You can sit right here and watch me." Or involve her in the folding, such as by letting her sort the clothes into piles by color.

Clinginess is one way a toddler shows anxiety. To deal with it, look for the cause.

Impatience. Here's a sound bite from your toddler's head: *"Hey, I've got a lot of things to do today, Mom! You can't expect me to lie still while you change this diaper and snap all those snaps back up, can you? Look—there's my favorite book, just out of reach. Sorry, can't wait forever for you to finish down there. I'm outta here!"* Even if you think you're an ace diaper changer, or juice pourer, it's probably not swift enough for your little mover and shaker. A toddler lives in the moment. That means, if she's thought of it, she expects it done—never mind that there's a reaction time involved. And never mind saying "Wait a minute."

You can't expect patience, but you can help minimize impatience. Responding quickly to requests for food or drink will help avoid meltdowns. (A healthy snack never hurt a toddler, even a few minutes before dinner.) If your child wants something that you simply can't provide right away, try to distract her. Patience gradually improves, so that between 2 and 3 you can actually say, "Wait a minute," and she will be able to.

Impulsiveness. Toddlers are insatiably curious. When they feel like trying something, they go for it, just for the sheer experience of swinging a bat in the house or removing a diaper all by themselves. How can you keep your child safe and set desirable limits without entirely squelching this wonderful

HOT TOPIC
Raising a Moral Child

Every parent wants a child who knows right from wrong. How do you instill these values in your child? The best way is through your example. Because toddlers are all eyes and ears, it's important to know that even at this tender age, their moral character is being shaped every day. True, when your child gets older you can have explicit conversations with him about your beliefs. But most experts believe that rote learning and rule making are not as effective in teaching morality as are subtle, everyday lessons. The fact is, kids of all ages identify with actions more than speeches.

Be a vigilant role model of good behavior. Say "please" and "thank you," and once your child is verbal, make it clear that you expect the same from her. Take care not to lie in front of your child; even an innocent white lie sends a mixed message about your standards. Older toddlers and preschoolers often lie, but this is a universal (and eventually outgrown) tendency that has to do more with an overactive imagination than deliberately defying what the child knows to be true. For this reason, it's best to be fairly indulgent about a child's lies in early childhood.

Another way to shape your child's character is to have firm expectations and limits that are consistently enforced. Restraints are a good thing, because they let a child know that he's not the center of the universe, which (regrettably for him) he isn't. And don't overlook bedtime as a wonderful opportunity for sharing stories that convey notions about right and wrong, whether they come from fairy tales, the Bible, or simple children's books.

curiosity? Your best tools are a watchful eye and a childproof space. Distraction is one of the best ways to redirect impulsive acts that pose a danger.

Being contrarian. You say yes, I say no. You say stop, I say go. Sometimes a 2-year-old truly holds an opposing view from yours. More often, though, he just likes to be different. It's another way of exercising control over his universe. It gets frustrating, of course, when you're trying to dash out the door and your child won't let you put his shoes on. Sidestep power struggles by remaining calm yourself. Don't let yourself get sucked into the whirlpool of an argument, because you can't win. Appeals to reason are lost, and your child may simply think it's a fun game to say the opposite of whatever you do. Instead, follow through firmly and consistently when it matters, and give in when it doesn't.

Rigidity. Stubbornness is hard enough to handle. But often it ossifies into inflexibility. That may mean your daughter insists on wearing dresses only, refusing even to look at the many pants stuffed in her drawers. Or your son demands that his bedtime ritual follow a very specific order, and if you say good night to Godzilla before Elmo, all hell will break loose. The child is smarter than he looks: He understands that by standing firm, he can (sometimes) make others bend to his will and do as he wishes.

The best course is to indulge such behavior whenever it's not really a big deal. Your child derives a sense of security from these extreme rituals. If the request is unreasonable or inappropriate—your child wants to watch television during dinner, for example—refuse him calmly but firmly. You may have to weather some tantrums. But ultimately, when it comes to your child's welfare, you're the boss.

Bossiness. "You put my shoes on." "Come here, Mommy!" "Wear this hat, Daddy." A toddler can issue marching orders as crisply and firmly as a commander in chief. And woe to the plebe (or parent) who ignores the command or drags her feet executing it. Your child sees herself as the center of the universe. It's only natural, therefore, that she believes all things—and all people—revolve around her. Besides, it makes her feel great to act like you, who (to her way of thinking) orders *her* around all day.

For these reasons, you can't entirely rein in the commands. You can, however, nip tyranny in the bud. Teach your child to couch her requests with the word *please* and a pleasant tone of voice. Accede to reasonable requests once she's asked nicely, but don't always jump just because she asks you to. Consider, too, whether nonstop orders are a bid for your attention. Maybe your bossy child is really asking you to put down the newspaper or stop fixing dinner and play with her.

Jealousy. The green-eyed monster that haunts adults is born in toddlerhood. This raging emotion can be triggered by something as seemingly inconsequential as your holding a friend's baby, or by something as life-changing as a new baby sibling. Either way, toddler jealousy is triggered by

---

WHAT IF...

My child is too shy?

Shyness is an oft-misused word when it comes to toddlers. In fact, most 1- and 2-year-olds are shy in some situations. Hanging back in new situations is common. Some children do have more reserved or slow-to-warm-up personalities. Labeling your child as "shy" tends to be counterproductive, however. Give a reserved child extra time to warm up to new people and new situations. Don't push.

MILESTONE

SHOWING EMPATHY (12-24 months)

You're upset, and your child pats your back. A baby starts to cry, and your toddler fetches her pacifier. Between ages 1 and 2½, children not only understand the rudiments of emotion ("I'm happy," "I'm sad"), they begin to see that others have feelings, too. While demonstrating empathy for others comes naturally, there are ways to encourage it. Point out emotions: "John is sad. How can we make him feel better?" Encourage your child to actively help other children they've wronged or upset—helping to rebuild a castle of blocks or wiping up spilled juice. And, of course, be a caring role model. Let your child see you treating others kindly.

---

a perceived threat. *Am I being displaced? Do you not love me anymore?* The thought of losing a parent's love is, to a toddler, just about the greatest threat of all.

Whether your child responds with howls and hitting or slinks away dejectedly, the best way to respond to jealousy is to show him how to channel the emotion. He doesn't have the language skills to express his fear. So give him words: "It must be hard to see me holding a baby when you're the one who needs a hug. Do you want to sit with me and help me hold her?" Reassurance of your affection through hugs and attention help, too. Sometimes a jealous child can be distracted. It's especially helpful to ritualize a new older sibling's special time with Mom and Dad, such as reading books or playing ball with one parent at roughly the same time every day, alone. This gives a jealous child something to look forward to, apart from the baby. But if nothing will tame the beast within him, be understanding. Stick to limits about antisocial behavior—no hitting, no biting—but don't punish him for a tantrum or crying. Let him vent.

Common Fears

Most children have one or more fears during the early years. After all, the world is new and they're not always sure what to expect from it or how to make sense of what they see or hear. A toddler is old enough now to develop a sense of what *might* go amiss—no matter how unrealistic such worries are. She feels small and powerless. Toddlerhood through age 5 is prime time for childhood fears. (They tend to escalate as a child's imagination flourishes, then subside as maturity brings newfound confidence and skills.) Temperament may play a role, too; some children are more fearful than others.

Often the cause is obvious—a neighbor has a new German shepherd, it's the first time at a pool. But don't overlook seemingly unconnected events, such as a new caregiver, a move, or a child's too-busy schedule, which are generally stressful. Other outside forces that can intensify a fear include something a child overhears (a TV movie showing someone flailing about in the water, for example) or is warned about (an over-protective parent constantly saying "Be careful!" at the jungle gym).

Fears are almost always outgrown. In the meantime, you'll want to buck up your child's confidence without pumping up the worry. Never ignore or pooh-pooh a fear. To your child, it's perfectly real, and your denial will only agitate him further. On the other hand, if you kowtow to a fear, it may never go away. Your best course lies in the middle: Respect that the child has a legitimate concern and gently help him to confront it. Overcoming a fear gives a child the same boost as mastering a skill.

It can be hard to judge when an acute fear goes beyond being age-appropriate and has blossomed into a phobia that might benefit from a professional's advice. Generally, this should not be a concern during toddlerhood, since fears are such a normal part of development at this age. Never hesitate to ask your pediatrician, though, if a fear seems so extreme that it's disrupting household routines.

Try these tactics for the following common fears:

WHAT IF...

I'm in a hurry and don't have the time to be patient while my child explores the leaves on the ground or learns how to put on his own shoes?

Once in a while it's okay to hurry your child if you've got to be somewhere, or to do things for your child even after she knows how. Not every experience has to be a learning one. Nor can your whole life run on toddler time. Do remember, though, that extra patience is essential with toddlers. Constantly rushing her causes unneeded stress for both of you. Plan ahead to simplify getting ready.

Fear of being left behind (separation anxiety). "Go away, I can't live without you" pretty much sums up how a toddler feels about his relationship with his parents. The child likes the idea of being his own little man (or woman) and is eager to discover where his newfound abilities and powers will take him. Yet he needs you as a springboard in order to feel safe enough to make these amazing discoveries. Separation anxiety begins in infancy, around 7 to 12 months, and begins to wane about age 2, though it can last until age 3. Some children are more temperamentally anxious, and separations are hardest for them. A change in your child's daily routine, such as an illness or a new caregiver, may make her more clingy than usual, too. While it's not necessary (or even healthy) to abandon your plans at the first whimper, you'll need to evaluate the source of the anxiety in timing your separations. For example, if you've been gone on a business trip and have a night out planned soon after, it may help a separation-anxious child if you postponed the latter.

Although often equally wrenching on parent and child alike, separations can actually be made easier on a child if they are relatively frequent. By briefly leaving a child with another relative or a sitter, she grows used to the idea that there are other caring people in the world besides her parents. Consider a slow warm-up to the arrangement, such as the sitter coming to the home for a few hours while the parent is still there, or the parent and child visiting a new day care together for a period of time. (For more tips, see Chapter 5, "Big Transitions," page 174.)

Fear of dogs. It doesn't take getting bitten to make a child afraid of Fido (or other large animals). This is a common, natural anxiety, even among kids who have never encountered a snuffling, pawing beast up close before. Role-playing with a stuffed toy helps them get used to the idea of a real animal. Never force a child to pet a dog. Let her decide when and where she feels comfortable about approaching one.

Fear of loud noises and thunder. All sorts of bangs and rattles—a balloon popping, a vacuum, a blow-dryer, fireworks, the backfiring of a car—can unnerve a child. Thunder is especially spooky since it seems to come from nowhere and is accompanied by bright flashes of light. The best course is to reassure your child with a hug and to act calmly yourself, so she sees that everything's all right. Explain where a strange noise comes from: "Thunder comes from the clouds when they fill up with rain. It can't hurt people." Encourage him to cover his ears if he wants to, which gives the child a measure of control.

Fear of the dark. It's no coincidence this fear lurks at bedtime. The real issue here is separation. Toddlers don't like to leave their parents, and they know full well that bedtime means the grown-ups will be hanging out downstairs (or down the hall) while they're alone with their Winnie the Pooh sheets. Predictable bedtime rituals—a bath, a story, saying good night to a dozen stuffed animals—help to ease this transition. After tucking the child in bed, tell her you'll be back in five or ten minutes to check on her, and then do it. That provides enough reassurance to allow her to relax. Don't fall for extreme measures, such as leaving the overhead light on. It's neither restful nor helpful in the long term. Far better: a flashlight or leaving the door open and a hall light on.

Fear of monsters, witches, clowns, and other characters. These figures can be real (as at Halloween) or imagined (as the ones that lurk under the bed or in the shadows on the walls). Hobgoblins of the more visible variety are often frightening because of their sheer size or unfamiliarity. A seven-foot Barney visiting the shopping mall looks so much bigger than the one your child saw on her TV screen, for example, as to be virtually unrecognizable. The Mickey Mouse on your child's pop-up toy or bedroom sheets will be nothing like the "real" one wandering around Disney World. Don't insist on a photo op or a hug. Better to encourage your child to wave from a safe distance and come away from the encounter feeling confident rather than cowed. Keep a fearful toddler away from scary Halloween masks, too.

Bedtime monsters show up closer to the preschool years. They creep forth for the same reason as fear of the dark—separation anxiety. Don't insist they're not real. Instead, try talking to them: "Okay, you monsters. Dylan has to get some sleep, so you need to fly out the window, now! Maybe you can come back for breakfast!" Some parents shake imaginary monster dust to make unwanted guests disappear, ring a bell, arm their child with a flashlight whose beam is guaranteed to send a gargoyle galloping, or simply close the closet door. There's a risk to these creative strategies, though. While they work for some kids, they tend to make the fear even more legitimate and persistent.

Bathtime fears. Many toddlers continue to love baths through toddlerhood. But 1-year-olds may turn into landlubbers when they see the water swirling ominously down the drain, have a single bath that's too hot or too cold, or get soap in their eyes. For some, outgrowing the bath chair can be a spooky transition. If this sudden change strikes your child, try switching to sponge baths while your child is standing next to the bathtub for a week or two, without making a big deal about it. Your child may forget his fright. Eventually run an inch or two of water, no more, into the tub. Your

WHAT IF...

My child is overly friendly to everyone he meets?

Count yourself lucky to have an outgoing, curious charmer. The unspoken concern here, of course, is that the child will be too trusting of a stranger who might prove to be dangerous. Toddlerhood is too soon, however, to instruct children in the sophisticated concepts of "good" and "bad" people. In fact, society has grown so generally hysterical about strangers that children lose out on learning such simple social niceties as saying "Hello, how are you?" Use your child's gregariousness to reinforce lessons about kindness and don't punish him for being friendly. As for stranger dangers, a toddler should never be out of sight in public anyway.

child may be enticed into playing while you wash her. More tricks: Bathe together, introduce the shower, or provide new bath toys, such as animal-shaped soaps or a baby doll that can get wet.

Fear of flushing toilets. Many 2-year-olds see their wastes as an extension of themselves. The whooshing disappearance of the water down the drain may make a child afraid that he'll get sucked down there, too. This is usually a short-lived phase. In the meantime, flush after your child leaves the room. Explain that a person is much too big to fit into a pipe. Invite him to use a potty instead of the big toilet.

Fear of doctors. At some point, most kids who greeted their doctors and nurses happily in infancy suddenly recognize the drive to the clinic and panic, or howl at the sight of a white lab coat. Often the memory of a shot or blood test triggers this reaction. Or a parent or older sibling says, "Oh! The doctor!" in an ominous tone. Reinforce the idea that your doctor is your child's friend, someone who wants to keep him healthy. A toy doctor's kit is a wonderful way to playact what will happen. During the exam, let your child sit on your lap, if possible. Never tell a child that a shot "won't hurt a bit." Be honest: "You'll feel a pinch and then it will be over." Never threaten your child that the doctor will "give you a shot if you don't behave."

Regression

Growing up doesn't happen in a straight line. Toddlers are especially vulnerable to backsliding into old habits you'd thought they'd outgrown, such as waking in the middle of the night long after they've been sleeping through, or begging for the bottle you discarded months ago after weaning to a cup. Sometimes toddlers lapse in one arena while they're concentrating on developing a new skill. Or it may simply take a while to fully absorb a new accomplishment, so the child takes two steps forward, one step back. The stress of change—a new sitter, a vacation, Mom going back to work—can trigger a dependency on familiar old ways, too.

The best ways to handle regression:

Look for the cause. Once you identify what's triggering the regression, you can address the cause directly and help your child express and manage his feelings of fear, confusion, or stress in other ways.

Be a Rock of Gibraltar. Provide security in the form of consistent routines and rest times.

Be blasé. Whatever you do, don't make a fuss over backsliding. It's an intrinsic part of development. Stick to a neutral nonchalance.

Go along. But make it clear that you're just playing along. Say, "You want to *pretend* to be a baby? Okay. Here's the bottle. That formula doesn't taste as good as your milk, does it?" Don't worry that a request to breast-feed or sit in a high chair once again will become permanent. Kids have an inborn drive to grow up and will soon grow bored of the behavior they left behind. In the rare event your child clings to the rediscovered regression, such as a bottle, set a limit: "Okay, you can try it again at dinner today and tomorrow, then we'll use your big-boy cup again."

Minimize pressures. Is your toddler engaged in too many different activities? Watching cartoons that may be frightening with an older child? Situations like these can cause regression also. Take extra care to reassure your child about what will change and how much will stay the same when stressful events such as a new sibling or a move are on the horizon.

Emphasize the good in growing up. Empathize with a child who says "I'm the baby" or "I wish I were a baby" by saying, "Of course you're my baby, and you always will be." Then subtly shift the conversation to mention the good things about being bigger. Babies can't ride tricycles or eat ice pops, for example, but big girls can.

Ask questions. If your child is very verbal, gently probe about the reversal. "You must feel very angry when you bite. But biting hurts people. Let's figure out a better way to act when you're mad. Did Sam do something that made you mad right before you bit him? What could you have said to him, or to me? Would it help if I was building the block tower with you?"

Never punish or chide for a regressive act. Don't say "Stop acting like a baby," even when you're sorely tempted. This is threatening and unsupportive—and anyway, in many ways your toddler still *is* very much a baby. If you harp on regressive behavior too much, you risk getting locked into a power struggle over it, which only prolongs the behavior. As your toddler navigates growing up, more than ever she's seeking your encouragement and reassurance.

Mental Development

Inside the Toddler Mind

Any parent who has ever watched a baby's solemn, unblinking gaze has said, "I wonder what she's thinking about?" Gaining ever more insights into your child's busy mind and how it works is a thrilling part of toddlerhood. The growing ability to communicate is the biggest way these thoughts are revealed to you.

Here's a peek at some toddler thought processes:

Why is she so curious about everything? Curiosity is your little discoverer's primary motivator. A toddler doesn't turn curiosity on and off at will; it's her nature. She's using all her senses to try and make sense of the world—what things are, what they do, how they work. Curiosity is the reason a 12-month-old uses her mouth and hands to investigate everything in reach. It's why an 18-month-old is drawn to a sandbox like a magnet. It's why a 2-year-old pulls the cat's tail, pours water out of the bathtub, tries to burrow in your cupboards, and beheads all the flowers in your garden. She can't help herself—at least the first time. She can, however, learn what's appropriate and what's not.

Does he have a sense of time? A toddler can't follow a clock or read a calendar. *Yesterday* usually means anything that happened in the past, whether it was really yesterday or six months ago. *Tomorrow* is an all-purpose word for the future. In fact, a child's notion of time doesn't resemble an adult's until second or third grade.

For the most part, your child exists in the here and now. Daily routines are the way he marks time. Even a 1-year-old knows that there is breakfast, lunch, and then dinner. If he is hungry and sees you rattling pans in the kitchen, he knows that dinner will be in a short while, even if he has no idea how long "five minutes" or "fifteen minutes" is. Naps help him pace the day, too. Keeping things as predictable as possible is enormously reassuring to your child. They help him know what's coming next in his day, providing the same relief that you may feel from checking your planner or glancing at your watch. Help your child gauge a sense of time by explaining sequences: "I will pick you up after you play, have lunch, and take a nap." "We will go on vacation after two more night-nights."

How much does she remember? More than you may think. Although many memories of toddlerhood are lost once we're adults, for reasons not completely understood, toddlers remember plenty from day to day. They can associate certain events (such as when you go to the bank, the teller gives your child a lollipop). They can begin to remember the steps involved in finger painting or a bedtime routine. Having a regular routine helps reinforce memories and builds your child's overall sense of security.

You can also encourage your child to use his memory skills by asking questions: "What did we see at the zoo?" In general, children tend to remember events that deviate from the expected. So rather than tell you about the lions and tigers and bears, your child may keep talking about how he dropped his ice cream cone. Toddlers also remember unusual events (such as a once-a-year zoo trip) more often than the details of routine ones (say, if a zoo excursion is a regular thing). Review the day together at bedtime. Help your child build on his memories by adding details: "Yes, the ice cream fell. But then we saw a peacock!"

As your child's language skills grow, his ability to organize and store memories increases exponentially. You may hear your child talking about a big truck he saw two weeks ago, for example. Or seeing a seashell may remind him of a beach vacation eight months earlier. Use pictures to preserve memories, too. Keep faraway relatives' snapshots visible on the refrigerator door, and look at family albums together, too.

How does his mind work? Toddlers are notoriously literal thinkers. They lack an

---

▄Milestone

IMITATING (12 months)

Even an hours-old newborn has been shown to imitate an adult sticking out her tongue. And around 6 or 7 months, a baby begins to mimic vocal sounds. But real imitation of others' behaviors doesn't start until around the first birthday. Your child may pat your back while you are patting his, for example. He may copy the way a playmate moves a toy car across the floor or leafs through a book. By 18 months a toddler starts to grasp the concept of task completion. They learn to echo an adult's satisfaction upon finishing a project; for example, they may try to help you empty the dishwasher or put all their toys into a box. By age 2½, much of toddler play is centered on imitation. Watch your child play house, grocery store, school, and driving.

understanding of the subtleties of language, context, and circumstance in order to see the nuances. If you say something like, "You're funny," your child may protest, "I'm not funny. I'm Sammy!" By age 2, your child will also develop more abstract thinking; an example is the ability to imagine something that's not there. One way that kids practice learning that things exist even if they're not there is by hiding objects, then going back to where they put them. Think of it as advanced peekaboo. You may find crackers under the sofa cushions or blocks in a kitchen drawer, for example. This helps a toddler build confidence as well as an understanding of object permanence—"Is it really still there?" Squirreling objects away is also a form of exercising control. In her own small way, your child is taking charge over a tiny portion of her universe because *she* decides what goes where. And indeed, only she may know where those crackers are.

Does he understand quantity? In a rudimentary way, your child gains a sense of amounts during his second year. A 1-year-old can understand the concept of "more," and even "big" versus "little." By age 2, your child may be able to count to two fairly accurately. Some bright 2-year-olds can recite their numbers from one to ten. But the ability to truly count more than two of something isn't generally achieved until age 3 or later. Counting songs (such as "Ten Little Indians") are great fun for toddlers and lay the groundwork for a later familiarity with numbers.

No joke: Toddlers' sense of humor may be primitive, but it definitely exists.

Does she have a sense of humor? Irony and late-night comedians' jokes go straight over your child's head, of course. A toddler's sense of humor is on the primitive side. But it's definitely there. Slapstick is a big favorite. Pretend to fall down, and watch your child howl. Incongruity is another favorite. For example, toddlers find it hysterical when you call their nose an elbow or pretend to wear a shoe on your head. Unusual noises, songs with silly lyrics, and even funny faces all count as highly entertaining. You can use humor to your advantage sometimes, such as to defuse a power struggle or to distract your child while getting her dressed or diapered. One rule of thumb: Always laugh *with* your child, never at her. (At least, not when she can see you.)

What You Can Do

Listen to what goes on in a toddler's brain while he's at play: "Hmmm, what does milk feel like? Will this bear fit into my pocket? What happens when I turn this basket of clothes over? How do the lights go off and on?" To you, this nonstop activity may look like play, or mischief, or one big mess. But to a toddler, it's all in a day's work—learning by doing. If you watch closely, you can see him repeating a task over and over. He studies cause and effect and the notion of gravity as meticulously as a researcher. Your child also learns by watching you. By observing and imitating, he begins to organize her world and understand how it works.

One way toddlers don't learn—or certainly don't need to—is through formal education. Sitting down with a child and saying "Now I am going to teach you to read" or "Let's learn colors" is not only unrealistic, it creates an unnecessary pressure to perform. The same is true of educational enrichment courses or other special brainpower classes aimed at toddlers. Your child doesn't even need fancy educational toys to learn. (Thomas Jefferson and Albert Einstein certainly didn't have them.) Flash cards, for example, are all right for a toddler to shuffle through or play with. But there's no need to drill her, even on simple concepts such as colors, shapes, sizes, and the names of objects. Your child will pick up these things naturally if you talk about them in everyday contexts: "Here are your yellow socks" or "Here's a small cup and a great big cup."

Spontaneous learning preserves a child's joy about discovering new concepts and skills. All you need to do is react and respond to this natural curiosity, and your child will learn plenty. More tips:

Step into your child's world. Slow down enough to observe what he observes, hear what he hears. Children learn best through their senses. So

---

WHAT IF...

I get tired of answering so many questions; is it okay to ignore them?

"**W**hat's that?" may be the number-one question in the second year of life, followed in the third by "Why?" Asking questions is one way toddlers make sense of a confusing world, so answering them is important. Your answers needn't be long. In fact, a toddler is looking only for a direct and narrow answer, not a lengthy monologue. To the question "Why do boys have penises?" for example, you need say only, "That's how boys go to the bathroom." You don't need to go into a long explanation of reproduction.

"Why" questions escalate at age 2. Sometimes asking "why" is a child's way of keeping the conversation going, since they lack more sophisticated language.

tune in to the textures, smells, and unusual sights all around you. Let your child pick up pebbles when you walk, count the stars in the sky, or smell the spices in your spice rack, for example. To help you figure out what something looks like from your child's perspective, crouch down to his level.

Use descriptions and comparisons in ordinary talk. At first your child won't understand all the adjectives you use—*big, cold, heavy, sweet, purple.* Use them anyway. She's busily trying to figure out and categorize everything around her, and these words will help her. Eventually the nuances of their meaning will become clear, first for obvious words *(small)*, then abstract ones *(exciting)*. It's a slow, gradual process. But a child picks up more in this way than you might think.

Tap into the learning experiences all around you. Sure, museums and symphonies make for wonderful educational outings—for older children. Toddlers will find just as many enriching fascinations right at home and around the neighborhood. The refrigerator is filled with exciting shapes and colors. The washing machine makes funny sounds. And the construction site on the corner is better than the Louvre, for a toddler. There's action,

NOT TO WORRY
Meltdowns

Toddlers lose it—a lot. Different from a temper tantrum, a meltdown is more of an extreme loss of control that's usually triggered by overwhelming feelings of fatigue or frustration (or both). The day is fraught with difficult tasks (taking off a sweater, making the toy train stay on the wood tracks) and frightening experiences (thunder, a creaking door). And your child lacks the speaking skills to make his needs, wishes, and feelings clear. When too much is too much, your child may holler, cry, whine, or lash out physically, including hitting and biting.

Stay calm yourself. Be empathetic. Instead of punishing or trying to reason with a toddler who's melting, move straight to a remedy. Try diverting his attention. Often physical activity, such as dancing or water play, is enough to soothe the distressed. A change of scenery can help, too, such as going outside. If your child snaps over very minor things, it could be time for a nap or a snack.

CHECKLIST
Fifteen Household Objects That Help Toddlers Learn

Toddlers don't need workbooks or fancy toys to learn how the world works. You can probably find most of these popular items in your drawers and cupboards already:

- Pots and pans
- Measuring cups and spoons
- Hand mirror (unbreakable)
- Playing cards
- A ball of string
- Cardboard boxes (large and small)
- Rolling pin
- Wooden clothespins
- Laundry basket
- Old magazines and catalogs
- Aluminum pie tins
- Wicker baskets
- Keys on keychain
- Adhesive tape
- Dustpan and brush

dirt, enormous machinery—and no one will tell you to shush or not to run in the halls.

Forgive messes. Your child moves from blocks to books to baby dolls—leaving a heap of puzzle pieces and crayons in her wake. Resist the impulse to demand that she clean up one thing before moving on to the next. Toddlers make messes because they are curious, not slovenly. Combine their zeal to explore with their brief attention spans and a yen to control their environments, and you have a recipe for chaos.

Read to your child. Not textbooks or first-grade primers, of course. But any age-appropriate book will open up a new world to your child's mind. Books also provide a natural springboard for conversations that teach. Choose both books that emphasize concepts (such as colors or shapes) and

WHAT IF...

We think our toddler is gifted?

Don't rush for the IQ tests yet. Some children are very early, fluent speakers; others seem precocious at counting or complex puzzles or athletics. It's common for a toddler to recognize letters or know the names of states, only to forget these things a few months later because they lack the complex understanding of the meaning. All children have notable gifts in one area or another. But even if your child is clearly months ahead of his or her peers in one arena, many of these skills level out later on; toddlerhood is too soon to label a child as advanced.

WHAT IF...

My child has a really short attention span? I can't get her interested in anything for very long.

Toddlers have plenty of interests, but it's perfectly normal for their focus on any one thing to last just nanoseconds. Don't expect more than a few minutes with any one book, toy, or game before she's on to something else. Long bursts of concentration (enough to stick with one activity for thirty minutes or more) don't begin until ages 3 to 5.

Like mother, like daughter: Imitation is a primary way toddlers learn.

those that entertain simply with wonderful stories, interesting language, and beautiful illustrations.

Learning Manners

One type of education that toddlers are ready for is basic manners. No, not the art of social introductions or which fork to use. It's time to lay the groundwork that will help your child grow into a polite, considerate person. How to do this?

Be nice yourself. It's obvious but simple: Little potatoes have big eyes. They watch everything you do, and through observation they absorb many lessons about how to behave themselves. Though toddlers are notoriously self-centered, they can begin to learn consideration of others' feelings through your example. Let them see you say "Hello," "May I?" and "Excuse me."

Show your child that actions have consequences in how they make others feel. For example, after an altercation you could say, "See how sad it makes Amber when you hit? Can you think of a way to make her feel better?" Use this approach to underscore the effects of positive behaviors, too. "Doesn't it make you feel happy when Aunt Sue gives you a hug?" "Let's give some of the flowers we picked to Mrs. Smith and see how it makes her smile."

Teach please and thank you. Your child will probably pick up *thank you* naturally, and at a surprisingly early age, if he hears you use it every time he gives you something. With *please*, at first you'll have to say it yourself, or prompt: "Can you say 'please'?" In fact, you'll probably keep prompting well past kindergarten. But eventually your persistence will be rewarded and the habit will become ingrained.

Know when to let it ride. Keep your child's developmental stage in mind. An 18-month-old is not ready to understand the concept of sharing his toys with a visitor, so don't expect him to be a gracious host in that way. And don't expect much civility of any kind when a toddler is tired, hungry, or ill.

HOT TOPIC

Computers

Ours is the first generation of parents to even consider computers in connection with toddlers. It's a reflection of how ingrained they've become in virtually every aspect of our culture. And since computer games and learning programs have the potential to amuse and benefit children all the way from preschool to high school, it's easy to extend the logic downward: Why *not* computers for toddlers? After all, a 1-year-old watches his mother at the keyboard and imitates her banging the keys. A 2-year-old can manipulate a mouse. Software abounds for even these tenderest years.

Nevertheless, there's reason to pause when it comes to toddlers and computers. Although special toddler learning programs can be engrossing, they provide no lasting academic head start for a 1- or 2-year-old. Toddlers learn best through three-dimensional exploration and play. The interaction a flat screen provides is limited. It can't be touched, mouthed, lifted, or thrown. And the lessons that toddler software emphasizes—cause and effect, colors, sorting, and so on—can just as easily be learned in other ways, through play. Some parents want their kids to be computer-literate as early as possible in life because these machines will play such a big role in their futures. Though well-intentioned, the fact is that there's no way today's toddlers will escape computer literacy. What computer know-how they haven't been exposed to at 2, they'll still pick up lickety-split by 4 or 5.

Language Development

The Power of Speech

Most parents can't wait for that first, precious, no-doubt-about-it word to spring from their baby's lips. It's hard to believe that by the time your child is a preschooler, you'll have a chatterbox who rarely stops talking (even though you sometimes wish he would).

The ability to talk is one of the biggest distinctions between a baby and a young child. Once, all you could do was guess at the reason behind a cry or a whine. But a talker can make his wishes clearer: "Me cold!" "I want a cracker, not a banana!" and possibly even "Change me!" Being able to communicate adds to the heady, swaggering independence that marks these years. The power of speech also lets a young child make sense of the world around him. He can ask "What's that?" or "Why?" And your answers will teach him more than he previously learned from just the use of his senses.

There are two parts to language development: understanding what is said and speaking. For a while, toddlers understand far more than they can say. In fact, studies have shown that 1-year-olds who aren't talking much can comprehend just as much as 1-year-olds with extensive vocabularies.

How Speech Evolves

Between 10 and 18 months is when most—but definitely not all—toddlers start talking.

At first, "ba ba" sounds the same as it has for months. Then you'll notice your child specifically using those sounds to indicate her bottle or a ball. The first

clear word may spring forth as early as 7 months or not until 18 months. It's often *Mama* or *Dada*, which are, not coincidentally, some of the same syllable combinations that she's been uttering since 7 to 10 months. First words typically are nouns that refer to an important object (*Mama, book, bird*) or descriptive words (*up, more*). The first word may also be social (*hi, bye-bye*). But listen closely. Sometimes the first word is woven into babbling: "Da da ba kitty." Most children begin to talk between 10 and 18 months.

From then on, your child's language skills explode, in both spoken words and comprehension. But the pace at which these skills develop is completely individual. For example, one major study found that the typical range for a 12-month-old's vocabulary is zero to forty words. By the time a child is 24 months old, she may still use only a few words, or more than six hundred. Sometimes a child acquires a new word every day. Just as often, she gets stuck on a vocabulary of only five or six words for months, followed by a burst of new words all at once. This spark, known as the naming explosion, can be fun. Often a child will point at object after object, or ask, "What's that?"

Early words are often simplified. *Ba* can mean "bottle," "Barney," "let's play ball," or all three of those things, at different times of the day. That's because toddlers tend to leave off the end consonants. Pronunciation can be tricky for them, too. You may also hear your toddler using a single word to stand for many different but related thoughts. For example, "juice" uttered in a cranky way near naptime may be her way of letting you know she's tired, if she typically has a cup of juice before her nap. Phrased as a question, "juice" may be her way of asking for more. If she spills the juice, she may say "juice" in a negative tone. Show that you understand by picking up on these utterances and expand on them for her: "Uh-oh, the juice spilled. We have to clean that up, don't we?" These are all signs of progress—she's learning about intonation, if not sentence structure.

Around 18 months a child puts two words together to help her express a thought. "Mama book" may mean "That's Mama's book" or "Will you read the book to me?" She'll also begin to describe objects rather than simply label them: "big cow," "wet pants," "blue shirt." Sentences follow between 24 and 30 months: "Look at the big cow," "My pants got wet." By the third birthday, the use of speech grows increasingly sophisticated. A 3-year-old

MILESTONE
STARTS TO SING (18-24 months)

It doesn't matter if neither you nor your toddler is on pitch. Singing is one of the pure pleasures of early childhood. Between the ages of 2 and 3, and sometimes earlier, your child will pick up repetitive choruses of familiar songs, such as the "E-I-E-I-O" of "Old MacDonald Had a Farm." It's worth investing in a CD or songbook of old classics just to refresh your memory.

Other popular beginners' tunes:

- Simple nursery rhymes set to music ("Hey Diddle Diddle," "Three Blind Mice")
- Finger-play songs ("The Itsy Bitsy Spider," "Ten Little Indians")
- Lullabies ("Hush Little Baby," "Twinkle Twinkle Little Star")
- Repetitive songs ("The Wheels on the Bus," "She'll Be Comin' Round the Mountain")
- Action songs ("I'm a Little Teapot," "Patty Cake")

uses tenses *(sleep, slept)*, plurals *(blocks, children)*, and function words *(should, who, would, some)*.

How You Can Help

A child builds his vocabulary on his own, but there are many ways you can encourage that process.

Talk to your child—often. Converse in the car. While you're pushing the stroller, talk about what you see. Talk about the food during meals. Name his body parts while he's getting dressed or having his diaper changed. In general, the more adult language a child hears, the better. Best of all is conversation directed at your child.

Describe what's happening. Narrate what's happening while you cook or go about everyday activities. "Now I'm chopping a carrot. Then I'll put it in the pot. Look at the steam!" This helps a child put words in their appropriate contexts.

Talk slowly. You don't have to exaggerate every word you utter, but do take pains to be clear and succinct. Stick to short sentences and fairly simple language.

Label objects. At first a toddler may not understand when you point to his coat and say *coat*, but as he hears the word more frequently, he'll get the idea.

Repeat and recast. If she says, "Go house," repeat it using proper grammar: "Let's go in the house." Echoing, "That's right. It's cold," signals to your child that he's been understood.

Expand on your child's conversation. If she says, "Bird," you can say, "Yes, look at the pretty red bird. The bird is sitting on a tree."

Make eye contact. The more a child can see your

face, the better he can learn how different sounds are made.

Use proper pronouns. A common parent trap is to refer to yourself in the third person all the time: "Let Mommy help you." "Daddy can fix it." But by using *I* and *you* properly, you'll help your toddler learn these important words.

Play word games. Help a young toddler link words and deeds. Say "I'm going to tickle you!" or "I'm going to pull your piggies!" and then do so. To help teach the names of objects, point to various parts of your body (or pictures in a book, or objects in a room) and say what they are. Eventually your child will be able to use the word when you prompt, "What's that?" And toddlers think silly mix-ups—calling a nose an eye, for example—are a riot. Games that involve talking—such as having pretend conversations on toy telephones—are another great way to make language fun.

> ### PARENT TIP
>
> #### Write those first words and funny phrases down!
>
> **M**ost parents jot their child's first word in the baby book. Here's an even better idea to use as your child's language skills advance. Buy a special notebook for recording his immortal early sayings. Keep it in a handy place with a pencil tucked inside. When something you hear makes you smile, jot it down. As the months—and years—go by, you'll be able to laugh at all the wild utterances you swore you'd always remember but inevitably won't, unless you've committed them to paper.

The Magic of Reading

Reading to a child is one of the most cozy, enjoyable things you can do together, and the benefits you reap are far greater than the effort required. A child who is read to often gets a head start on talking, thanks to this added exposure to words. He's learning to make connections between words, sounds, and meaning, as well as absorbing the cadences and emotional expression of language. You're also embedding a lifelong love of books and the stories, adventures, and answers within them.

When to begin? Experts say it's never too soon to read to a child. Certainly by a child's first birthday, you should be having regular reading sessions. Bedtime is ideal, because storytelling is calming and can become part of your going-to-sleep ritual. But books should also be available to a toddler throughout the day, right there with his toys. At first you may barely get through a single volume. Your child will want to turn the pages—fast. Or she may want to chew on the book, or fly through one after another. Don't be discouraged by this—it's good. The whole idea is to make books familiar, fun, beloved objects. Actually following a simple story line will come eventually.

Some ways to make reading pleasurable for both of you:

Choose books with toddler allure. Best are those that have bright, uncomplicated artwork that varies a lot from page to page, and brief, captivating stories. Repetition and rhymes are favorites. For a 1-year-old, so are books that simply label pictures of objects. Board books encourage a young child to thumb through them easily on his own (or taste them). But variety adds interest: Also make available plastic or cloth books, pop-ups, oversized volumes, and those with textures. (Go easy on the electronic "talking" books, however. Not only are they annoying to listen to, but the noises they make distract a child from fully absorbing the richness of language.) Pick subjects your child shows a special interest in, be it dinosaurs or construction equipment or teddy bears. Older toddlers will begin to enjoy tales on everyday themes they experience, such as going to the doctor or using the potty.

Make time every day to read with your toddler.

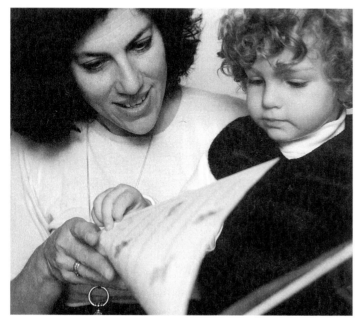

Snuggle. The best place for a toddler to hear a story is right in your lap.

Tell stories apart from books. Repeat nursery rhymes, tell simple Mother Goose stories (like the Three Little Pigs), sing songs, or make up your own funny sagas featuring your child as a character. Some children like to listen to books on tape during quiet time or in the car.

Attend story hours in public places. Many libraries and bookstores hold them for free. A

True Toddler Tales

The Silent Type

One by one, Kim Hurley began noticing the other children in her play group beginning to talk. Not her son, Cameron. At 1 year he sometimes babbled but hadn't uttered a word. "As I became aware of how little he was speaking, I became more concerned," recalls the Troy, Michigan, mom. She couldn't help but compare the boy to his sister, Kailyn, whose first words came very early, around 7 months.

Her pediatrician ruled out hearing problems with a basic test and told her not to worry. Cameron understood people very well. He could follow directions. When he wanted something, he'd point and grunt. Or he'd whine, leaving Kim to run through a list of possibilities. "When I'd figure out what he wanted, like juice, I'd tell him, 'Say "Mama, I want juice." ' " Kim tried working with him on speech, but it seemed to make Cameron edgy, and he'd lose interest. She labeled things he was pointing at and made a simple ABC book with familiar family pictures that she'd hoped would encourage him to talk.

Cameron was 13 months old before he even said "Mama" and "Dada." It was another six or seven months before he added more words. "Now at 22 months, he's saying a lot more and no longer seems behind," Kim says. "There are children out there who are just not verbal."

Kim's tips for parents of a nontalker:

- **Let your child interact with other kids.** "Join a play group or a mother's group. Your child will see and hear others speaking."
- **Get a professional opinion.** "It's especially helpful if you're worrying every day. A doctor can rule out a speech or hearing problem." Don't merely assume your child will "grow out of it" if you are concerned.
- **Simplify your speech.** "He'll be less overwhelmed and more ready to learn."
- **Focus on today.** "Try not to look too much into the future. It's easy to worry about development, but deal with your child the way he is today, and let nature take its course."

younger toddler won't sit still, but a 2½- or 3-year-old may. Before going to a reading where life-size book characters, such as Clifford the Big Red Dog or Barney, make special guest appearances, prepare your child first—their very size may thrill or terrify a tot.

CHECKLIST
A Beginner's Library

These toddler-perfect titles will be read again and again. Many are available as sturdy board books. Look for other classics by these same authors.

✓ Jez Alborough: *Where's My Teddy?*

✓ Byron Barton: *Boats; Planes; Trucks; Dinosaurs, Dinosaurs*

✓ Margaret Wise Brown: *Goodnight Moon* (the perfect bedtime book); *The Big Red Barn*

✓ Eric Carle: *The Very Hungry Caterpillar; Brown Bear, Brown Bear, What Do You See?*

✓ Nancy White Carlstrom: *Jesse Bear, What Will You Wear?*

✓ Eileen Christelow: *Five Little Monkeys Sitting on the Tree*

✓ P. D. Eastman: *Go, Dog, Go; The Best Nest*

✓ Mem Fox: *Time for Bed*

✓ Eric Hill: *Where's Spot?*

✓ Crockett Johnson: *Harold and the Purple Crayon*

✓ Ruth Krauss: *The Carrot Seed*

✓ Dorothy Kunhardt: *Pat the Bunny*

✓ Sylvia Long: *Hush Little Baby*

✓ Helen Oxenbury: *All Fall Down; I Hear; Friends*

✓ Richard Scarry: *Busy, Busy Town; Richard Scarry's Color Book*

✓ Dr. Seuss: *There's a Wocket in My Pocket; Dr. Seuss's ABC*

✓ Cindy Szekeres: *Things Bunny Sees; Kisses*

✓ Rosemary Wells: *My Very First Mother Goose; Max's Breakfast; Max's First Word*

✓ Pat and Eve Witte: *The Touch Me Book*

Let your child see you read. Toddlers love to imitate.

Never withhold reading time as punishment. Not even at bedtime when you're at wits' end. Books should have nothing to do with discipline—ever.

Late Talkers

For every 20-month-old chatterbox, there is another child the same age whose speech is limited to just a few words. If your child seems to talk less than his peers, should you worry? Although late talkers tend to make their parents anxious, patience is important. Many children simply talk later than

VERBAL MILESTONES

7–12 months	May say first recognizable words. Begins to mimic the cadence and tone of adult speech.
12–18 months	Uses a word to stand for a thought or sentence: "juice" means "I want juice," "bye-bye" means "I'm ready to go." Understands many more words and phrases than says.
18–24 months	By 18 months, can say about fifty words. By 24 months, may know as many as two thousand. Puts two words together: "big dog." Begins to use verbs. Starts to use pronouns, not always correctly: "me hungry." Adds several new words to working vocabulary each day.
24–30 months	Regularly uses sentences that are several words long: "No go sleep," "Want cracker now." Understands correct use of *me* and *you*.
30–36 months	Vocabulary continues to grow. Uses word order and phrase structures similar to adult speech. Describes in accurate, vivid detail. By 3 years, uses *I* correctly and can carry on a conversation.

others, and this trait has no bearing on their health or intelligence. Avoid pressuring such a child or quizzing him incessantly, which can backfire and cause feelings of inadequacy.

Before 24 months, it's hard to pinpoint whether there's even a problem. In fact, experts can't agree on the point at which delayed speech should warrant worries. By age 2, you'll certainly want to see definite efforts to communicate through gestures, sounds, or facial expressions, at least. A child who's not doing some of these things by 1 or who doesn't have a vocabulary of at least twelve words by 1½ should be examined to rule out physical or developmental problems.

WHAT IF...

No one can understand my child except me?

It's not unusual for the person who spends the most time around a child to best understand the idiosyncrasies of his or her speech. It can be frustrating for the child when Grandma or Daddy doesn't know what he wants. Help others understand by echoing what the child has said. And be patient. Lisps tend to disappear and enunciation will gradually improve.

NOT TO WORRY
Stuttering

All toddlers stammer a bit. It's a by-product of learning to communicate. Your child's excited thoughts may be flying faster than she can lasso them into words. She may be unconsciously stalling for time while searching for a way to describe something. Tiresome though these endless jerky repetitions can be to hear, have patience. Interrupting to rush the speaker along won't help her find the right words any faster. If she really gets stuck, gently invite her to take a deep breath and start over.

Stammers disappear as children grow more fluent and confident as speakers. It's very rare that a permanent stutter will develop, and toddlerhood is too soon to diagnose such a problem.

Several factors may be responsible for a slow-to-talk toddler:

Hearing problems. If your child doesn't look in the direction of sounds or hasn't uttered a single word by 14 months, tell your pediatrician. A hearing evaluation can identify any problems that may be interfering with normal speech. Persistent ear infections, even if they have ended and the child's hearing is now normal, may delay speech. Sometimes speech therapy is recommended to help such a child catch up.

Heredity. Research has shown that some children inherit a tendency to late speech development and a generally laconic manner. So if you're naturally tight-lipped, your children may be, too.

Birth order. Later-borns are sometimes slower talkers, especially when they are close in age to older siblings. This may be because firstborns tend to get more undivided attention—and hear more adult conversation. There's also more time to carefully model conversation for beginning talkers. Older siblings often do the talking for the younger ones, too.

Being a multiple. Twins, for example, sometimes develop their own communication system of

WHAT IF...

My toddler calls all men "Daddy"?

It's called overgeneralizing. And every toddler does it. Your child knows that isn't *his* daddy; he just means that he sees a man *like* Daddy. Some kids call all animals "doggie" or anything served in a cup "juice." Don't correct the mistake; just put it in a helpful context: "Yes, there's a man who looks like Daddy. Your daddy is at work."

made-up words, gestures, and facial expressions. Children who are multiples may also receive less individualized attention.

Gender. Boys and girls learn to talk at about the same pace, overall. But at the extreme ends of the spectrum, it's true that the earliest talkers tend to be girls and very late talkers tend to be boys. Researchers are not sure why this is so.

Activity level. It's not uncommon for a child to abandon his talking efforts amidst newfound zeal for walking and running. This usually changes once he masters the physical skills.

A bilingual household. Generally, a child who grows up hearing two languages initially says fewer words in either language than a child exposed to only one. Eventually the bilingual child catches up, however, and can become fluent in both languages by the preschool years.

Prematurity. A preemie's language skills may lag through the third year. By the school years, however, most children who were premature speak as well as their full-term peers.

A developmental disorder. Some children understand language but have trouble getting their mouths to form the proper sounds for coherent speech. This can be corrected with therapy. Others have language disorders that make it difficult for them to understand words. If your toddler isn't talking by 30 months—or if you're worried before then—insist on a professional evaluation by a physician or a speech-language specialist.

WHAT IF...

My toddler mispronounces words or uses the wrong grammar? Should I correct her?

Not directly. Constantly correcting a budding talker can be deflating and may undermine her confidence. It's better to simply echo what your child has said, but using the correct pronunciation or grammar. If you use the right forms yourself, she'll eventually pick them up.

MILESTONE
FIRST SENTENCE (18-30 months)

A few months after the first word combinations ("more juice," "big book"), the typical toddler strings together a series of words that approximates a sentence: "Me see kitty," "Read Chris book." This is an exciting leap forward. Don't count on consistently perfect grammar or word order until the third or fourth year.

CHAPTER TWO

Everyday Routines

Eating. Sleeping. Dressing. Keeping clean. These are the day-in, day-out necessities of toddler rearing. Although everyday routines are basic, they shouldn't be taken for granted. For a 1- or 2-year-old, regular rhythms build a vital sense of security. There's also growing evidence that predictable routines and repetition enhance learning during the first three years of life.

This chapter explains the importance of everyday routines to healthy development. There are effective ways and less-than-effective ways to manage them. That's especially true when you're dealing with a frisky 1- or 2-year-old who has plenty of her own ideas on what constitutes lunch or how many books and back rubs are required to fall asleep at night. Get the daily rhythms down pat, however, and the whole household tends to run less contentiously. In addition, you'll find time- and parent-tested tactics for making mealtimes, bedtimes, grooming, and dressing less stressful—and therefore more pleasant—for everyone.

Why Routines Matter

Familiarity Breeds Contentment

Put yourself in your toddler's slipper socks. Every day her world is changing. She's growing bigger, stronger, and able to do more things on her own. One day she can walk, the next she's running. Everything has a word to describe it—so many to learn! Even mealtimes bring wonders anew, with different colors and textures on her plate to explore and taste. Then there's a spoon to master, and eventually a fork, a coat zipper, a tricycle, and more.

Your child is discovering, too, that he's his own little person, with likes and dislikes, moods, and a personality all his own. And he's figuring out the many ways he can express that individuality. He's learning that complying achieves one result, crying brings about another. And when all else fails, there's this marvelous tool known as the temper tantrum.

All this novelty and power is intoxicating—and often overwhelming. That's where routines help. A predictable order to the day is one of the greatest gifts a parent can give to a toddler. Routines provide essential, reassuring structure. They're a reliable oasis amid so many new things, a refuge in the storm of emotions that marks a typical day. Daily rituals build trust, too. They help a child relax, knowing his basic needs will be met. Since a toddler can't tell time by a clock, routines also provide a framework by which he can pace out the day.

Parents benefit from routines, too. A better-adjusted, well-regulated child is an easier one to live with. Without a gentle sense of order for the day, life with a mercurial toddler can quickly dissolve into chaos. Regular ways of doing things serve as unspoken rules. Arguments over when a child needs to sleep, for example, are minimized when they're part of a predictable pattern expected by both parent and child.

Some parents use a schedule with their babies almost from the start. Others fall into routines gradually, as their infants grow hungry and sleepy at the same times every day. Routines are meant to evolve naturally, along with your child. If you haven't initiated regular routines into your family life yet, toddlerhood is a wonderful time to start.

PARENT TIP

Do You Feel Like a Slave to Your Child's Schedule?

Routines are supposed to make your life easier, not harder. Don't mistake them for carved-in-stone, never-can-change commandments. Give yourself a break occasionally. If you can't bear the twenty-five steps involved in your child's bedtime, it's probably too complicated. If you don't feel like making the daily excursion to the park, stay inside. The best routines build in flexibility.

Little Rituals Matter, Too

Routine refers to the general order and pattern of activities throughout the day. You provide the basics of life at the same time and in the same way, more or less, day after day. Your child should have a routine whether he's exclusively cared for at home or attends out-of-home care. For a 1-year-old, this may mean a schedule like the following: Wake up at seven; get dressed; eat breakfast at seven-thirty; play; eat a snack; nap from ten-thirty to eleven-thirty; wake up and eat lunch; run errands with Mom; snack; nap from three-thirty to four-thirty; play inside; eat dinner at six; watch a video; have a bath; read books; go to bed at eight-thirty. A 2-year-old's day is roughly similar, with the exception of the morning nap; instead, he may take an earlier (and longer) afternoon nap.

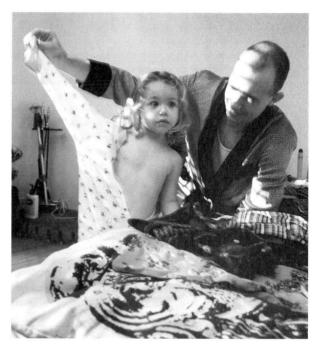

Doing things in a particular order, like getting dressed before eating breakfast, provides an invaluable sense of security.

Peppered throughout the day are apt to be many little rituals shared by you and your child. A *ritual* is a specific action or activity that's done in a certain way. Toddlers love rituals as much as they need routines. Often of the child's own concoction, rituals are a way for a child to exert control over the general helplessness of his life. They're reassuring, too. A ritual might involve choosing a certain place mat for lunch, or the special order in which the child likes the parts of his body to be scrubbed in the tub.

Toddlers often get stuck on rituals that seem peculiar to grown-ups. Because Daddy sat in a certain chair one night, for example, the child insists Daddy must sit there *every* night, and woe to the visitor who tries to perch there instead. Or a child may insist that you address her a particular way, such as "Mary, Mary, Quite Contrary" rather than merely Mary. Rituals tend to escalate in their elaborateness. One night you're sweetly bidding good night (with a kiss and a hug) to your child's favorite stuffed animal. Before long he wants you to kiss each and every animal in the room, and in a very specific order.

It's best to humor rituals. More than whims for a young child, they are tangible forms of security. That's not to say they should be limitless. Indulge routines *within reason*. Nobody wants to (or should) spend forty-five minutes

My child has a hard time making the transition from a weekday schedule to a weekend one?

Grown-ups welcome the weekend downshift. But for your child, the more similar all of his days are, the better. If your child attends day care or is with a sitter during the week, you should be familiar with the entire pacing of your child's day, including when quiet activities and outdoor play are scheduled. Try to approximate the same schedule at home. It's tough, especially when errands and special events crowd weekend calendars. But at least stick to consistent mealtimes, naptimes, and bedtimes. If something disrupts your plan one day, bounce back to it the next.

kissing every stuffed member in a toddler's menagerie. Instead, tell the child to pick three favorites whom you'll tuck in with him.

An underlying need for routine remains throughout childhood. Fortunately, however, the absolutism and redundancies that are so characteristic of toddler routines will begin to wane as your child grows older and more confident.

When Routines Are Disrupted

Inevitably, your daily schedule will require variations when you can't stick to the habits your child expects. Family vacations are a prime example. Or one parent may need to go on a business trip, a relative may visit, or the holidays bring a burst of parties and late-night events. How will your child weather such changes? Fairly well, if he is prepared. Kids are surprisingly resilient. Let your child know in advance when there will be a deviation from the norm. Tell him what will probably happen instead: "The baby-sitter will give you a bath and read you three stories just like I do, and then tuck you in bed, and when you wake up in the morning, Daddy and I will be home." Or "When Grandma visits, she'll be sleeping on the extra bed in your room. But we will move your crib into Mommy and Daddy's room, and all your pillows and blankets will be there." It's best to keep the basics of the day as close to normal as possible, even on vacation. Provide

NOT TO WORRY
Over and Over and Over

"Again!" It's perfectly normal for a 1- or 2-year-old to want to read the same book night after night (or several times on the same night). It's not a sign that he lacks curiosity or imagination. Following a specific sequence, insisting on a certain lullaby, and other repetitive rituals provide the order he craves. Give in as much as is reasonable. Use your child's fondness for a particular book to introduce others by the same author or on the same topic.

GOOD ADVICE

Easing Transitions Between Activities

"No one is in the room but Danae and me when I put her to sleep. I talk to her about bedtime. I brush her teeth, give her a bath, change her clothes, wrap her in a blanket, and hug and kiss her."

—Debbie Dinderman, Texarkana, Texas

"When we end an activity, Benjamin and I say goodbye to it. Even with something as simple as a slide, we say 'Bye-bye slide' when we're finished playing with it. He usually walks away fine when we do this."

—Sheryl Kingstone, Framingham, Massachusetts

extra love and attention during times of change. TLC helps buffer the stress of the change.

Whatever you do, don't attempt to reassure your child by making promises that you can't follow through on. It's unfair to tell him that he can have a certain kind of food at a restaurant if you're unsure whether it's served (unless you bring it along). Likewise, saying "Don't worry, I'll tuck you in at bedtime" when you know you won't be home on time is not something a 1-year-old will soon forget. But neither should you worry that straying from the established pattern of your child's life will cause long-lasting upset. A routine that's disrupted for a spell can easily be put back into place when the conditions are more suitable. All routines should be flexible.

Household Rhythms

There's one kind of routine that many parents fail to consider at this age—or rather, that they do for their child almost unthinkingly: household chores. Certainly with a 15-month-old, you're more concerned with keeping her clothes on her

Letting your child help you with an interesting task helps him learn and sows the seeds of responsibility.

GOOD ADVICE
Helping Around the House

"When Kaytlyn, 18 months, makes a mess with her toys, she has to clean it up. I hand her each toy and tell her where to put it away. It may sound like it takes more time than it's worth, but she's learning. She claps and says 'Yeah!' when she knows she's done it right."

—Melissa Cajeton, North Charleston, South Carolina

"Aidan, 27 months, really enjoys unloading the dishwasher. I take out the sharp knives and put the silverware tray on the floor. He hands me the spoons and forks so I can put them in the drawer."

—Dawn Gold, Seattle, Washington

"Madison is 2½. She helps me set the table. It looks messy, but she loves it. I'll say, 'Do Mommy a favor and put this plate at Daddy's place.' I give her just one plate at a time. Then I give her forks and spoons."

—Lisa Kent, Tucker, Georgia

body than with teaching her to pitch them in a hamper. But as she approaches 18 to 24 months, she's ready to begin taking part in the household routine. In fact, the sooner you start giving a child responsibilities appropriate to her developmental level, the more she'll come to think of them as normal, no different from eating or sleeping.

Bear in mind, however, that for toddlers the word *chore* is to be used only loosely. You can't expect a child this age to do these things regularly, nor should you enforce them as assigned responsibilities yet. That's not a good idea until your child approaches kindergarten or the early elementary-school years. Your toddler is ready to begin to learn about such tasks, nothing more.

Toddlers love to imitate adults. In their play, for example, they love to cook at a stove and put babies to bed. They can mimic you in realistic ways as well. When milk spills, don't rush to mop it up yourself. Give your child some paper towels. You'll certainly need to finish the job, but not before you've imparted a fun lesson in taking responsibility and bestowed a sense of pride and accomplishment. The key is to make these things fun—not tasks. Don't expect your child to execute them perfectly, or even to finish a job.

True Toddler Tales

"How Routines Helped Us Weather a Move"

"**T**he whole day was pretty predictable," says Kathy Barron of life before a move to Boise, Idaho. Kathy would go to preschool with Jake, then 5, and Eric, then 2, and stay in Eric's class awhile. The school provided a regular schedule of snacks, naps, and indoor and outdoor play. On the days that Kathy, a nurse, had to work, her husband, Jeff, picked up the boys from school in the midafternoon. Afterward they'd take an outing to somewhere, perhaps a park, and dine at five-thirty. Then came a bath, reading time, and a nine o'clock bedtime.

Before their move, Kathy and Jeff prepared the boys by talking about the new area and by reading books about moving. They told them about the house they were going to build and the new friends they would make.

To ease the move, they tried to reestablish their old routines. Eric took naps and went to bed on the same schedule, with the same tape player he used in his old home. They spent time at playgrounds and toy stores similar to those in their old town. At first Eric didn't attend a school and Kathy didn't work, so she thought up new activities for the two of them. Although he was scared by so much that was unfamiliar, it took Eric only a few weeks to adjust to his new life.

Kathy's tips for easing a move:

- **Plan ahead.** "I wish I'd had more information about schools and other community resources before we moved. I could have set up schedules closer to what my boys were used to at home."
- **Be organized.** "I couldn't find certain things that weren't packed well. It took days to find the pots and pans, for example, so we couldn't cook at home right away. That didn't promote a family atmosphere."
- **Make time to spend with your child.** "When Mom and Dad are running around stressed about moving-related errands, it's easy to forget to sit down and tune in to your children."
- **Stick to the usual pacing of the day.** "A routine was comforting to Eric because it was something he could predict when so much else was unpredictable."

More things toddlers can do:

- ✔ Water a garden
- ✔ Pick up playthings
- ✔ Help you use a small broom and dustpan
- ✔ Help cook (cutting out cookies, adding ingredients to a pot)
- ✔ Help feed a dog or cat
- ✔ Dust (unbreakable objects, of course)
- ✔ Help empty nonbreakable items from the dishwasher
- ✔ Put napkins on the table
- ✔ Wash her own hands
- ✔ Begin to feed himself
- ✔ Begin to dress herself

Feeding Your Toddler

Nutrition Needs Now

Nutrition and nurturing are deeply intertwined. Feeding a baby is a source of deep pleasure for most parents—snuggling to breast-feed, offering a warm bottle as you rock in a chair, those cute little baby food jars, the eager, O-shaped mouth awaiting the next spoonful of brightly colored mush, the first messy graham-cracker smile. Toddlerhood brings plenty of changes to mealtimes, including more food choices, the advent of self-feeding, and newly defined tastes and opinions. It's little wonder, in the face of developments like these, that your onetime pleasure over the primal act of feeding may ripen into worry, frustration, and the occasional standoff. In fact, more feeding problems are thought to begin during the second year of life than at any other point in childhood.

The first question most parents have, once their child's food intake is no longer easily measured in bottles and jars, is how much is enough? The answer is less than you may think. The first year of life was one big growth spurt. Your child nearly tripled her birth weight in her first 12 months—gaining about a pound a month—and doubled in height. But the

WHAT IF...

My toddler wants to nurse in public?

Breast-feeding in a restaurant, at a shop, or on a playground becomes a challenge as your child gets bigger, mostly because toddlers are so darn distractible. Also, some moms who never thought twice about lifting their shirts in public places for a baby begin to grow more self-conscious when the hungry child is doing the lifting for them.

If you don't want to nurse away from home, tell your child you'll nurse as soon as you can find a more private place. Then follow through. Distracting your child with a song or game buys a little bit of time. Some mothers create a special word or signal for their child to discreetly use instead of screaming, "I want Mommy juice!"

pace of growth drops off now, and so, correspondingly, does a toddler's appetite.

By the time your toddler is playing with his meal more than eating it, he's finished. Parents often overestimate how much food kids this age really need.

What should a toddler eat? A balanced diet can be elusive at this age. Good luck, for example, trying to orchestrate meals that are carefully constructed from all the food groups. If you have a hearty, curious eater who welcomes whatever you set before him, thank your lucky stars. Most toddlers' appetites are more whimsical. Your child may insist on a cheese sandwich every day for lunch and dinner for weeks at a time. He may refuse all fruits. He may devour something one day and sneer at it the next. He may go through a growth spurt and eat like a lumberjack, then seem to live on air for the next few weeks. These tendencies have little to do with your own modeling—even gourmands have kids who eat nothing but American cheese on white bread.

Relax. Studies show that if they are offered a healthful variety of foods, toddlers have a remarkable innate ability to self-select just what, and how much, they need to survive. In fact, their total intake may veer from a few hundred calories at one meal to as many as a thousand at the next. What your child consumes over the course of a week or two is more important than the nutrient breakdown of a single meal, or a single day's meals. The right balance averages out on its own.

What follows is a description of a toddler's overall nutritional needs, in very general terms. Keep in mind that the typical toddler serving is much smaller than that of an adult. The general rule of thumb is that a serving equals about one tablespoon of each food per year of age (that works out to one tablespoon for a 12-month-old, two and a half tablespoons for a 30-month-old).

Dairy. No more than twenty-four ounces of milk in twenty-four hours, or about two to three cups per day, for 800 total milligrams of calcium per day.

MILESTONE

USING A SPOON (12-15 months)

If you haven't already given your child her own spoon, now's the time. The best type is molded plastic (soft for teethers), with a short, wide handle (for easy grasping). Use two spoons at first—one for her to hold and one for you. Give her the opportunity to feed herself. Don't expect her to get the food in— or even near—her mouth at first. But let her work at it awhile, and then help her finish up. Yes, some food will be wasted this way. By about 24 months, though, she'll get the hang of it. (A fork isn't necessary until closer to 2. Start with a child-sized, plastic scooper shape with rounded, not sharp, tines.)

Practice makes perfect when it comes to mastering flatware.

Most children switch to whole milk (from breast milk or formula) at 12 months, or begin to supplement breast milk with whole milk. By age 2, your pediatrician may advise a switch to milk with a lower fat content, but don't do so unless you're so advised, as this recommendation depends on the individual child's overall health and diet. Remember that calcium is found in cheese, yogurt, and ice cream, too. Some toddlers can be cajoled to drink milk to which a little chocolate syrup has been added—not harmful in small amounts. Pediatricians recommend that toddlers' milk not be served in a bottle, to prevent overfeeding.

Proteins. Two to three servings per day in the first year, then four to five servings. Options include meats, fish, eggs, cheese, tofu, and beans. A serving may be less than one-fourth of an adult-sized portion, or about one ounce.

Fruits and vegetables. Three to five servings a day. Remember that fruits and vegetables can be mixed into other foods, too (such as berries in muffins or grated zucchini in spaghetti sauce). Limit juice to eight ounces per day (which can be diluted). Any 100 percent juice is fine, but don't rely on juice alone for this food group. Whole fruits and vegetables provide added fiber and vitamins. Note that some orange juice brands have added calcium, helpful if your child dislikes milk or cheese.

Grains. Three servings daily in the first year, then four servings. Includes breads, hot or cold cereals, teething biscuits, crackers, rice, and pasta. Serve healthier 100 percent whole-wheat products as much as possible to orient your child's taste to them.

Fats. Roughly 10 percent of daily total. Includes butter, oils, and peanut butter. (Spread peanut butter thinly, as it can be a choking hazard—it's not recommended for the under-2 set.)

Most of these foods should be chopped, mashed, or pureed versions of what the rest of the family eats. You may also use stage-three baby foods, although as they get more teeth, many older babies suddenly rebel against anything they can't pick up themselves, which means the mushy stuff is out. It's useful to keep on hand a few jars of the toddler-style baby foods, especially if you don't cook a lot. Their textures are like adult foods and provide variety in a pinch.

Should you give your child a daily vitamin? That's a call for your pediatrician to make. In general, it may not be necessary if your child enjoys a wide variety of foods and is a good eater. If, like many toddlers, however, your child is finicky, goes on food jags, or refuses a food group (such as vegetables, fruit, or milk) altogether, a multivitamin can provide a nutritional safety net. Select a brand formulated for children. A younger toddler needs liquid vitamins. After about 18 months (depending on how many teeth your child has),

CHECKLIST
Fifteen Healthful, Easy Snacks

- Rice cakes
- Fruit-filled cereal bar
- Wheat crackers and cheese
- Graham crackers with peanut butter
- Goldfish-shaped cheese crackers
- Cheese sticks
- Cold cereal
- Shredded apples, sliced bananas, berries
- Soft, ripe avocado or tomato slices
- Pretzels
- Hard-boiled egg
- Quick bread: banana, pumpkin, zucchini (or make it in muffin cups)
- Cooked broccoli with dip
- Soft-cooked carrot sticks
- Yogurt

a chewable kids' vitamin may be prescribed. In addition to having the proper nutritional composition, fun colors, flavors, and shapes ensure they'll be eaten. Because they can look like candy, however, avoid poisonings from overconsumption by storing all vitamins out of reach of children.

MILESTONE

FROM HIGH CHAIR TO BIG CHAIR (18-30 months)

The broad age range for this milestone reflects the myriad of tables and chairs available. Between 1½ and 2 years is a good time to bring a toddler to the table proper. Your child sees you sitting in a big chair and wants to join in. Since many ordinary kitchen chairs are too low for a young child to comfortably reach the table, many parents use a booster seat. Choose one that straps securely to the chair. Or you can bring the high chair right over to the table (without the tray) and use it until age 3 or beyond.

Smart Mealtime Routines

In theory, things are supposed to get simpler now that your child can help feed himself. Yet fretting over food is a leading concern that parents bring to their pediatricians during their child's second and third years of life. Why the disparity? Because parents, in their concern about rearing a healthy child, tend to fixate on this very visible, controllable part of life. Keep telling yourself: *My toddler won't starve or suffer malnutrition.* Let his own natural appetite be his feeding guide. If you focus on making eating pleasant and avoid power struggles, everything else should be, well, a piece of cake.

Here are the golden rules of feeding toddlers:

Feed 'em when they're hungry. It's obvious but important. Don't try to teach a toddler patience when it comes to food. This is not the right time for such a lesson; the only thing she'll learn is that you're ignoring her basic needs. If it's close to a meal, give her a quick nutritious snack—such as a piece of bread or a bowl of applesauce—to tide her over until everyone sits down together.

Exception: If your child is continually hungry just twenty or thirty minutes after a meal has ended, she's not eating enough at meals and may be relying on snacks too much. Try making her wait until the next set snacktime or meal to curb the habit.

> ## WHAT IF...
>
> ### The only seat my child wants at meals is in my lap?
>
> **S**nuggling is delicious—within limits. It's neither comfortable, convenient, nor necessary at the table. Build the association that your child's chair (or high chair), not your lap, is the place to sit when eating. Be consistent about putting her back in her seat. Don't let her sit on your lap during snack time, either. Consider the possible causes of the habit: Sometimes a persistent lap cat is trying to tell you that she needs more one-on-one time. If you've been absent or particularly busy, try to make up for it in other attentive ways.

Introduce the idea of regular feeding times. You shouldn't ignore a toddler who's spiraling out of control because his little tummy is howling with hunger. At the same time, for your own sanity and for your child's benefit, establish a feeding schedule of three meals and two or three snacks, all at about the same times every day. Eating on a predictable schedule helps pace a toddler's energy and underscores a sense of security. A child is also more likely to eat well at meals and try new foods if he hasn't been snacking all day. For safety's sake, serve food at the table or high chair. This also prevents the habit of your child noshing while doing something else.

Don't isolate 'em. Although your child's small tummy may not be in sync with the rest of the family's, that's no excuse for serving him all of his meals segregated from everyone else. He should be seated with the family for breakfast, lunch, and dinner. Even if he's had his meal earlier, let him have dessert or a snack while everyone else eats. By dining together, you're modeling a healthy attitude toward a variety of foods, as well as basic table manners. Another good reason to start the habit now: Studies have shown that adolescents who eat five or more dinners a week with their parents tend to be better adjusted, do better in school, and are less involved with drugs than their peers who don't eat with their family. It's the companionship and communication of this nightly routine that appear to make the difference.

Make mealtimes something to look forward to. Talk, tell stories, ask questions. No yelling, criticisms, radio, or TV—not even any *Sesame Street* videos "to keep him quiet." That can come *after* the meal. Don't, however, expect a 1- or 2-year-old to sit at the table as long as everyone else. When he begins to get restless, turn him loose.

Keep portions small. Little bits at a time are more appealing for a child, not to mention less messy for you. If your child wants seconds, let her ask for them. Never demand that your child join the "clean-plate club" (to which you may have belonged as a youngster). Also outdated: cutesy here-comes-the-airplane gimmicks. They might work to get an easily distracted diner to finish a few more bites, but once she's signaling that she's full, don't force more. Cajoling by hand-feeding is also time-consuming for you and doesn't promote self-feeding.

Nor should you restrict portions. By only giving your child "this much and no more," you risk fueling an insecurity about having enough to eat, which can backfire into overeating. Unsure when he'll get to fill up again, the child begins to stuff himself whenever the opportunity for unrestricted dining presents itself. Left to their own devices, toddlers are naturally able to stop when they're full, even in the middle of dessert.

Don't push, but don't stop trying, either. If your child turns up her nose at a new food, don't give up on it. Serve it again a week later. Some toddlers must see a food two dozen times or more before it becomes familiar enough to be acceptable. (The opposite is true, too: Sometimes a well-liked food inexplicably loses favor.) Realize, too, that some children are more generally averse to all things new. At a later meal, offer another tiny

---

PARENT TIP

It's Only a Meal

Probably the biggest mistake parents make concerning kids and food is trying to exert too much control. Here's a list of what food should never be used for: rewards, punishment, bribes, consolation, demonstrations of love. A meal is a meal is a meal. Nothing more, nothing less. When we make a bigger deal out of feeding a child than is warranted, the usual result is tension, power struggles, and a sense of failure. Squelch feelings of guilt or rejection about the way your child chooses to eat. Don't take it personally. It's not a reflection on you (no matter what your own mother says). Don't impose your own value system on food, either. If you're preoccupied with your weight, expect your child to eat like a grown-up, or make up arbitrary rules about meals ("You must clean your plate" or "If you eat this, you'll make me happy"), your child will pick up on these loaded signals. Bite your tongue.

portion of it. The food may have grown strange because the child hasn't seen it in a while, or it could just be a phase. Vegetable hating—the sudden dislike of anything green or orange that grows in the ground—commonly sprouts up at age 2 and can last for several years. Don't insist. Just keep serving them in a low-key way. Be prepared to admit temporary failure.

Let 'em try to feed themselves. By the time your child is a year old, he should have his own spoon, plate, bowl, and sippy cup. Plastic or melamine dishes eliminate the fear of breakage, and decorated children's dinnerware sends the message that meals are enjoyable. For very young toddlers, dispense with the plate (which is liable to get overturned) and put food directly on the high chair tray, or in a dish that has suction cups on the bottom.

Certainly there will be some foods that you need to help out with (such as soup). But your days of spooning every single mouthful should be over. It's important to give your child practice in feeding himself. At every meal, provide lots of finger foods cut or broken into easy-to-grasp morsels. Most kids naturally gravitate to such foods. Don't insist that he use a spoon or fork to eat foods that are normally consumed this way.

Ignore the mess. Toddlers are naturally sloppy eaters. They overturn the fork before they can successfully navigate it into the mouth. They dump. They drop. They smear. They squash. Expect this. In fact, remind yourself that making like a scientist or a modern artist at the table is a good sign. Messy self-feeders are practicing their dexterity and learning to love food as they explore it with their hands. Not least, they're having fun, which is always good.

Make cleanup easier by using bibs or smocks that are larger than those left over from baby days. Look for bibs made of molded plastic, waterproof backings, and styles that cover the entire shoulder. Cover the floor below the high

---

WHAT IF...

My child flips out when his cookie breaks in two and refuses to eat it?

The waste and the irrationality drive parents berserk. But there's a developmental reason behind your child's penchant for perfection. A toddler holds very definite notions about things. A cookie, for example, is round and whole. A graham cracker is rectangular. Any deviation is very upsetting because the child is such a literal thinker. He can only see the object as whole or broken. This is different from a 4-year-old, who is capable of seeing the cookie in a more multifaceted way— "yes, it's broken, but it's also chocolate and my favorite kind and tastes great with a cup of milk, and it will break when I bite it anyway." A baby will mouth anything you give her. But the fact that a toddler sees only that the cookie is broken is a sign of her early consciousness of how things are supposed to be.

chair with yesterday's newspaper or a washable plastic splat mat.

Set limits, however. When your child is clearly finished eating and is just swishing or tossing food for the heck of it, end the meal.

Let 'em eat what they like. Nobody likes everything. Respect your child's individual food preferences, which she begins to establish now. If she likes eggs, serve them for dinner occasionally, or in egg sandwiches or as French toast. If she refuses all vegetables, try concealing them in omelets, spaghetti sauce, or soups. Or if a plain bowl of cereal is preferred for dinner, so be it. One trick to gaining a child's acceptance of a food is to give her some ownership of it. Let her help prepare it or pick it out at the store. And if her particular palate rejects everything you serve? Don't cook an entirely separate meal. But do offer an easy-to-fix alternative, such as a PB&J sandwich or a bowl of yogurt and fruit.

Don't use food as a reward. Many parents swear by M&M candies as incentives for potty training. Or they promise checkout-line candy at the grocery store if the child behaves well during a shopping excursion. The treat is well intentioned and the effect, at least in the short term, may be great. But by using food as a reward or bribe, you're setting up an association with food as a source of comfort, praise, and love. Better: Offer treats "just because."

Because they're so tactile, toddlers love foods they can pick up with their fingers.

Snack Time: The Favorite Meal

You can't expect a toddler to be satisfied on three squares a day. Their stomachs are small and their energy needs are constant. That's why snacking is an important part of the toddler diet. Your challenge is to make it healthful.

Don't, however, let your child snack at will all day long. That bad habit can lead to lack of appetite at mealtimes, tooth decay, and obesity. Provide one snack between breakfast and lunch, and another between lunch and dinner. Some kids may also need to eat before bed. Make this last snack light and digestible, so as to not interfere with sleep. (Milk and a cookie or some cereal is good.) If heavy snacking becomes a habit, reexamine what and how much your child eats at meals. It may be that he likes the snack food

CHECKLIST

Fun Finger Foods

Offering foods that your child can pick up easily promotes self-feeding. Need some ideas? Try these:

- Fun-shaped or colored cooked pasta (bow ties, rotini, radiatore—)
- String cheese
- Cubed meatloaf
- Quarter-size pancakes, or large pancakes rolled up
- Grilled cheese sandwiches cut in finger lengths
- Steamed broccoli "trees" (the florets)
- Green beans (canned or well-cooked fresh)
- Grilled-ground-beef-and-mashed-potato balls
- Large-curd cottage cheese
- Hard-boiled egg or deviled egg
- Orange or pear slices with yogurt dip
- Steamed carrot spears or cauliflower with cheese dip

better than the meals, or simply that he's not eating enough at meals.

In general, a snack should be lighter and smaller than a full meal but similarly nutritious. Snacks should also be served at the table. Kids who eat in front of the TV are more likely to grow up to be sedentary and overweight than those who don't indulge in this habit, studies show. Don't start bad habits early. Of course, sometimes snacks on the go are downright handy. A cracker or cookie that keeps a toddler momentarily occupied in the grocery store or in his stroller can be a lifesaver. Stash a few in resealable plastic bags in your purse, car, and diaper bag for just such emergencies.

What snacks should you feed your child? Make them interesting and fun. Snack time shouldn't mean one dry teething biscuit every afternoon at three. But remember that *snack* and *junk* aren't synonymous. In fact, a good snack for a toddler might be indistinguishable from one of his meals—soup or a half a sandwich is just as good as crackers or a sliced apple. Sweets are okay, too, in moderation. Choose cookies or breads with nutrition that's been

True Toddler Tales

"My Adventuresome Eater"

Ander Thompson is a rare toddler—he relishes new and healthful foods. "He's always tried anything we put in front of him," says his mother, Dawn, who lives in Aurora, Colorado. Among the 2-year-old's favorites: lemons, limes, pickles, spicy salsa, waffles, yogurt, and dark rye bread.

Ander has sampled Mexican, Thai, and Ethiopian fare. He even eats sushi (though not with raw fish, because of the bacteria risk). "If he doesn't like something, he'll make faces or pick out what he does like," says Dawn. "But usually he'll at least try it once. And when he finds something he enjoys eating, he flaps his arms about and says, 'More!' "

Dawn's tips for raising an exploratory eater:

- **Start early.** "Introduce a wide range of different foods as soon as your child can eat them."
- **Be creative.** "Experiment with textures and tastes. Or try disguising the food. Try it cooked, raw, or in a casserole. Presentation doesn't matter much to a toddler."
- **Stick with fresh.** "Fresh vegetables have more flavor, without the sugar and sodium of processed foods."
- **Don't be obsessed.** "We try to stay away from fried foods and limit fat and sugar. But my son doesn't eat only healthy things. If you don't give him something like sugar, he will find it somewhere else. It's okay sometimes."

sneaked in, such as those that contain oatmeal, carrots, or figs. Take your child's overall nutritional balance into account when planning snacks. If he hasn't had much calcium, then cheese cubes might be a good idea. If he wolfed green beans at lunch, a few Oreos with milk won't hurt at bedtime.

What about junk food? To many adults, chips, pretzels, and candy bars are the definition of the word *snack*. Dole these empty calories out sparingly to a young child, though. You don't need to blacklist them entirely. (Exception: Avoid hard candy or trail mixes with nuts, which can cause choking.) In fact, there is some evidence that children who are completely denied "forbidden" foods often discover them with a vengeance eventually. It's better to okay the occasional treat that is less than a paragon of perfect nutrition. Just don't overdo it.

CHECKLIST
Foods That Can Cause Choking

Toddlers should *not* be served the following:

✔ Whole grapes

✔ Raisins

✔ Hot dogs, unless diced or cut lengthwise in thin pieces

✔ Raw carrots (unless grated or thinly julienned)

✔ Raw celery

✔ Chewing gum

✔ Popcorn

✔ Hard round candy (sourballs, gum balls, malted milk balls)

✔ Caramels

✔ Nuts (including peanuts)

✔ Thickly spread peanut butter (or spoonfuls of it)

Parents' Common Complaints

The way children eat drives many parents crazy. Yet, ironically, it's rarely cause for concern or alarm. Psychologists often suggest that grown-ups get so caught up in food fights because food is an integral part of nurturing. We tend to take eating quirks personally. We also worry about our children growing properly and developing lifelong good habits. Not least, feeding times come so often—and are so visible, so messy!—that one can hardly avoid becoming obsessed. Whatever the motivation, you're not alone if you wonder and worry as you watch your toddler eat (or, more typically, not eat).

Some often-seen problems and how to handle them:

The child who doesn't eat anything. *Why it happens:* Toddlers don't require many calories. It's normal for their appetite to drop off as compared with infancy. They're also maddeningly slow eaters. Consider the serving sizes that you offer as well. If you put too much on your child's plate, she may pick off just what she needs, leaving what looks like a great amount. What looks like nothing to you is often plenty to meet a 1-year-old's nutritional needs. And some kids snack so frequently between meals that they are simply not hungry at mealtimes.

What you can do: Consider your child's overall food consumption rather than getting hung up on how much passes his lips at a single meal. If he truly

69

WHAT IF...

My child still uses a bottle?

A 2-year-old brandishing a bottle is a common enough sight. But most pediatricians and the American Academy of Pediatric Dentists strongly recommend weaning a child off the bottle by the first birthday. Why? Falling asleep with a bottle is the number-one cause of tooth decay in kids under age 3. An overdependence on liquids, which are easily taken by bottle, can also interfere with a toddler's natural need to consume more solid foods, impeding growth. Drinking too much milk can cause obesity and anemia. Anyway, it's much easier to break the bottle habit early (between 10 and 14 months) than nearer to age 2, when the habit is even further ingrained.

To break the bottle habit, you can either gradually phase it out, or switch cold turkey to cups.

To wean your child from the bottle, start by introducing your child to a cup. Choose an easy-to-grip or double-handled no-spill type. Some parents like to make the switch cold turkey, rounding up all the bottles and tossing them on a given day and from then on serving all liquids in the cup. Don't be wishy-washy or permit relapses, though, which prolong the switch.

Another tactic is to eliminate one bottle-feeding every few days until you've completely shifted to the cup. Serve the bottle only in the high chair—no wandering around with it and sipping at will. This makes the bottle far less interesting.

refuses to eat even one bite, take a hard look at his snacking habits. Cut back on the frequency or amount of snacks, or serve more fruits and vegetables then, rather than starches such as crackers, which can be very filling. (On the other hand, if he eats healthful snacks, there's no harm in continuing the pattern.) Remember, too, that your doctor monitors your child's growth at checkups. If your child is growing steadily, he's obviously consuming enough.

The picky eater. *Why it happens:* Fussiness is a natural part of toddler development. Some kids are simply more extreme than others, perhaps as a function of their inborn temperament. It's also a way of exerting control. Some indifferent diners are simply imitating their parents' quirks. Picky eating can manifest itself in a thousand different ways. One child won't eat his potatoes if they touch his peas. Another eats only yellow cheese, never white. A third refuses anything that seems to have "ingredients," such as visible bits of onion or parsley. A fourth child might have all of these quirks.

What you can do: Have a sense of humor—and patience. Respect your child's whims within reason. Don't get into power struggles by insisting a fussy diner taste something he doesn't want to. Nor is it usually effective to go to great lengths to tempt tempestuous taste buds. If you find yourself telling your child how hard you worked to make a particular dish, for example, or laboriously cutting pancakes and sandwiches into alluring shapes with a cookie cutter, you're probably trying too hard. Some picky eaters outgrow the tendency by the preschool years, but many diehards will remain this way their entire lives.

The food jag. *Why it happens:* A toddler doesn't hold the same general culinary outlook as an adult. We savor flavors and textures, relish variety, get enthused about new recipes. To a child, food is what they eat when they

Don't worry if your child is stuck on only one kind of food.

are hungry and what they play with on their plate when they are not. Repetition is comforting. For some kids, this translates to pasta seven nights a week, for months on end. Their inflexibility can also be a form of rebellion: "This is what I like and you can't make me change."

What you can do: Nothing. You can't make a child eat. Serve what he likes. Embellish it, if you can—serve some sauce with the noodles, on the side, for the child to sample as he likes. Offer foods that have a similar texture to the favorite; for example, a child who adores applesauce may also enjoy yogurt or oatmeal. Eventually—and yes, it may be many months—your child will move away from the jag, possibly on to another one. This, too, shall pass.

GOOD ADVICE
Coping with Eating Quirks

"I give Jacob, 22 months, one thing at a time on his plate. He's not a big eater, and if he sees a plate filled with food, he gets overwhelmed. Jacob likes seaweed and it has a lot of nutrients, so I give it to him."

—*Wendy Hart, Mississauga, Ontario*

"We give Meredith, 16 months, a smaller portion of what the rest of the family is eating. If she won't eat it, she has to wait five minutes before I make her a peanut-butter-and-jelly sandwich. She now tries almost everything."

—*Amanda Bluemel, Bakersfield, California*

"When Lauren, now 2, won't eat something, my first instinct is not to bother again. But when I continue to offer the same food, almost every time she eventually comes to like it."

—*Elise Myers, Seattle, Washington*

"I've learned to present the food in different ways so Bonnie, who's 2, doesn't get bored. If I'm serving a cheese sandwich, one day I will cut it into strips and the next time I'll cut it into triangles. Once I told Bonnie that a plate of spaghetti was a bunch of worms. Then I asked her to pretend she was a baby bird. She ate it all."

—*Elizabeth Margolis, Bethesda, Maryland*

The indecisive diner. *Why it happens:* Mostly this is a bad habit that's been reinforced. You make meatloaf. Your child wrinkles his nose. You say, "How about macaroni and cheese?" He agrees. But then, when the macaroni is set before him, he makes a face again and insists he doesn't want it. Then one of you makes a third suggestion, and you head back to the stove. He might eat this third item, or he might toss out yet another culinary whim.

What you can do: Offer limited choices. If the child balks at the meatloaf everyone else is eating, provide a single easy-to-prepare alternative that you know he likes. If he balks again, say, "I see you're not hungry," and end the meal. Remember, your child will not starve.

The vegetable hater. *Why it happens:* Vegetables are an acquired taste. Most are not naturally as sweet or flavorful as items in other food groups. Children tend to avoid some or all of them at one time or another, especially at age 2.

What you can do: Get sneaky. Serve foods that conceal vegetables. Examples: omelets with spinach or finely diced mushrooms or green peppers, spinach lasagna, broccoli soufflé, meatloaf (with diced vegetables or baby-food purees), eggplant parmigiana, pumpkin muffins, sweet potato pie, tomato bread, chocolate cake made with grated zucchini, carrot cake or cookies, or blends of carrot and fruit juice. Try finely grated yellow squash in spaghetti sauce. Make vegetables fun, too, by serving them with yogurt or cheese-based dips. Call broccoli "trees" and cooked carrots "pennies."

Experiment with form. If boiled potatoes are a dud, maybe mashed potatoes will be a hit. Take care not to overcook. Broccoli, for example, tastes much less bitter when it's still got some crunch. Serve pureed soups or vegetable-soup broth in an easy-to-handle cup, rather than a bowl. Don't forget that pizza, stews, fresh salsa, and casseroles can contain vegetables, too. Above all, don't force the issue. A toddler who refuses to eat a single vegetable can get plenty of comparable nutrients from fruits and vitamins.

HOT TOPIC

Fat Control

American adults have come to see fat as the enemy. We look for "fat-free" on food labels, count fat grams, and strive to adhere to health guidelines that say our fat consumption should be limited to 30 percent of our daily calories. But applying that thinking to a toddler is a mistake, and very possibly dangerous.

Small children need fat for their bodies and brains to grow. In fact, before age 2, you don't need to limit fat intake at all. That means serving whole milk when your child has finished with formula (usually around 12 months)—not fat-free or low-fat. And even from 2 to 3, you need only be aware of your child's overall fat intake. Consult your child's doctor before making any significant dietary changes. A skinny, finicky eater, for example, may benefit from continuing on whole milk after age 2, rather than switching automatically to fat-free.

It is a good idea, however, to limit saturated fat (the kind in coconut and palm oils, store-bought cakes, butter, and cheeses made with whole milk or cream) to about 10 percent of the daily total. Cook with polyunsaturated fats (vegetable oil) or monounsaturated fats (olive oil, canola oil). Limit fast foods such as french fries, hamburgers, and fried chicken. Avoid feeding a toddler products containing the fat substitute olestra (Olean), which may cause side effects such as bloating or gastric distress.

NOT TO WORRY
Sugar and Hyperactivity

Too many sweets and sodas pose plenty of drawbacks to a young child's diet. They have no nutritional value, cause cavities, and tend to make a small tummy too full to take in the good foods it needs. But there's one accusation of which the sweet stuff has been cleared: Sugar does not cause children to become supercharged with energy. Numerous studies have disproved the sugar-hyperactivity link. Rather, it's more likely that sweets are on hand at times when kids are already pumped up, such as at a birthday party or a holiday. The occasional treat, in moderation, won't adversely affect a child. (Exception: sweets that contain caffeine, such as some sodas, *can* cause jumpiness.)

The dessert lover. *Why it happens:* Many dietitians believe that withholding dessert as a hostage until vegetables and meats are eaten elevates its importance. A child learns that it must be far better than that other stuff. What's more, human beings naturally have a sweet tooth. Kids know what they like.

What you can do: It's best not to use dessert as a threat or reward. That's why some experts advise against insisting a child clean his plate before he can indulge. Better, they say, to place dessert on the high chair right along with the rest of the meal, to equalize the values attached to each food. (Remember that dessert can be nutritious as well as sweet, such as fruit or oatmeal cookies.) On the other hand, dessert *is* a treat, not a dietary necessity. If your child gobbles the dessert and refuses to touch the other foods, set up some rules. Tell a tot who craves dessert that she needs to eat some of her meal first.

The allergy-prone child. *Why it happens:* Food allergies are actually rare. And most of the commonest ones, including milk and eggs, are outgrown by age 5. Just 2 percent of all adults have food allergies. But if your child is vulnerable, such statistics can be of little comfort. The eight most

WHAT IF...

My toddler adores fast-food kids' meals?

While "everything in moderation" is the best guideline for toddler (as well as adult) diets, fast food is one area where it's smart to tilt to the *very* moderate. The main reason is that this is not a particularly healthful habit. So why start it so early? A typical small serving of fries gets more than half its calories from fat. A children's cheeseburger at one restaurant contains a whopping 770 grams of sodium.

That said, a kids' meal every once in a while won't hurt. Opt for milk instead of a carbonated drink, hold the mayo, and split the fries.

common food allergens are responsible for 90 percent of allergic reactions: peanuts, other tree nuts (almonds, pecans), dairy products, soy, wheat, eggs, fish, and shellfish. A child is usually born with a tendency to become sensitive to certain foods, generally having inherited it. Some of these children may be vulnerable to too-early exposure to the allergens in peanut protein or egg whites (usually in infancy), predisposing their bodies to allergic reactions.

What you can do: Don't attempt to diagnose a food allergy on your own. You may be mistaking the child's reactions and depriving him of nutrition. Your child's doctor, sometimes in conjunction with an allergist (some of whom specialize in food), can properly pinpoint a food allergy and suggest the right diet. If you are allergy-prone yourself, get your doctor's advice before introducing that food to your child. Generally, in such cases, the longer you wait before giving the problem food, the better for your child; she may avoid developing a total intolerance for the food and may even be able to eat it without problems when she is older.

Once your child's allergen(s) has been identified, you'll need to be vigilant in anticipating its possible presence in the foods he is served. Many processed foods contain peanuts or peanut oils or milk proteins, for example. Read labels,

HOT TOPIC
How Much Juice?

For toddlers, juice is practically its own food group. They love the stuff. The problem is that drinking too much juice has been shown to reduce the absorption of nutrients and add empty calories to a young child's diet, stunting growth. In excess, it can also cause diarrhea. So how much should you serve? From 6 to 12 months, up to four ounces daily. From 1 to 3 years, up to eight ounces daily—about as much as one bottle or one and a half sippy cups.

Dilute juice with half or one-third water to reduce its sweetness and extend the number of servings. Be sure to check labels carefully. Look for the words "100 percent juice." You'd be surprised how many popular brands and old favorites contain mostly water and sugar. Orange juice is a good choice because it's lower in diarrhea-producing sugar alcohols and an excellent source of natural vitamin C. Fresh and concentrated orange juice are comparably nutritious. Don't overlook tomato juice or blends of carrot and fruit juice. Always choose pasteurized juice, which has undergone a process to kill bacteria. Not all organic juices or brands sold in health-food stores or roadside stands meet this requirement.

ask about food preparation at restaurants, and inform caregivers (at home as well as at day care) about precisely what your child can and cannot eat. A caregiver also needs to be informed how to respond in the event of an allergic reaction. Begin to teach your child which foods are off-limits for him as well.

Fortunately, many nutritional equivalents are available; a child who is allergic to wheat can eat oat- or rice-flour products, and meat and cheese proteins can be used if your child is allergic to eggs.

Sleep Time

Good Sleep Routines

If there were one surefire way to raise a good sleeper, that information would have been handed out at the hospital when your child was born, as part of the biggest public-service campaign ever. Some children doze peacefully right from birth. Others are more restless or susceptible to disruptions in routine, causing bedtime to be more fraught with challenge. It's also common for fairly reliable sleepers to begin having problems for the first time in toddlerhood. Separation anxiety peaks now. So does a growing awareness that the fun goes on in the living room after his good-night kiss. Or the transition to a big bed can mean more independence than he's ready to handle.

Sleep needs vary quite a bit by individual; a child who was a light sleeper as an infant will likely continue that way.

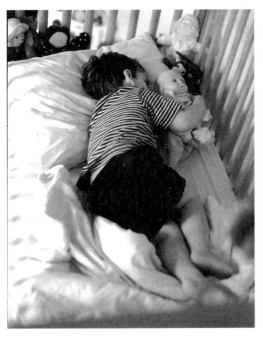

The good news: Virtually all children have the ability to sleep well. It's a matter of instilling healthy sleep habits, understanding what's normal, and persevering with appropriate solutions if problems crop up.

A 12- to 18-month-old needs about thirteen hours of sleep total, including naps. This amount drops off to about eleven to twelve hours by the preschool years (between 3 and 5 years). But these totals are merely averages. There's a fairly broad range of what's normal; some children need more sleep, and some less. (A child's overall tendency usually establishes itself in infancy.) One gauge of whether your child is getting enough sleep: Does she rise on her own or need to be hustled out of bed every morning? There are plenty of reasons to make sure your child gets her quota. Children who get adequate sleep are less likely to have behavior problems and wild mood swings. They have longer attention spans and better memories (long-term and short-term). They're even physically better off, tending to bounce back more quickly from illness and growing larger than do kids who sleep poorly. That's because human growth hormone is produced during sleep.

To help your child get adequate sleep, learn to recognize his sleepiness signals. Not everyone yawns and begins to nod off. Indeed, most toddlers who are overtired seem to wind *up* rather than down. They bounce off the furniture and the walls, run in circles, and persist in annoying behaviors that convince their parents they're just not sleepy. Don't be fooled. Crankiness and full-throttle zaniness by the time most (grown-up) mortals would be sacked out on the sofa are the hallmarks of a worn-out tot. And if your child is always running at full throttle? Then rely on the clock to tell you when he needs to rest.

The best ways to establish good sleep habits:

MILESTONE

FIRST PILLOW (18-30 months)

A child's first pillow should come with his first bed. Babies and young toddlers simply don't need them. Anything big and fluffy in a crib—and that goes for large stuffed animals and down comforters as well as pillows—presents a smothering danger under age 2. In addition, such objects could be used to give the child a boost up and over the side of the crib.

Holding off on a pillow until your child sleeps in a big-kid bed can help make the transition more enticing: "Mom has one, Dad has one, and now I do, too." (In truth, not even adults need pillows for healthy sleep.) Avoid down or feathers, which could cause an allergic reaction. Washable cotton is handy. Avoid fancy trims that could be a choking hazard or scratch the child's face. Some parents prefer small, firm pillows (often called "crib pillows," though they should not be used in a crib), which can be easily transported on trips.

Stick to a consistent schedule. You owe it to your child to make sleep as predictable a part of her day as meals. By toddlerhood, this means that your child should rise, nap, and go to bed at approximately the same times every day. Of course there are going to be exceptions: special occasions, illness, rainy days when she's cooped up, and vacations can all throw a schedule off. It's also natural for the schedule to evolve as your child grows; by 36 months, she needs about one to two hours less total sleep time than at 12 months.

Have a bedtime routine. Don't let your child run around until he collapses in exhaustion. Follow a predictable pattern of events at bedtime. If you don't already have one, 12 months is the perfect age for initiating a bedtime routine, the order of events that signal to your child that sleeping

CHECKLIST
The Making of a Good Bedtime Routine

✓ *Best place:* The child's own room (or bed)

✓ *How long:* Fifteen to thirty minutes

✓ *Best time:* At about the same time every night; give warnings a half hour and ten minutes beforehand

✓ *What works:* A predictable order of events; calming activities (a bath, drinking a cup of milk, brushing teeth, using the potty, reading, listening to soft music); a night-light; a favorite blanket or soft animal to cuddle

✓ *What doesn't work:* Fluctuating bedtimes; roughhousing before bed; leaving on an overhead light; allowing the child to fall asleep in front of the TV; keeping a radio or TV on in the child's room

✓ *How you can tell if your routine is too elaborate:* If you can't explain it to a baby-sitter or you don't have the energy (physical or mental) to face it every night

✓ *How you can tell if it works:* Bedtime is pleasant for everyone

time is coming next. Reading is ideal. It's the reason so many wonderful children's books, from *I Am a Bunny* to *The Big Red Barn*, end with a good-night scene, the main characters tucked into bed. Other good winding-down activities: singing lullabies or reviewing the day and all the interesting things that happened.

WHAT IF...

Teething keeps my child up?

It's a myth that teething causes ongoing sleep problems. A fitful night or two is about the most you could blame on new teeth. On the other hand, chronic ear infections could seriously disrupt sleep. If you've ruled out a behavioral explanation for poor sleep, ask your pediatrician for advice.

Aim for long-term healthy sleep habits. One of the biggest bedtime mistakes parents make is going for the short-term solution just to get through the battle at hand. For example, they rationalize, "Oh, it only takes me five minutes to get up and put the binky back in his mouth," or they lie down next to the child to help him fall asleep. What seems like the quickest route to peace, however, can grow wearying over the long haul. But by then, a firm association has been established for the child, which is all the harder to break.

It's best not to let such associations start. But what if you're already in a bedtime trap—say, your child wakes in the middle of the night because she's lost her pacifier? Stop it now. In some cases you can go cold turkey when making a switch, though the process will take a week or so and probably involve some tears. You can also try to gradually withdraw the habit. One thing's certain: The longer a bad bedtime habit continues, the tougher it will be to break.

More bad bed habits: (1) Letting your child go to sleep with a bottle. Juice and milk can cause cavities; even water is unnecessary and will interfere with later toilet training. Better: a bedtime blanket or beloved toy. (2) Wrestling with Daddy when he gets home late, just as bathtime is about to begin. Substitute quieter play for stimulating play, or let Daddy give the bath and read the bedtime stories. (3) Following an endless bedtime ritual or keeping your child up later than he can handle in a quest to squeeze in more time together. It's hard if you get home at six and bedtime is eight. But toddlers desperately need ten to thirteen hours of rest every twenty-four-hour day. If the child is staying at home in the morning and can (and will) sleep late, this may not be a problem. But if you need to rouse him at six or seven to get out of the house on time, he isn't likely to make up the lost sleep at naptime. That's because the naps he already takes are necessary, and aren't likely to be lengthened as much as would be required to compensate for the missed nighttime sleep.

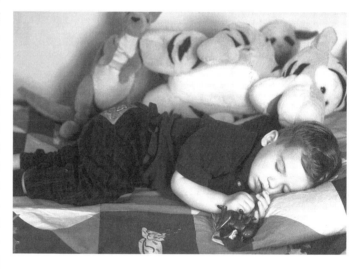

The regular presence of special friends can comfort a reluctant napper.

Encourage comfort objects. You can't force a child to love a certain blanket or bear, but you can build an association between sleep and an object your child already seems fond of. Encourage her to hold the object during your bedtime routine, such as when you cuddle to read at bedtime. It will pick up a little of your scent as well, another plus. Place the toy or blanket in her arms when you tuck her in. The idea is that when she wakes up in the middle of the night, the blanket or doll is the surrogate you, whom she can cuddle and then drift back to sleep with.

Expect changes. Departures from the usual routine can disrupt sleep patterns, whether the change is good (a vacation), bad (an illness), or somewhere in between (the birth of a sibling, toilet training). The silver lining to these relapses: They aren't permanent. Just as a routine can fall apart swiftly, good sleep habits can be quickly relearned. Usually you can get your child back on track again in just a few days.

Parents' Common Complaints

Here's how to handle some typical toddler sleep busters:

Bedtime procrastinating. *Why it happens:* Separation anxiety is the main reason it can take a child so long to say good night, which typically doesn't become a problem until the child moves from a crib to a bed. With a procrastinator, delaying tactics become an art form: "I need water." "One more story." "You forgot to rub my back." "I forgot to tell you you're beautiful, Mommy." Falling asleep alone can be anxiety-provoking. But parents can fuel this behavior by responding eagerly. Maybe you've been working all day and feel conflicted about not having spent enough time together. Or you feel that not responding promptly to every request is somehow neglectful. It can be hard to judge when enough really is enough.

What you can do: Try to identify the cause of the separation anxiety—is it just the normal stage all children go through, or are added stresses in your child's life making him extra clingy? Having consistent bedtime routines helps raise his comfort level.

To nip callbacks in the bud, remind your child ahead of time about the nightly drill: "After we take a bath and brush our teeth, I will read two books and sing you a lullaby. Then I'm going to tuck you in and give you and Mr. Bear a kiss." Before you leave the room, ask if your child needs anything else. That way you can retrieve the inevitable last cup of water without your child roaming around to ask for it. Make consistency your mantra. Stick to the prearranged limits and be firm about them. If you give in to a third book and three songs one night, you can be sure your child will expect a repeat

---

WHAT IF...

My child keeps climbing out of the crib?

The crib mattress should be at its lowest setting. Also check to see if your child is using stuffed animals as a booster, or if he can climb out without help. Clear out all toys and pillows. *If your child can climb out of the crib on his own, however, it's time to move him out of it immediately.* He risks a dangerous fall. Some parenting experts advocate lowering the guard rail to make entrances and exits easier, but this isn't the safest course. Better to switch to a regular bed with a guard rail or a mattress on the floor. Don't put it off.

performance the next. If he is unusually wound up because of something like a holiday or visitors, you can firmly negotiate: "I'll read three books tonight because your birthday is tomorrow, but then we'll go back to just two the next nights because that is what we always do."

Jack-in-the-box roaming after bedtime. *Why it happens:* She's in bed, she's out. Pop her back in bed, and she pops back out again. Making the transition from a crib to a big bed spurs this exasperating behavior. Your child is now free to roam her room, and the rest of the house, at night. It's hard for a toddler to be alone, and the ability to hop out of bed makes wandering irresistible. Your child may also simply be curious about what you're doing, once she realizes she's the only one going to bed.

What you can do: Indulging this behavior tends to prolong it, so it's best to return the child to her bed right away. Be kind but firm: "Everything's going night-night—the birds, the trees, the toys—and now you must sleep, too. I will come back and check on you in ten minutes." Often this promise is reassurance enough for the child to drift off. Every time she gets up, firmly and calmly lead her back to bed. Say, "Back to bed" every time in a matter-of-fact monotone. Over and over. Eventually, she will learn that popping up is no fun after all.

If the problem gets out of hand, gate the child's room at bedtime. (Use a child-safe gate of the same type used to cordon off stairways. Never simply close and lock the door.) Don't think of it as "jailing" your child. Rather, sleep experts recommend this tactic because it's a matter-of-fact statement: "You're too young to have the responsibility to stay in your bed, so I'll do it for you." In essence, the entire room becomes the child's crib. Expect the child to stand at the gate and cry at first. Every five or ten minutes, return to the room and reassure him that everything's all right, but don't relent. It's not fair, and somewhat dangerous, to leave a gate on a child's door at night. Always remove it before you go to bed.

WHAT IF...

I have an early riser who gets up at 5 A.M., ready to play?

You can't force her to sleep longer, of course. Nor is it usually effective to try putting your child to bed later in the hopes that she'll sleep later. Odds are that she'll still rise before dawn but be crankier than usual. You may be able to prolong *your* rest, however. Try placing a few books in (or next to) her bed after she's fallen asleep and before you turn in. If you're lucky, they may occupy her attention for as long as a half hour before she calls for you in the morning. Teach your child how to know when it's time to get up—there will be light outside the window, the alarm clock sounds, and so on. You can also try bringing her to bed with you to snuggle, at which time she may fall back to sleep. If all else fails, start perking the coffee for yourself.

WHAT IF...

My child out-and-out refuses to nap?

It happens. Especially around 2, after a child is well adjusted to a solitary afternoon siesta, he may begin to rebel against it. Fear of separation and the sheer willfulness of this stage fuel this development. You can't force sleep, but you can insist on a quiet time. Make the child's pillow and blanket available if the place you designate for quiet time (a sofa, the floor) is not his own bed. Some days he may not sleep at all. Other times he'll be snoring within minutes of declaring he won't. Some kids outgrow the need for any nap as early as 3.

Middle-of-the-night visits to your bed. *Why it happens:* It's common to wake several times during the night. Everyone does it. But while most children and adults learn to go right back to the land of Nod, perhaps with the aid of a thumb or a beloved blanket, some kids rely on a crutch that's unwittingly reinforced by compliant parents. The child needs Mom's or Dad's very presence to calm himself back to sleep. And the desire to be with you outweighs even that creepy traipse across his room and down the hall.

What you can do: How you react depends on how you feel about a child sleeping in your bed. If you don't mind a size-six foot in your face in the morning, you don't need to do anything.

Sleeping in Mom and Dad's bed is a quick-forming habit, though. If you have reservations, it's worth squelching the habit before it settles in. This is very hard. The first time you find your warm pillow hog curled up between you, it will be tempting to let him stay all night. He's so cute and cuddly! Trouble is, you're apt to find him there the next night, and the next. Unless you're okay with this, it's best to return your child to his own bed immediately, reassuring him that he's safe and cozy there. Keep it quick and sweet. Do this repeatedly if necessary. It may work to let him fall back to sleep with you, and then carry him asleep to his own bed. The risk with that method, however, is that he may grow frightened when he next awakens and finds himself not where he expected to be.

There is a middle ground. You can let the child sleep with you but set certain parameters, such as "You can come in our room once it starts to get light outside" or "You can come in once you hear the clock radio come on." Be flexible, of course. If your child is sick, very frightened, or under significant stress (such as divorce or a move), his need for added security probably outweighs your momentary discomfort. What's important is that *you* are the one deciding where he sleeps.

Ultimately, you want your child to see his own room as a secure haven so that he can fall back to sleep on his own when disturbances strike. This may seem like a tall order, but there are plenty of things you can do to reinforce security. Bedtime rituals set the soothing tone. Beloved stuffed animals,

True Toddler Tales

"Sleeping Through the Night (Finally)"

Pam Clark and David Smith know what it's like to be tired. Really, really tired. Their daughter, Jencie, wouldn't sleep through the night. For the first five months, she slept reasonably well in a bassinet next to their bed. When she was around 8 months, they moved Jencie to a crib in her own room. Then the problems began. "We would put her to bed at nine-thirty, and four hours later Jencie would wake up screaming," says Pam, who lives in Frederick, Maryland.

They tried everything. "We left the lights on. We tried feeding her and singing to her and minimizing outside noises," she says. They tried rocking Jencie to sleep, sometimes as long as half an hour. But as soon as she was lowered into the crib, the howls began anew. "We were tired, frustrated, and at our wits' end," says Pam. "We didn't know what to do next."

Their doctor told them to let her cry it out. "We couldn't do it—it just wasn't for us," Pam says. "Once she cried for three hours." Then they brought Jencie into their bed. Forewarned by their pediatrician that it might lead to problems in getting her to sleep alone (because they were setting up an association that she needed her parents to sleep), they tried it anyway. It worked until she was 1 year old. Then Jencie began to literally push her parents out of bed. "She was an active sleeper who needed room to move around. We realized that she wanted her own bed. But the crib was too confining for her. She would hit her head on the wood edges and get her arms or legs stuck between the rails," Pam says.

Finally they bought a double bed and put soft plastic guard rails around the edges. Jencie also got her own pillow and blanket. "One of us slept in her bed with her for the first week. We were concerned about her rolling off the bed. But the soft gate protected her head without waking her if she hit it." At 19 months, Jencie sleeps from 9:30 P.M. to 7:30 A.M.

Pam's tips to help your toddler sleep through the night:

- **Do what you need to do.** "I wish someone had told me to move her into her own bed sooner, or to try a single mattress on the floor. Friends said that she should stay in a crib until 2½, and I believed it."
- **Trust your instincts.** "Professionals told us the cry-it-out technique didn't work because we didn't try hard enough. It just didn't work for us."
- **Keep trying.** "Figure out what's effective for your child, not just what other people do."
- **Be creative.** "Don't be afraid to try unconventional methods, like letting the child sleep with you or moving her to a bed early."

favorite blankets, night-lights, or a hall light left on provide continual reassurances.

Middle-of-the-night crying. *Why it happens:* Like the middle-of-the-night snuggler, this child wakes regularly throughout the night. All kids do this. But instead of running for your bed, she waits for you to come to him. And how does she get your attention? Simple: by crying and screaming. The habit is reinforced by parents who tend to rush to their child's cries at the first whimper.

What you can do: The persistent middle-of-the-night crier, like his counterpart the middle-of-the-night snuggler, has a sleep association that must be broken. This habit is typically born in infancy. The baby cries, and the parents rock him back to sleep, all through the night. By age 1 or 2, the zombielike parents are so tired of these wee-hours awakenings that they're finally motivated to do something about them.

To change the behavior, don't rush right into a crier's room. Wait. Three, five, even ten minutes won't hurt. Often a child cries out during sleep and then settles back on his own. (Again, this advice is for chronic criers. If night waking is unusual for your child, you should investigate promptly.) After three to ten minutes (whichever interval you can stand) is up, go to your child. Offer reassurance that you are nearby. Give gentle hugs, pat his hair, readjust the blankets, sing a quick lullaby. When the child begins to calm, kiss him good night and leave. Don't go overboard with comfort measures, however. If you rock your child back to sleep for a half hour, or offer a pacifier, you're merely setting up a new sleep association that involves your assistance. Firmly tell him that it's sleeping time now and that you will see him in the morning. He may begin to cry again once you leave the room. Repeat the process. Gradually lengthen the amount of time you're away.

PARENT TIP

Don't Send 'Em to Their Room

Avoid using a child's bed or crib in connection with punishment. You want your child to have pleasant associations with these places, not punitive ones, so he'll go there willingly at bedtime.

Yes, it's grueling. Yes, it's a variation of the cry-it-out techniques often prescribed for getting babies to sleep through the night. If you're thinking, "Oh, I could never do that," then you may not be as sleep-deprived as you think. If you don't mind constant wakings, it's your prerogative to let them continue. But by 12 months, there's no medical or developmental reason for a child to disrupt the entire household (or the one beleaguered parent who gets up)

HOT TOPIC

The Family Bed

Most parents come to an opinion on this topic during the first year of life. Either you like sleeping together with your child, or you don't. Still, the issue crops up anew at several points in toddlerhood, such as when your 12-month-old begins having trouble sleeping through the night or your 24-month-old flees his new big-kid bed to come cuddle with you.

Should the family bed continue in toddlerhood (or beyond)? Those who like to sleep *en famille* find the custom provides another opportunity to bond with their child. They don't see any reason to be separated from their children day or night. Advocates believe that the family bed fosters a child's sense of security and, in turn, helps him develop trust and strong self-esteem.

Though co-sleeping is a convenience when breast-feeding a young baby, opinions are sharply divided about whether all-night access to the breast is necessary for a 2-year-old. There is also disagreement about whether co-sleeping creates a dependency in the child. (What happens at night when you have to be away, for example? Can the child comfort herself back to sleep?) Also on the potential downside is the quality of sleep that everyone receives. Finally, some parents see their bed as their refuge, the night hours as theirs alone (except in a crisis)—an attitude that's understandable, given how demanding daytime with a toddler can be.

Whether three's company or a crowd in bed depends on many factors.

Whatever you decide, it's important that both parents are comfortable. If one of you finds co-sleeping stressful, that tension will carry over into the waking hours. Think through when, and how, you plan to have your child make the transition to her own bed.

If you feel it's time for a child who slept with you as a baby to move to her own bed, start by discussing the change with her. Tell her that her own bed is an important part of growing up, and reassure her that she'll sleep well there, too. Be firm; if you act wishy-washy about the change, she'll pick up on it. Institute a comforting bedtime routine if you don't already have one; routines are particularly comforting for kids who are about to embark on something new.

Expect the change to be hard, though. Co-sleeping with a baby sets up a powerful sleep association: The child needs *you* in order to nod off, both at bedtime and when he wakes in the middle of the night. The transition may take a week or two.

My child naps at day care but won't nap on the weekends at home?

This phenomenon is common with older toddlers. At preschool or day care, there's a whole roomful of nap mats and snoozing playmates. Chances are good that the teacher also dims the lights and plays soothing music—and does so at exactly the same time every day. Try patterning home naps around the same time. Use a wind-down routine. Nevertheless, it's possible that your child just won't go for it. In that case, you'll have to settle for thirty to sixty minutes of enforced quiet time in lieu of a total nap.

night after night. Some parents find that after teaching their child to sleep well on her own, an illness disrupts this, and they're right back to frequent wakings. This is normal. Once the child is healthy again, just repeat the process.

Some children wake occasionally at night because they're cold, hungry, or wet. Warm sleeper pajamas, even in summer if you use air-conditioning, can help, since most young children regularly kick off blankets but cannot replace them on their own. A bedtime snack (not a bottle taken to bed) can ward off hunger. If a wet diaper upsets your child, look into extra-strength varieties marketed for nighttime use.

Realize that an episode of night waking, for most parents, is a fact of toddlerhood. It's not realistic to expect that your child will sleep as soundly as you do. For many parents, it's stress-relieving just to know that this is normal. Your goal should not be to eliminate all night wakings, but to minimize them so that your whole life is not disrupted.

Note: If a child has been sleeping fairly well and suddenly starts waking often during the night over a period of several weeks, let your child's doctor know. Long-term sleep problems can be a sign of a health problem. Ruling out any illnesses can give you greater peace of mind.

Nightmares. *Why it happens:* Most common in almost-3's and pre-schoolers, bad dreams are the result of a high-octane imagination. But even in younger children, stress or exaggerated versions of the day's events—a new child care situation, a scary segment on the TV news—can invade sleep, triggering nightmares.

What you can do: A comforting bedtime routine builds security, which may in turn make a nightmare less likely. Nightmares often linger with a child, so don't pooh-pooh them. After a nightmare, patiently explain to your child that dreams are not real, even if they sometimes have the power to scare us. Remind your child that she dreams about nice things, too; encourage her to concoct a favorite scene about which she can "dream"—like a ballerina dance or a special farm for baby animals. Limit exposure to scary movies, TV programs, and books, especially if your child seems sensitive and suggestible.

Night terrors. *Why it happens:* Also called confusional arousals, night terrors typically strike during the first two to four hours of sleep. Though rare, this is when humans cycle out of deep sleep into a lighter phase. A young child might suddenly whimper or scream, sit up, or thrash around. An episode can be terrifying to a parent, especially because the child seems unresponsive, often staring vacantly ahead even while physically appearing upset. They're no cause for alarm, however. The child falls back asleep comfortably after ten to fifteen minutes and has no memory of the incident. (Rarely, they last thirty to forty-five minutes.) About 5 percent of kids experience night terrors, usually when they're overtired, sick, tense, or off their usual schedule—such as during the

> **PARENT TIP**
>
> ### Point Out That Magical Moon
>
> **M**any young toddlers are transfixed by the moon. Shining, shifting, it seems almost alive. "Mr. Moon" or "the man in the moon" becomes the child's personal friend, to be looked for, waved at, and blown kisses to. *Moon* is often among a child's first words. Given the egocentricity of a toddler, your child may believe it lights the sky for her alone, her own personal night-light. This is comforting, and a relationship worth encouraging. Add some of the wonderful children's books about the moon to your bedtime routine, such as *Goodnight Moon* by Margaret Wise Brown and *Happy Birthday, Moon* by Frank Asch.

phase when they give up the morning nap. A child might experience them several times a week, or just once or twice in her life. They're typically outgrown by grade school.

What you can do: In fact, there's little that can be done during a night terror. Trying to help the child awaken and snap out of it will only prolong the episode. So might soothing talk and pats. While it's happening, it's really best to stand guard and make sure the child doesn't fall down or bump something, perhaps keeping a hand on a shoulder or leg, but otherwise minimize your interaction until the episode passes.

Consider your child's schedule to see if you can account for the night terror. Perhaps putting him to bed earlier, once the morning nap has been abandoned, will provide more and better-quality sleep. Kids who have willy-nilly schedules are also at greater risk of night terrors—another reason predictable hours are best.

Sleepwalking, sleep talking. *Why it happens:* Like a night terror, walking and talking while asleep occur during the shift from deep sleep to lighter REM (rapid eye movement, or dream) sleep. About 15 percent of people sleepwalk, mostly children under age 12, and it tends to run in families.

What you can do: Remember that your little wanderer is, in fact, still asleep. Don't try to wake her, as it can confuse the child or prolong the episode. Safety is the most important thing: Be sure she can't trip over toys in her room or fall down the stairs. Put up a gate by the stairs at night. Follow the same preventative advice as for night terrors, above.

Teeth grinding. *Why it happens:* Sometimes it's an idle habit that develops, just like hair twirling or foot jiggling. It may also occur when a child is under stress.

What you can do: Nothing. It's rarely damaging, even though it sounds awful. If the habit is persistent, mention it to your child's dentist when you visit, so he or she can check that the teeth are all right.

Head banging. *Why it happens:* Some children repeatedly knock their head against the side of the crib or a wall at bedtime. They do so to help themselves fall asleep, just as others suck their thumbs or stroke the satin edge of a blanket. It's seldom the sign of a serious disorder if it's done only at bedtime. And it's rarely likely to cause injury.

What you can do: A crib bumper might soften the blows, but its use must be weighed against the risk of your child using one as a step to climb out of the crib. Talk to your child's doctor if the habit is severe or also done outside of bed, to rule out a developmental disorder.

Napping Know-How

For toddlers, one or two midday slumbers are as important as the nighttime stretch. There's a good biological reason kids crave them: Their metabolism slows and body temperature declines around 2 to 3 P.M., the same way it does at 2 to 3 A.M. (This happens to grown-ups, too. We just tend to get slow and cranky, without being lucky enough to actually nap.)

Nap needs are highly individual. No two children require exactly the same amount or follow the same schedule. And conditions can change from day to day. Naps typically range in length from forty-five minutes to more than two hours. The morning nap usually falls between 9:30 and 10:30. Afternoon naps are best scheduled after lunch, around 1 to 2 P.M. (to coincide with the natural energy dip that occurs around 2 P.M.). Wait too long to start your child's nap—say, 4 to 6 P.M.—and you'll probably have an overtired youngster all afternoon, and one who will be too refreshed for a reasonable bedtime.

As with going to bed at night, a routine is useful. It shouldn't be as elaborate or time-consuming. Nevertheless, you need to signal to your child that a nap is about to take place. The easiest way is to follow a repetitive series of activities, such as lunch followed by cleanup, followed by a short video or story time. Slow the pace. Don't schedule a nap right after playground time without some sort of wind-down transition in between. Having a familiar routine helps make napping a little easier when you're away from home, too.

MILESTONE

MOVING TO A BIG-KID BED (18-30 months)

Most kids switch between 2 and 3 years. But there are many factors to consider. Are you expecting another baby? Start the transition several months before your due date so the toddler won't feel jettisoned out of her property. Has your child begun to complain that "cribs are for babies"? As the third birthday approaches, many kids rebel against the bars, even if they sleep well there. Can your child vault over the sides of the crib? If so, no matter how old, make the switch *today* as a safety step.

Most kids are excited and nervous about a big bed. Some toddlers voluntarily begin to sleep in it if one has always been available in their room, along with a crib. Make the change more inviting with spiffy new sheets and a first-time pillow. Time the graduation for a calm period when your child isn't undergoing other big changes (a new baby-sitter, giving up the pacifier).

Which bed is best? Some parents start with a toddler bed, which is smaller-scaled and uses a crib mattress. (Some cribs convert to toddler beds.) The downside is that you'll need to invest in yet another bed in a few years. If you're worried about your child tumbling out of bed—which you should be, unless she is nearly 3—try a mattress on the floor (crib or twin), a futon, or adding a bed rail (available where baby or kids' furniture is sold). Skip waterbeds, which have inadequate support, and bunk beds, which pose too much risk for a child under 3.

Beware of catnapping. Some kids fall into the habit of stealing short naps in the car, in the stroller, or while watching TV. But these short sleeps that last less than thirty minutes aren't usually taken in a comfortable place where the child can stretch out and sleep well. Also, a day riddled with catnaps becomes choppy. It's hard for the child's natural biological rhythms to flow properly, resulting in a child who may rise unusually early or be wide awake at 11 P.M. Try to steer a catnapper toward a predictable schedule by placing her in the crib when she seems sleepy and leaving her there to play quietly even if she's awake. If she wants to doze between scheduled naps, engage her in some kind of absorbing play to help her hold off. Avoid running errands at these times so she doesn't nod off in the car seat or stroller.

Remember that sleep needs vary. Some children tend to be heavy sleepers who put in ten or more hours at night along with a couple of two-hour naps by day. Other children simply demand less. The way your child slept as a baby is a reliable predictor of how he'll sleep in toddlerhood. Almost all toddlers under 2 will put in at least some nap time, at first twice a day and then dropping to once in the afternoon. But there are a few who will abandon napping by 24 months. Most children outgrow naps by age 4, although some not until almost 7.

Grooming and Dressing

Keeping Clean

Finger painting. Mud pies. Sandbox play. Playground tumbling. It's one of the ironic challenges of toddler rearing that just when your child can get messier than ever, she's also more resistant to cleanup. One factor working in your favor, however, is the toddler's drive to imitate Mommy and Daddy. Your child wants to be like you. Watching you go through the motions of hair brushing and hand washing encourage her to try the same.

More advice on turning personal care into good clean fun:

Bathtime. It may sound like heresy, but a toddler doesn't need a daily bath. In fact, with regular face cleaning, hand washing, and bottom wiping, you can get by on just one or two baths a week, unless the day's activities involved something like wallowing in the mud. That said, most toddlers relish the tub. Nighttime is the right time. A warm soak provides a soothing downshift before bed.

Some toddlers are bath-resistant, however. They may go through a fear-of-water phase, or dislike one aspect of the bath, such as getting scrubbed or having their hair shampooed. Tub time also tends to involve a lot of commands: "Get in," "Hold still," "Get out now." An independent-minded toddler will naturally resist such controls. The best tactic for such a child is to make it short and sweet and keep the child actively involved in the process.

Let him choose which bath toys he wants to play with tonight, or which color of soap he'll use to scrub.

To ease fears, have him stand in the tub in just an inch or two of water and wipe him down with a wet, soapy washcloth. With each subsequent bath, increase the amount of water in the tub. Another possibility: Some toddlers will take showers with you. Be careful, however, since a hard, wet floor and a wet, slippery child are a dangerous combination.

Your child will probably soon become too big for the bath seat he used as a baby. But he won't outgrow the need for bathtime vigilance. *Never leave the bathroom for a second*—even if the telephone and the doorbell are both ringing. Provide a bath mat (the type that attaches with suction cups to the tub) for him to sit on without slipping. If he refuses to sit, it's okay for him to stand if you hold him at all times. For extra traction, try special beach shoes made for water. Teach him the right way to get in and out of the tub: always with your assistance, and never by placing one foot on the side of the tub as a step—it's too slippery. He should always step over the side right into the tub.

A bath before bedtime is a soothing way to wind down.

If your daughter is having vulvar redness or itching, it might be because she is sitting in bath water containing irritating shampoo or bubble bath. Avoid bubbles when your child (boy or girl) has an irritated diaper area, and shampoo right before exiting the tub.

Hair washing. Continue using mild baby shampoo during toddlerhood. A conditioner or detangler can simplify combing out wet hair, but it's necessary only if your child has long hair and is prone to tangles. You don't need to blow-dry, which can irritate a toddler's tender scalp.

Another reason to make shampoos the last step in your bath: It tends to be kids' least favorite part. Make a game out of working the shampoo into the hair and rubbing the scalp by sculpting silly shampoo hairdos, spikes, and triceratops horns. (Keep a hand mirror within arm's reach so your child can see.) The main objection to shampoos is the unexpected rush of water down the child's face during rinsing. Give warning: "Okay, here comes the water at the count of three. One, two..." Or teach your child to pretend to be a coy-

CHECKLIST

Fun Bath Toys

Rotate items like these to keep bathtime amusing:

✔ Puppet washcloths

✔ Special soaps (bars in animal shapes, in unusual colors, or made of clear glycerin with a visible toy embedded inside)

✔ Soapy "crayons" for drawing on walls

✔ Stacking cups or plastic containers

✔ Measuring spoons, basters, funnels

✔ A baby doll that "wets"

✔ Boats that float

✔ Rubber duckies

✔ Action figures, dinosaurs, or other plastic figurines

✔ Bathtub books with vinyl pages

✔ Shapes and letters that adhere to the side of the tub

✔ Plastic play food

✔ Paintbrush to "paint" walls or tub

PARENT TIP

Use Bathtime as Break Time

At your wits' end? Rainy day? Too pooped to march in another parade? When you need a break and are running out of ideas, put your tot in the tub. It's a contained, safe space, and a pleasant change of scenery for your child. To make a bath a fun activity as well as an exercise in hygiene, add something special: bubbles (bubble bath or the kind you blow), shaving cream, or plastic toys to "wash" that don't normally go in the tub. Or put your own feet in the tub and let your child scrub them. Your child can play as long as the water stays warm. There's no truth to the old belief that he needs to come out when his fingers turn wrinkly.

ote: head tilted way back and howling. That position allows you to rinse hair without the water streaming into the eyes. Wearing a rubber visor or swim goggles serve the same purpose. If your child is very resistant, consider the drastic measure of a short haircut.

Hair cutting. Hair growth varies tremendously. Some kids begin getting shorn during babyhood, while others may make it nearly to their third birthday with nary a trim. Haircut phobias are common among toddlers. In part, they find it hard to sit still for the duration of the styling, however brief. The word _cut_ may inspire fear of getting hurt. To minimize anxiety, look for a salon or stylist specializing in kids. Bring a favorite toy, a juice box, or even a snack to occupy your child. A child-friendly stylist will be able to work around the inconvenience. You may even need to let your

HOW TO
Give a Home Haircut

Home haircuts are cheaper for you and less scary for your child. The only tools you need are special hair-cutting scissors no longer than 5¾ inches (available at drugstores), a fine-tooth comb, and a spray bottle filled with water. Seat your child in a high chair (strapped in). A tray full of toys or a video helps minimize resistance. Even so, you may not have a lot of time. Aim for the hot spots: those bangs dangling over her eyes, or the tail poking into his shirt collar.

The basic steps:

1 Use a spray bottle to dampen the hair. (If the spray frightens your child, just dampen the hair with a wet towel.) Then comb down the section that needs cutting.

2 Extend the pointer and middle fingers of your nonwriting hand and slip them around the hair near the roots. Slide your fingers to the desired length. (If your child has curly hair, slide them an inch or so past this point, because curls cause the hair to look shorter when it's dry.)

3 With your writing hand, grasp the scissors with your thumb and middle finger so the blades are horizontal, and the bottom blade is resting on your pointer. In one smooth motion, carefully snip the hair below your fingers.

NOT TO WORRY

Bathwater Cocktails

Young toddlers still use their mouths to explore the world. A warm, bubbly tub of water can be irresistible. It's unlikely, however, that your child will drink enough so that the dirt or the soap cause any harm. Still, you don't want to encourage bathwater sipping. Calmly tell her that soapy water can make her sick. (Yelling will simply give her a delightful reaction that prompts her to do it again.) Make it a tub rule: If the child drinks water or splashes water out of the tub, she must come out. Matter-of-factly follow through. Removing cups and scooper toys from the tub can help eliminate the impulse.

child sit on your lap the first time or two. Try having the stylist snip a lock of your own hair first, to prove that it's not painful. It also helps to return to the same salon or barbershop every time. Most kids calm down after the first few haircuts.

WHAT IF...

My child doesn't like toothpaste?

Just use water. There's little need to use toothpaste before your child turns 3.

Tooth brushing. Most toddlers lack the coordination to brush well. But don't let that stop you. It's important to clean the teeth and to ingrain the habit during toddlerhood. So brush at the same times every day, such as after breakfast and at bedtime. Choose a soft toothbrush with rounded bristles, sized for an infant or child. Letting the child pick the color or characters on the brush help kindle interest. Don't use an electric brush for a child under age 4. Toddlers tend to swallow toothpaste, though, especially the kiddy flavors, so apply no more than a pea-sized dot (toothpaste is not even necessary at this age).

To brush, have your child sit in your lap with his head against your chest. Gently hold her head with one hand while you brush with the other hand. Or, since toddlers love to imitate parents, start by brushing with your child. Make it a game. Let her try on her own awhile and then finish up for her. Praise her efforts: "Your teeth are sparkling! Let me get this one spot you missed." If your child refuses to let the brush pass her lips, try letting her brush your teeth first, then reverse. More tricks: Have your child open her mouth and imitate you as you make a series of exaggerated sounds as she brushes. Or suggest that the child work hard to chase out the sugar bugs that are lurking in their mouths.

Ideally, your child should brush for two minutes. That's an eternity for a toddler to keep his mouth open while you poke a brush around, however. For a fun way to keep track of time, use a timer, a two-minute hourglass, or a special tooth-brushing clock or musical tape. Some brushes make music, too. Or just do the best you can to clean all surfaces. Flossing isn't necessary.

Ear cleaning. Clean the outer ear with a washcloth, but don't worry about the orange-yellow waxy buildup you see in your child's ears. Called cerumen, it's a naturally produced substance that helps keep the ear free of dirt. Don't use a cotton swab or anything else to remove the wax, or to clean farther into the ear than you can see. You risk puncturing an eardrum. Mention the wax to your child's doctor, who can verify whether there's too much and take appropriate steps. A clogged ear canal can cause temporary hearing loss, which may lead to delayed speech.

Hand washing. Model frequent hand washing yourself. Do it together before you eat anything. Invest in a solid step stool to help your child reach the sink. Show her how, beginning around 18 months. Emphasize getting the soap all over the hands. Colored soap, soap shaped like animals, or liquid soap can make the job more enticing.

General germ prevention. By 1½ or 2, your child is ready for the basics: Cover your face when you cough or sneeze. Better still, cough or sneeze into a tissue or toward the ground (so the germs won't spread from the child's hand all over the room). Remind

---

MILESTONE
FIRST DENTIST VISIT (36 months)

Professional opinions vary as to when it's best to go for that first dental checkup. Some pediatric dentists want to see their patients during infancy. The American Academy of Pediatrics thinks age 3 is fine for a first visit, some dentists wait until age 4. Professional cleanings aren't necessary before then.

Do consult a dentist or your child's doctor before the third birthday, however, if your child's teeth appear discolored. White or brownish spots are a sign of serious tooth decay, typically caused by too much contact with juice or milk. Also called baby-bottle mouth, it's most common in children who are put to bed with a bottle or who carry one around during the day. Sometimes topical fluoride can remedy the problem. Sometimes a tooth must be removed. Speckled teeth may also indicate that the child is consuming too much fluoride, which is uncommon but may occur if, for example, unnecessary fluoride supplements are being taken.

Frequent hand-washing helps prevent the spread of infections.

your child not to put her fingers in her mouth or to rub her eye—a common entry point for colds and other viruses. Demonstrate how you blow your nose. (Exaggerate to make the point.) You'll need to repeat these lessons over and over, but repetition and good example are the best teachers.

Getting (And Staying) Dressed

Remember the days when you carefully selected the most adorable outfits to show off your beautiful baby, and baby wore them ever so agreeably? Those days are about to change, if they haven't already. Clothes become a bigger issue for some toddlers than others. But nearly all kids, at one time or another, fall into one of the following categories:

The naked ape. *The problem:* "I'm fast, I'm free, I'm my own person. And I don't have the time or inclination to bother with anything as confining as clothes, thank you." Young toddlers heady with newfound independence and mobility are most likely to resist getting dressed.

What you can do: Make dressing as speedy as possible. Keep their outfits as minimalist as possible. Skip garments with the zillion snaps and complicated straps. Slip-on pants and leggings are faster. And if it's warm, indoors or out, who needs clothes, really? Sometime between 12 and 24 months, your child may begin to take great interest in clothes. Give her plenty of opportunity to work zippers or pull on socks all by herself. She won't be able to perform many fine motor tasks well until the next year, but it's wonderful practice.

The streaker. *The problem:* You get her dressed, but she doesn't stay that way for long. Deft toddlers even learn to unfasten their own diapers.

What you can do: Here the fun lies in shedding the clothes. It's your toddler's way of saying, "Look, Mom, I can do it!" She likes to practice newfound skills, such as pulling off sleeves or unfastening buttons. So she does these things at every opportunity—that is, whenever she has clothes on. The repetition is both absorbing and satisfying. There's no harm in around-the-house nudity. Your child probably likes the way it feels. (Although, unless you're very brave or beginning potty training, you may wish to draw the line at running around diaper-free.) *Don't* make a fuss, or your child will also begin to see removing clothes as a big game that's sure to rile you. Distraction is the best way to handle the situation. Some children enjoy special skill-building dolls whose clothes feature zippers, buttons, and snaps on which to practice. Overalls or one-piece rompers with back zippers—clothing that's hard for a child to take off—may also help a streaker lose interest.

The mismatchmaker. *The problem:* Checks with plaids, stripes with polka dots, lime green with mauve. Or three kinds of florals, none of which quite go together.

What you can do: Unless you're heading to a formal occasion such as a wedding or you're having your child's portrait taken, do nothing. Mismatched clothes are a by-product of learning to dress. Some toddlers, show an interest in their wardrobes as early as 18 months. Independent dressers are expressing their personality and mood, too. Don't give a second thought to what others might think, including your child's day care teachers. (They've seen it all. Besides, they're uniquely positioned to appreciate the creativity at work in your child.) Nor should you apologize for bizarre costumes.

Offer explanatory praise instead: "Janey picked out her clothes all by herself today! She's getting so big!" It can be hard for mothers who took pride in their baby's attire (and who are conscious about their own appearance) to let

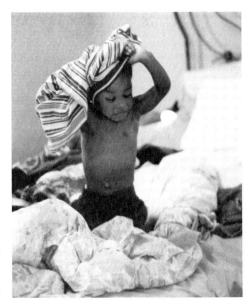

"What will I wear today?" Some toddlers take that question seriously at an early age.

go. But fighting over her efforts is deflating to the child and not worth the trouble. If it really bothers you, color-coordinate your child's wardrobe—buy all primary colors, for example, or all solid pants and print tops—to minimize eyesores. Many toddler clothing lines offer cute mix-and-match separates.

The sensitive type. *The problem:* The tags are "too itchy." The sweatpants are "too fuzzy." The seams in socks are "too bumpy." Kids may also rebel against body-hugging clothes, complain that turtlenecks are "choking," or simply murmur "no, no" but be unable to articulate the trouble.

What you can do: Take your child seriously. Many of these complaints are legitimate. Tags *do* often feel rough against tender skin, fleece pants get hot, and sock seams

MILESTONE

SELF-DRESSING (24-36 months)

Many toddlers begin to insist on dressing "all by myself" after the second birthday. It may take another year, however, before they can get by without any help from you. Further the cause by buying easy-to-manipulate clothing. This means elastic waistbands (no zippers or buttons), pull-on shirts and sweatshirts, and shoes with Velcro closures. It's a wonderful convenience when your child finally masters self-dressing—no matter what combinations he chooses to wear. But getting to that point is time-consuming.

While he's learning, build in extra time for your child to wrestle himself into his clothes. Don't criticize the results, either. When he puts things on inside out or backward, let it go if possible. Or use praise and humor to correct the mistake: "Wow! You got your pants on all by yourself. But look! This silly tag snuck around to the front when it's supposed to be in the back. Let's help that old tag go back where it belongs!"

positioned the wrong way on a foot can hurt when you walk. Complaints tend to escalate in winter, when skin is drier. Some children, particularly those with a history of allergies, simply need to wear soft-to-the-touch fabrics. Don't bother forcing your child to wear something just because you've spent good money on it, painful though this may be. That only sets up a power struggle. Better to let it rest a few weeks and try the item again later. Some parents of sensitive children launder new clothes repeatedly with fabric softener to break them in. Others seek out well-worn hand-me-downs from friends or at resale shops. Cottons are generally more comfortable than synthetics.

Some kids, however, are just naturally more inclined to whine no matter what you do. In that case, all you can do is make reasonable amends (snip tags, don't buy turtlenecks) or stock up on acceptable favorites, and endure the complaints.

The fanatic. *The problem:* This little absolutist goes on fashion jags. This week his wardrobe is 100 percent purple. Next week it's the Big Bird shirt, every day. Some girls go on extended jags in which they refuse to wear anything but dresses, even on the playground, and the fancier the better. Her mirror image is the girl who will wear only pants, including to parties or church.

What you can do: Go along. A little purple or a lot of dresses never hurt anyone, even if it drives you crazy to see all those things you've bought hanging unworn in the closet. For some kids, clothes become a security blanket. Wearing the same thing over and over makes them feel good. Explain that a favorite shirt must get washed and that it might wear out one day. Encourage your child to pick a backup favorite for wash day.

The weather-or-not kid. *The problem:* When it's sunny, she picks the yellow slicker. When it's snowing, only a short-sleeved shirt will do. Kids mix up

True Toddler Tales

"My Daughter, the Fashion Queen"

At 18 months, Isabelle Carbone began voicing opinions about which clothes she wanted to wear. At 2, she became more definitive about what was acceptable and what wasn't. If she didn't like an outfit, she'd cry and try to pull her clothes off. If she *really* didn't like it, she'd pitch a tantrum or run away. Her favorite look: T-shirts, bicycle shorts, and leggings, just like her two older brothers and her mother, Alison, wear.

"For everyday outfits, I say, 'Okay, wear whatever you want.' But I give her guidance, like 'How do jeans sound?' or 'If you don't like this, how about this?' " says Alison, who lives in San Rafael, California. For special occasions, she gives advance notice to let Isabelle get used to the idea. "I'll say, 'Tomorrow is a big-girl party and you have to wear a dress. I'm going to wear one, and So-and-so will be wearing one, and you'll want to wear one, too.' She's allowed to pick between two dresses I offer, so she's still part of the decision."

"Instead of buying dresses that I always wanted my daughter to wear, I've learned to compromise on choices that work for both of us," she says. "It's been a process of elimination, figuring that out. But battles over clothes aren't worth the frustration."

Alison's tips for dealing with opinionated dressers:

- **Try distraction.** "Sometimes when nothing seems to work, I have to distract her from what she was objecting to. We go do something else and come back to getting dressed fifteen minutes later when we're both in a more positive frame of mind."
- **Use advance preparation.** "Give extra notice for when the child needs to wear an unusual mode of dress. Your explanations will set expectations."
- **Find a balance.** "Sometimes giving your child total freedom will work. Sometimes you need to give limited, appropriate options."
- **Give the child control.** "Clothing is a good way for kids to express themselves, and it's nice to give them that freedom. If an outfit doesn't potentially affect her health, don't make a big deal about it."
- **Enlist others.** "Sometimes her dad or brothers will say 'Wear this one' or 'You look pretty in that' to help me get Isabelle to wear something she doesn't want to."

HOW TO
Put on a Jacket

A child as young as 18 months can learn to put her own jacket on. How to do it:

1. Lay the jacket on the floor with the sleeves spread out and the body opened up a little.

2. Teach your child to stand with her toes touching the tag along the neck. (The jacket will appear upside-down to the child.)

3. Have her bend down and reach her arms into the sleeves.

4. Next, with her arms burrowing into the sleeves, she lifts the jacket over her head, and *voilà!* Ready to go!

occasions as well as weather: "Why can't I wear my party dress to the playground? What's wrong with my sweatpants for church?"

What you can do: Help your child make winning choices. When cold weather sets in, store bathing suits and seersucker out of sight, and stash the wool sweaters in summertime. When you're faced with a situation specifying a certain type of clothing, explain why it's appropriate: "I love your tutu, too, but people don't wear them to weddings. I'll help you put it back on tomorrow, when the wedding is over." Let your child choose between two outfits you've set out. (Too many choices are confusing.) But be sure the choices are things your child likes. Some parents find it useful to negotiate an outfit with their child the night before. It's a time-saver, if it works. Be prepared for your child to have a change of heart the next morning, however. If you stand firm, you'll just be drawn into a power struggle of another sort. A toddler won't understand the promise she made the night before.

Finally, consider these practical suggestions for easing the task of dressing toddlers of every stripe:

Abandon thinking of your child as an extension of your image. Toddlers rarely care how they look, at least by your standards. That's fine. As

WHAT IF...

My child refuses to wear her jacket even though it's cold outside?

Forcing tends to make everyone miserable. Better to say, "Well, it's pretty cold. Why don't we bring it along just in case?" This gives an entrenched toddler some wiggle room. Ask again when you get outside: "What do you think?" If it's truly cold, she'll opt for the jacket (or mittens or hat) after all. This issue isn't always negotiable, of course. If there's a foot of snow outside, you have to simply make it a rule: No going outside to play in snow without jackets.

long as they have some clothing on, that should be sufficient. Everyone wishes their child would look as clean and adorably attired as the cherubs that fill those fashion catalogs, especially when they're out in public. But they're not accessories. They're people.

Choose roomy, easy-on play clothes. They encourage self-dressing and make play comfortable. Better to buy a little large—you can always roll up cuffs. Front-zip or front-button coats are easier on a toddler than pullover jackets. Choose shoes and boots with Velcro straps rather than laces. Opt for mittens over gloves. Use mitten clips to keep them securely attached to coats. Avoid small buttons, frilly dresses that may scratch, pants with zip flies, rough seams or trims.

Encourage early attempts at self-dressing. Even a 15-month-old can try to do certain things by himself, such as put on socks or shoes. Make it fun, and don't let the attempts go on until they lapse into frustration. It takes extreme patience on your part, but most kids can begin sooner than their parents think.

Make potty training easier. Avoid overalls and snap-crotch shirts once you begin, so that your child can get to the potty with as little delay as possible.

Beware long scarves, drawstrings, or ties. Most new children's clothing manufactured since 1994 no longer has these strangulation hazards, but beware with old clothes. Remove hood and neck drawstrings from jackets and sweatshirts or sew a seam through the drawstring at the middle of the hood and neck so that neither end can pull out and catch on an object. Don't let your child wear any sort of string or necklace around her neck, especially on the playground.

WHAT IF...

My mighty wriggler won't hold still for diapering?

A toddler on the go hasn't the time for something as trivial and time-consuming as a diaper change. What's more, he sees your insistence on the task as another way you're trying to control him. To make changes quicker and easier on all: First give your child some forewarning, to help him segue from his current activity to the diaper change. Divert his attention with a special toy you keep at the diaper station. Or keep him involved—say, by having him open the diaper tabs or hand you the wipes. Changing diapers on the floor or a low ottoman is safer than hauling an active child up to a changing table. If he resists lying on his back, make the change while he's standing up.

CHAPTER THREE

Playtime!

All the world's a toy box to a toddler. A 1- or 2-year-old's endless capacity for fun is one of the most pleasant surprises of this age. Increasingly, your daily grind of feeding and diaper changing is balanced by sweet rewards as you gain more and more glimpses into your child's mind and heart. As a toddler's ability to move and communicate improves, she notices more, her attention span lengthens, and her laughter flows. She finds humor and delight in the smallest and most ordinary things.

Better still, you get to play along. When was the last time you tried to taste a snowflake? Walked like a monkey? Made mud soup? Led a parade?

This chapter gives you insight into the many ways that play benefits your child. It also provides helpful, age-appropriate guidelines now that so many new toys, friends, and opportunities for play enter your child's life. Best of all, you'll find lots of fun ideas for things toddlers love to do.

How Toddlers Play

Learning by Doing

It's often said that "play is a child's work" because it's a child's main preoccupation. Far from a trivial time filler, play is vital to learning and growth. Play enhances all aspects of a child's development: social, emotional, mental, and physical. During these seemingly idle hours, a child fine-tunes motor skills, broadens language abilities, practices social interactions, improves memory, better understands how things work, and finds an outlet for feelings ranging from anger to glee to fear. Importantly, play provides a way for toddlers to exercise control in a world where they're generally at everyone else's mercy. Safe in their own circle of toys and make-believe, they can experiment with actions and reactions of their own choosing. Being the boss reinforces confidence. Play also plants the seeds for creativity and imagination, which will continue to flourish as your child grows. Not least, play feels good.

For toddlers, a more fitting adage might be that "play is a child's *life*." A toddler makes few distinctions between what is playtime and the rest of his day. He finds as much pleasure in a trip to the grocery store as he does at the playground. The novel sight of a telephone repair crew's cherry-picker truck is as fascinating as a new toy. Singing and dancing are great entertainment; so is exploring the broccoli on his tray. Even getting dressed in the morning can be a game. Every experience holds the capacity for fun.

You don't need to go overboard in making your child's play a learning experience. Buying only fancy educational toys, for example, isn't necessary. Select a particular puzzle because it's simple and has a bright, funny picture, rather than because it purports to teach a child her colors. A stack of measuring cups are fun to mouth and bang and fill, without a lecture about their relative capacities. Sing songs and play games that make you and your child happy, rather than those that stress an underlying lesson. That's not to say that counting games or "The ABC Song" aren't worthwhile. They're great. In

---

WHAT IF...

My child develops an obsession for one type of toy?

A child's individual tastes first become clear during toddlerhood. One child may go crazy for toy cars, another for teddy bears or balls. Sometimes, in our marketing-crazed country, it's a favorite movie or TV character that becomes idolized, in forms such as a doll, a small action figure, a puzzle, and so on. The familiarity of these icons is comforting to a young child. Often these early preferences stick; sometimes they're merely passing fancies. Such favorites are driven both by the child's natural interests and by the sense of security they provide, the same way a comfort object like a blankie makes the child feel better. Encourage your child's love of a particular type of toy, even if it's something offbeat like keys or boxes. But also make available a wide array of different playthings.

fact, many such favorite forms of toddler play have built-in lessons. Just don't get too hung up on making sure that your child is "getting something" out of her activities. There's plenty of time for formal learning in the years ahead. For a toddler, almost all learning comes through play, and it comes quite naturally.

Safety First

Now that your child is more agile and curious than ever, reassess your home to be sure that playtime is free of unnecessary hazards. Consider the following:

A safe play space. Even if your child has her own bedroom or playroom, you'll probably find that she won't play there by herself. She wants to be where you are. Be sure that all the areas in which your child plays, including the kitchen, living room, and backyard, have been toddler-proofed.

MILESTONE

FIRST TRICYCLE (24 months)

Once your child has been walking and running well for a few months, she's ready to try a trike. A low-slung model made of plastic and designed for toddlers will feel most comfortable and be safest in the event of the inevitable tumble. Don't be surprised if it takes a while for your child to figure out how to pedal. Most kids master this between 2 and 3. Safety basics: Watch beginners at all times, in case of spills. Never let a toddler ride on the street even if supervised; she's too small to be seen by drivers. It may seem a little overzealous for a big-wheeler, but a snug-fitting helmet is a must: It protects in case of spills and ingrains this safety habit early.

Safe toys. Thanks to eager relatives and endless holidays, as well as your own desire to add age-appropriate playthings to your child's life, a constant stream of new toys will enter your house. Throw away the plastic wrappings right away. Inspect each new object for safety before giving it to your child. Remove labels and tags from stuffed animals and examine each one to see that there are no removable parts, such as loosely attached eyes. Check the recommended ages on toy boxes and adhere to them. Your child may seem mature or bright enough to play with a certain toy, but it may have small parts that pose a danger to her.

Reexamine toys periodically for dangerous signs of wear, and toss or repair anything questionable. The edges of wood toys, for example, can splinter. Metal outdoor toys can rust or weaken.

Safe toy chests. Kids age 2 and under are at highest risk for injuries from unsafe toy boxes, according to the CPSC. The lids can fall on the head, neck, or fingers. Suffocation is a danger if the child climbs into an unsafe chest and becomes trapped. The best toy caches have no lid, a removable lid, or a hinged lid with a safety catch so that it stays open in any position. (All chests made since 1984 should have child-safe lids.) A good toy box should also have ventilation, such as a space between the closed lid and the side of the chest. If you already own a chest with an unsafe lid, it's best to simply remove it. You might also be able to install a spring-loaded lid support, available at hardware stores.

Alternatively, skip a toy box altogether. Large laundry baskets or plastic bins hold toys without any safety risk, and they're inexpensive enough to station all around the house. Because plastic tubs or baskets are lower than most toy boxes, they're also more easily accessible to a toddler. A series of smaller plastic containers on shelving is another way to keep toys organized. Paste a

GOOD ADVICE
Clutter Control

"We keep all of Randi's toys in different containers. If a box is for Duplos, we glue a Duplo on the outside of the box. We keep three boxes out at a time. The big items, like her farmhouse, are kept in a closet. I hope she'll get used to seeing everything organized, so when she's old enough to clean up on her own, she'll know where everything goes."

—*Robin Johnson, Coon Rapids, Minnesota*

"Kaytlyn, 2, has one room just for her toys. She can make as much mess as she likes as long as it stays in the toy room. She can take the toys out of the room, but she must carry them back after she finishes playing. We clean up the toy room together about once a week."

—*Melissa Cajeton, North Charleston, South Carolina*

"Hayley, 2½, goes into each room like a tornado. I used to follow her around and pick things up, but it was so tedious. Now we do one big tidy-up at the end of the day."

—*Robin Curtin, East Weymouth, Massachusetts*

picture of the contents (blocks, toy soldiers) on the outside of each container to help your child stay organized.

Safe sleep toys. Double-check bedtime playthings, too. Your child is too old now, for example, to have a mobile or a crib gym stretched across the top of the crib. These infant amusements pose a strangulation risk once a child can push up on hands and knees (usually by 5 months). Plush toys in a crib pose a suffocation risk in sleep, even for toddlers.

One-Year-Olds' Favorites

These are some of the forms of play that young toddlers tend to prefer:

Imitation. A keen observer, your child notices nearly everything you do. And he delights in mimicking your actions, whether it's the way you brush your hair or how you read the newspaper during breakfast. Even everyday chores are fun for a child who is mimicking the grown-ups in his world. Give your child a whisk broom and let him sweep along with you, for example. Enhance this kind of play by providing child-sized versions of adult paraphernalia, such as toy telephones, plastic tools, and soft brushes.

Two-year-olds enter a world of fantasy that dominates much of their play.

Repetition. Repeating an activity over and over is a good way to master it. And that's exactly what your child is doing when she spends a half hour pouring sand in the sandbox, dumping and refilling a basket of toys, or banging the table with a plastic hammer. She's practicing hand-eye coordination. In part, she's also looking for confirmation that the same results will happen each time she attempts to pour, stack, or pound. That knowledge inspires confidence. Most likely, as she plays she's also subtly

My son likes to play dress-up?

Sartorial switching may seem jarring to some parents, but in fact it's a sign of a healthy imagination. Dress-up—whether in a cowboy hat or Mom's old cocktail dress—is a form of make-believe. Young kids believe in magic, that they can be anything or anyone they want to be. Cross-dressing is born of simple curiosity ("What's it like to be a princess?") and pretending ("This time I'll be the mommy"). It's not a sign of gender confusion or poor self-esteem. It's best to let it pass without comment from you. The fad usually wanes during the preschool years, when peer pressure and other factors tend to narrow a child's play along gender lines.

varying her efforts. First she'll pour the sand slowly, then quickly. She may pour it into a cup and then into her hand to see how different these activities feel. This kind of play can go on for surprisingly lengthy intervals. Don't discourage it, however frustrating or boring it may be for you. On the contrary, view repetitive play as a sign of healthy development.

Sensory exploration. Children learn through all their senses. Their drive to explore in this way often defies adult sensibilities. A toddler thinks nothing of tasting dirt in a garden, reaching to touch a candle flame, or plucking every petal off a flower in order to smell them. He can climb or crawl almost anywhere to get to an object that catches his eye. And you can bet he's not censoring his wishes with thoughts of what's appropriate or breakable or safe.

Mouthing is a particular danger. Toddlers instinctively put almost everything in their mouths, so you need to be especially vigilant, not only about toys but also about unexpected dangers such as sticks and pebbles on the playground or everyday household objects like coins. Don't expect your child to catch on the first time you say no—or even the twentieth time. The rules about sensory exploration are confusing to a child. Think about it: Your child can taste this new thing called an ice pop, but he can't taste the flower. He can touch this wooden bowl but not that china one. It takes a long time, and much parental patience and persistence, for a child to figure out these complexities.

Weighing and measuring. This type of learning is a form of sensory play. Toddlers love to fill objects with water, sand, rice, or small objects and then empty them out again, over and over. Not only are the motions satisfying, but the child is collecting important information about size, bulk, and the ways objects relate to one another.

Physical play. Movement is pure joy for a child who's recently learned to walk and to run. You'll see your child push, pull, lug, dump, knock down,

NOT TO WORRY

Imaginary Friends

The sudden presence of a friend whom only your child can see is common among preschoolers. But some particularly imaginative and verbal toddlers may invent such friends as well. Imaginary friends are born of creativity. They're not indicative of an unhappy nature or an inability to make real friends. On the contrary, kids with imaginary pals tend to be more sociable, cooperative, and well adjusted, and less violent and bored, than children without them. These characters can be a way for a child to navigate scary waters, such as a new school or a new sibling. Tolerate them (and, to yourself, laugh at them), but you don't need to go overboard in adopting them. In fact, if you ask about imaginary friends too often, your child is apt to clam up. Such friends are creatures of his own invention and best left to his own devices.

run, and climb. More than just fun, active play helps develop muscles and rehearses coordination. Build in opportunities for physical play several times during your child's day. Go outside, to the backyard, or to a park. Take walks. Put on some music and dance. Toddlers also love to experiment with motion, making them entranced by playground equipment such as slides, swings, and low jungle gyms. Provide toys that encourage a range of motions: a mop for pushing, wagons for pulling, balls for throwing, pillows or cushions for climbing, plastic hammers for pounding.

Two-Year-Olds' Favorites

As your toddler grows older, she'll add some new modes of play to her repertoire:

Make believe. Pretend play escalates after the second birthday. Instead of merely carrying a baby doll around, your child will begin to treat it like a real person, feeding it and putting it to bed, for example. He'll stage elaborate journeys or spectacular crashes for his toy cars. Often a child narrates his invented story line as he goes along. The props a child uses to further this play don't have to be real. A shoe can become the car's garage. A wicker basket serves nicely as a diaper bag. A stick found on the ground is used as a gun or a fairy wand. This type of play lets a toddler exert control over his environment. He's also practicing motor skills, and often verbal skills as well, as he directs the action and narrates the activity at hand.

Role playing. At first a toddler imitates his daddy shaving. Eventually he pretends that he *is* Daddy. He invents all sorts of activities for his adopted persona, including some that he's never actually seen Daddy do. He may pretend to work in an office, for example, or fly to the moon. In addition to the familiar role models of Mom and Dad, a toddler may make believe that she is a puppy, a zoo animal, a favorite superhero, a fairy princess, or a character in a cartoon. Trying on these roles lets a child more fully understand them. She can safely practice such emotions as anger or empathy. Role playing also helps her conquer situations that might make her uncomfortable. "Go to sleep!" the child, as Mommy, might tell her dolls. "There's nothing to be scared of. There are no monsters under the bed." If your child involves you in such play—asking you to be the baby while she is the mommy is a favorite—go along with it. Resist the temptation to lead the skit or advise your child on the way a real grown-up might do something. Let her be in charge and follow her lead.

Music. Even as infants, children like music. As your child grows, she begins to move to the sounds and sing along (albeit not in perfect rhythm or on pitch). Her fine motor skills also improve, enabling her to make music by banging on a toy xylophone or drum. Sharing music with a parent helps a child feel relaxed and happy. There's even some evidence that exposure to music in the early years can improve a child's abilities in language, math, and science. This is true even if you don't spring for fancy instruments or Suzuki violin lessons. Use pot lids for cymbals or rice-filled canisters for shakers. Wrap rubber bands around a shoebox with the lid off to create a homemade dulcimer (or cut the lid into the shape of a handle, tape it on one end of the box, and call it a guitar).

Singing is a form of music, too. Introduce your child to old classics that you remember from your younger days, or make up silly songs of your own about the things that happen during the day. Many childhood nursery rhymes, such as "The Itsy Bitsy Spider," feature fun hand movements that you can teach your child. Listen to CDs or the radio as background music during playtime or in the car. There are dozens of child-oriented selections, from Raffi to Disney tunes. But don't underestimate your child by playing nothing but kid songs. It's equally beneficial for a child to listen to classical, jazz, or pop tunes (not to mention easier on parental sanity).

It's the process rather than the product that counts when it comes to toddler art.

Art. Like music, art has been shown to improve a child's mathematical abilities and language skills. The tasks involved rely on basic reasoning—comparing thick lines to thin ones, or one texture to another. Even scribbling in a coloring book allows a child to improve fine motor skills. For a toddler, paints and glue pots are tactile adventures. What he sees in the clay or on the paper spurs the imagination. Also, open-ended art projects provide an all-important measure of control. The child decides which colors to use or when the work is finished, for example. That's why every child should be exposed to art during toddlerhood. You don't need to set him up in his own fully equipped garret. The kitchen table or a child's easel will do nicely. Stock up on a few basics: chubby washable crayons and markers, paints (watercolors and tempera), colored chalk, drawing paper, colored construction paper, play dough, and collage materials, such as paste, leaves, shells, and fabric scraps. Always supervise your little Picasso's efforts for safety's sake; he probably won't be able to resist chewing the Crayolas or licking the paste pot until the preschool years.

Sorting and classifying. As a child takes in more information about the world, he begins to organize in his mind the ways that things are alike and different. During toddlerhood your child is gaining his first understandings of such concepts as large and small, grown-ups and children, colors, counting, and classifications of things such as animals and clothes. No longer are all four-legged animals called "dog," for example. Now he can begin to see the differences between different kinds of animals, and between

Natural treasures for little collectors abound right in your own backyard.

different breeds of dogs. Many of the activities that you view as everyday chores are fun opportunities for your child to practice his budding analytical skills. For example, you could empty a toy bin and ask your child's help in sorting out the different types of items, such as balls, cars, and blocks. Even mundane activities such as helping you sort socks or put the napkins on the table before dinner are exercises in the principles of organization.

Collecting. Hand in hand with this newfound discrimination between objects is the older toddler's love of collecting. There's no telling what object your child may take a shine to. During the fall, he may become fascinated with the different shapes and colors of leaves. At the beach, he may begin a seashell collection. The particular merits of each cherished specimen may be lost on you—for example, your child may pick up broken shells as well as perfect ones, or homely clamshells along with gorgeous conchs. Even if it seems like junk to you, try not to direct his passion or simply trash the stuff. Instead, encourage his efforts. Talk about what he finds, such as pointing out the different colors of the leaves or the different shapes of the seashells. Your child may get proprietary about his collection. Let him store them in a special place; a cardboard box or empty diaper wipe container are perfect. Other popular objects of desire: sticks, rocks, feathers, or a certain type of toy (such as action figures).

Solo Play

"Mama!" You hear the familiar wail, feel the insistent tug at your leg as your child tries to pull you down to his level. As fun as playing with your child can be, you'll eventually find yourself longing for the day when he can amuse himself all alone, at least for a short while. The ability to play inde-

Toy Guns? Barbie Dolls?

Sooner or later, if you have a boy, you'll encounter the question of toy guns: Should you allow them, or shouldn't you? And for many parents of girls, a similar hot-button question will center on Barbie, the buxom eleven-inch fashion doll.

The argument against both toy guns and fashion dolls goes like this: They're inappropriate. Toy guns, in effect, sanction violence, some people believe, and make children overly aggressive. As for Barbie, her big hair and astronomically unlikely proportions are felt by many parents to provide an unrealistic image of womanhood for young girls to aspire to, warping their own self-image.

Many parents choose to sidestep the issue by simply not exposing their children to such toys. That strategy works, at first. But as children grow, they develop their own toy preferences. They watch TV, are exposed to marketing ploys in fast-food kids' meals, and check out friends' toy boxes. Nature as much as nuture influences the differences between boys and girls. In fact, it's been shown that as early as 18 months, children begin to make toy choices according to gender.

In fact, both kinds of toys can be terrific instruments for creative play. A toy rifle may be just the prop that turns your child into a cowboy, a space explorer, or a battle leader. Similarly, dolls let your child try on adulthood for size.

"All things in moderation" is as good advice regarding toddler toys as it is about food. If your son is crazy about guns, adding such toys to his repertoire isn't going to lead him to a life of high crime. Much of the latest research indicates that gunplay does not make boys more aggressive. Rather, it provides an outlet for natural feelings and helps them make sense of violence and fears. Consider compromises such as purchasing less-realistic-looking water guns or ray guns. Instill rules: No guns in the house, or no pointing them at people.

If your daughter desires a Barbie, remind yourself that it's only a doll. Your daughter will form her self-image based on the input of many images. Especially at this age, she sees the doll as the representation of a grown-up (unlike her baby dolls or stuffed animals) and a wonderful chance to act out being big, rather than as a symbol of sexuality. Deemphasize Barbie's accent on appearance by helping your child play with her in ways that go beyond simply changing clothes. Remember that you have an enormous role to play in the messages your child receives about values.

You can also counter the impact of such toys by limiting how many you buy. Balance toys you have qualms about with lots of traditional toys, too.

Ultimately, of course, toy choices are yours. Many parents prefer to avoid certain toys during toddlerhood, which at least postpones the issue. It's not until age 2 or later that most kids begin to covet certain items. But by preschool you'll find the question inescapable.

WHAT IF...

My child always makes a huge mess when she plays?

Everything is an exercise in cause and effect for a toddler. "What will happen if I knock over these papers?" she may wonder. "What would this chair look like upside down?" "What happens when I dump out this basket of blocks?" Toddlerhood is too soon to demand neatness. For one thing, a toddler moves too quickly, in eager curiosity, from one thing to another. Eventually, though, you will want your child to learn to clean up one activity before embarking on another. Periodically make a game of cleanup, such as before you make the transition to lunch or to outside play. But basically, it's best to tolerate a degree of clutter when you have a 1- or 2-year-old in the house.

pendently doesn't come naturally for most children until the preschool years. It's not developmentally appropriate, anyway, for all of a toddler's play to be completely self-directed. A 1- or 2-year-old needs a grown-up to introduce and initiate games, to be a role model in terms of behavior, and to talk to. Some children are more temperamentally inclined to amuse themselves. Later-borns are also often better than their older siblings at self-entertainment, because they escape the constant scrutiny that most first-time parents can't help but direct toward their eldest.

Still, even a toddler is capable of short bursts of self-amusement. And it's sheer wonderful relief when your child can go a full thirty minutes without you or the tube for entertainment. Independent play also fosters self-confidence, self-reliance, good self-esteem, and an active imagination. It's believed that children who can amuse themselves are more attentive in school because they're experienced in concentrating. They tend to require less discipline because they're not as apt to get into mischief as an attention-getting ploy. Now's the ideal time to begin accustoming your child to the idea of solo play. Some tips:

Build solo time gradually. When you notice that your child seems engrossed in an activity, excuse yourself for a minute or two. Tell your child that you'll be right back. Leave the immediate area for just a few seconds, then return. When you do this repeatedly over time, your child learns to expect your return. You can gradually lengthen your "right back" time and begin pursuing activities in another room. (If you simply disappear, though, you'll only teach your child that whenever he plays nicely, you'll take off.)

Be a base. A toddler playing alone will repeatedly check in with her caregiver (the supervising parent or a sitter), either verbally or by making eye contact. For this reason, as well as for safety's sake, it's essential that you stay nearby rather than leave your child entirely to her own devices. Give occasional gentle pats or touches as you pass by, but don't necessarily talk. If you intrude too often with words of praise about how nicely your child is playing by herself, you risk interrupting her activity and refocusing her attention back on you.

Don't hover. It can be hard for parents of firstborns, especially, to disengage themselves from their children. After all, you've just spent a year perfecting the art of tuning in to your child's every cry and need. His every action is a marvel, and you love to entertain him. Backing off, however, has its place. You shouldn't feel guilty. Solo play is a skill like any other that your child will gradually master. Or look at it this way: If you're constantly there selecting your child's toys and pushing the buttons on the pop-up toy, you're interfering with the learning process.

Provide on-my-own toys. Books and simple puzzles are good examples of toys that engross a child. Rotating playthings to retain their fresh appeal is another attention extender. Be sure that some of your child's toys are always readily accessible to him, such as on a low open shelf or bin.

Play wholeheartedly when you do play together. Twenty minutes of your undivided attention may be enough to satisfy your child to then go off on her own for another twenty. Many children cling and clamor because they don't receive enough focused attention from their parents.

WHAT IF...

I've always used a playpen? When do kids outgrow them?

The old name, playpen, has been discarded by manufacturers in favor of play *yard* because many people objected to the prisonlike implications of the word *pen*. If your child is content enough to play in one once she's learned to walk, you're lucky. Many toddlers reject the confines of the play yard outright. That can be unfortunate, especially if you grew accustomed to it in your child's babyhood. A play yard can be a handy safe zone when you need to fix dinner or use the bathroom, for example. Be sure it's still in good working order, with no broken hinges or dangerous tears in the mesh or padding. Never let one side down so that your child can move in and out of the playpen. Rotating the toys inside can also keep it an interesting play place. But be careful not to overuse the pen as your child grows. A toddler ought to have plenty of opportunities to walk around and explore a larger, more stimulating space. Definitely put the play yard away once your child can climb out of it.

115

BEST TOYS FOR TODDLERS

For 1-Year-Olds

Action toys	Balls (a variety of sizes except very small), push toys (shopping carts, doll carriages, lawn mowers), pull toys (on a string), tricycles, small rocking horses, foot-propelled ride-on vehicles, swings, tunnels for crawling into
Toys for imitation play	Child-scaled kitchen gear, brooms, hairbrushes, toy telephone, simple musical instruments (especially for banging), play tools, steering wheel
Stacking toys	Nested plastic cups, wood or cardboard blocks, plastic rings on a spindle
Building toys	Duplo-style plastic blocks, hollow cardboard boxes or bricks, empty diaper wipe boxes
Toys to manipulate	Wooden beads on dowels, simple puzzles of two or three pieces with knobs, radio (play or, under supervision, real), activity boxes attached to crib or playpen (not activity gyms that are suspended over the child), simple shape sorters, pop-up toys
Open-ended playthings	Dolls and simple doll accessories, stuffed animals, trucks and cars, dinosaurs, puppets, large cardboard cartons

For 2-Year-Olds *(in addition to the toys recommended for 1-year-olds)*

Action toys	Slides, realistic-looking ride-on toys (trucks, tractors), pedal tricycle, light wheelbarrow, wagons, climbing structures, spinning seat
Toys for imitation play	Tea set, plastic cash registers, toy grocery cart or basket, more realistic musical instruments (including horns and whistles)
Toys to manipulate	Boxes with clasps or locks, dump trucks, puzzles of four to twenty pieces (also called play trays), large beads for threading, lacing cards, special dolls that feature zippers and buttons for fine-motor practice, blocks (Duplo-style and wood)
Toys that create patterns	Colorforms, felt boards, magnetic boards, peg boards (with large pegs), colored blocks, simple matching games
Make-believe play	Play sets (such as farm, castle, pirate ship), cars and a racetrack, dress-up costumes, puppet theater
Open-ended playthings	Realistic dolls (representing all ages) and doll house, realistic-looking stuffed animals, popular character figures and dolls, action figures, dinosaurs, large cardboard cartons

First Friends

Do Toddlers _Need_ Buddies?

Watch two 15-month-olds play together and, well, you're not likely to see much togetherness. More likely at this age, the children engage in parallel play—each child pursues her own activity, playing close to each other without interacting. A young toddler tends to see another child like another toy to look at or touch, but she's not developmentally ready to interact much more than that. This indifference to playmates continues until about 18 to 24 months, when a child gains an awareness of other children as individuals like herself. This is when first friendships often develop, as children gain the ability to engage in interactive play (such as pretending to be puppies together, chasing each other, or rolling a ball back and forth). Kids often develop preferences for one or two best friends over others now, too, especially if they see each other often, as at day care. The preferred pals may visibly brighten when they see each other, go off together to use the same toys, name their dolls after each other, or mimic behavior, such as selecting the same color of paper.

Many parents whose children have not been in a group environment, such as group day care, begin to wonder whether they should expose their toddler to other children. Certainly there's no need to schedule play dates for a 1-year-old or to enroll him in a play group or nursery school program if exposure to other children is the only consideration. A 2-year-old can grow up quite normal and well adjusted without these types of activities, provided he receives plenty of attention and stimulation from his parents and other close individuals, such as a caregiver, grandparents, or older siblings.

That said, however, many toddlers enjoy the company of their peers. Unlike siblings, where one child is older and another younger, playmates of the same age have a better balance of power and share similar perspectives on the world. Peer play is another step in social development, just as a child is learning to communicate through language and

---

WHAT IF...

My child doesn't seem to enjoy other kids?

Don't worry that he'll be a wallflower for life. Some children are naturally more reserved. Others mature later and have little interest in a social life until they approach 3 or even 4. Look for gentle ways to involve him in group play, such as joining along in the activity yourself or letting him participate from the safety of your lap. Sometimes a little encouragement is all a reserved child needs to feel more confident. Tread easy, however. Pushing a child to interact with others tends to be counterproductive. Eventually he'll find his way with peers on his own terms.

Don't Forget Free Time

In a zeal to expose your child to enriching experiences, it's possible to overdo his schedule. Yes, even toddlers today are at risk of getting overbooked. The possibilities are endless: play dates, mothers' groups, lessons, classes, nursery school or day care, everyday errands. In fact, toddlers have lower thresholds for social interactions than older children. A little goes a long way. One to three social activities a week is plenty.

Watch for these signs of overwhelm:

- Your child displays excessive crankiness or clinging, especially in new situations
- He shows diminished enthusiasm for activities that once were thrilling
- You have to spend a lot of time cajoling your child to get somewhere
- Your child is fatigued (hard to wake up)

nonverbal actions, like hugging and grabbing. It's a way to practice getting along with others.

If you're not lucky enough to have the perfect same-age child living right next door (or twins of your own), there are many other playtime options. Playgrounds and parks are usually full of children, although your child could be overwhelmed if there are too many big kids around, or if they're too boisterous. Many parents schedule one-on-one playtime with parents of toddlers similar in age. One- and 2-year-olds will be happy to play with a child of either gender, although you may discover through trial and error that some children have temperaments that don't mix well, such as one child who's outgoing and aggressive and another who's quite reserved.

Check your neighborhood association, church or synagogue, or pediatrician's bulletin board for information about play groups (also called mothers' groups, since it's the mothers who mostly benefit, in infancy and early toddlerhood, from the camaraderie of other women at the same place in life). Some churches and day care organizations sponsor mothers'-day-out programs, which are an abbreviated type of child care in which you leave your child in a group setting once or twice a week.

Another option is a more formal class for mothers and children. Those geared to toddlers typically have an exercise or music theme (such as swimming classes, Kindermusik, or Gymboree). Check your phone book or local YMCA/YWCA. Such programs aren't widely available for this age, however, since it's hard to get a group of toddlers to do anything together and on command. Finally, look into nursery schools and preschools. Those of high quality offer many wonderful benefits to a toddler. But, again, they're not necessary to a toddler's social development.

Finally, as your child grows, friendships with other adults are as important as peer relationships. Exposure to relatives and neighbors helps your child learn that there are many loving grown-ups in his world. Different people bring different social gifts. Grandma or Grandpa, for example, may possess infinitely more patience when it comes to the endless tea party or toy car race.

Peer Play Pointers

First friendships are no different than the first efforts at many new skills: They require lots of time and patience. Complicating matters is the complete lack of social graces in a toddler's repertoire. Without the language skills to express her feelings, a child may quickly resort to biting or hitting. You shouldn't expect too much of your child's early forays into the social whirl.

To make early play dates go more smoothly:

Keep it small. Three can be a very big crowd for toddlers. That's not to say that mothers' groups, in which as many as four or five moms get together with their children, are a bad idea. You can, however, expect more spats, more wildness—and less conversation for the grown-ups—with a group.

Stick around. While preschoolers do just fine when they're dropped off at a pal's house for the afternoon, toddlers are too immature and mercurial to be left without their parents or caregiver for very long.

WHAT IF...

I don't believe in corporal punishment but another mother in my play group does?

You can't insist on how a parent disciplines her own child, but you do have every right to make clear how you want yours handled. Be sure that you discuss this topic with the parents of the children your child plays with regularly. Explain the whys behind your viewpoint, and ask the other parents to respect your views. Some play groups address this issue by making each parent responsible for addressing her own child's behavior only.

NOT TO WORRY
Kids Who Won't Share

You can't expect toddlers to share. They're too young. A 1- or 2-year-old is naturally self-centered, in a positive way. She's developing a sense of who she is. And to her mind, her belongings are an extension of herself. Her blanket or doll or truck is a part of her. No way is she going to give it up just because you tell her to.

Although a toddler can't yet understand give-and-take or taking turns, you can plant the seeds of these concepts. Don't insist she give up a precious object, but praise her when she does so voluntarily: "Look how happy you made your friend when you shared your cookie." Rather than stepping in to break up a tussle, try saying, "When you are finished with that toy, then you can give it to Hannah for a little while." You may be surprised to see how calmly Hannah stops grabbing for the toy and how easily your child hands it over once *she* has decided it's okay to do so.

Time it right. Schedule play dates when both children are rested and fed. Best times include first thing in the morning or soon after the afternoon nap. Cancel if your child skipped her nap or seems like she's coming down with something.

Avoid the big buildup. It's best to tell your child less than an hour before the appointed time that he'll be getting together with a friend. Otherwise you risk your child becoming overly keyed up in anticipation.

Keep visits short. An hour is a long time for a young toddler. For 2½-year-olds, the best length of time for a play session with a friend is forty-five minutes to two hours. Keep your eye on the kids rather than the clock, though. When the happy mood evaporates and either the guest or the host seems to flag, it's time to call it a day. Best not to wait for the tears to flow.

Provide easy-to-share toys. Circumvent arguments over who gets the toy telephone or another choice plaything by making lots of fun communal objects available. Examples: multipart sets (such as blocks); multiples of the same item (balls, cars, or buckets); large objects (a plastic slide, a sandbox). Group activities are a good idea, too, such as blowing bubbles, dancing to music, or making an art project.

Ease up on the controls. Let the kids play at their own pace. It's great fun to get down and tumble with toddlers, but take care not to become overly involved in the activity or spend too much time directing it. Make suggestions or introduce a new toy to get things rolling, then sit back. You usually won't need to intervene unless one of them is in physical danger. Even a tussle over a toy can often be resolved by the children themselves, provided the grown-ups just hang back a few minutes. By leaving kids alone, they're better able to practice language skills and social repartee. But do keep a constant eye on the action. Toddler moods can change faster than the weather.

WHAT IF...

Play takes some violent turns?

Watch a child play long enough and you're apt to be startled by some uncharacteristically rough scenes. A toy farm is bombed repeatedly by blocks. Cars have spectacular wrecks, complete with loud crashing sound effects. A doll is spanked and sent to bed without any supper (even if you've never spanked your child). Resist the temptation to read any particular meaning into violent play. Your child may be safely acting out angry, pent-up feelings. He may be mimicking something he chanced to see on the evening news or overheard someone say. Or it may simply be experimental play. It's harmless, so long as real people go unhurt.

Distract and prevail. When the inevitable fight escalates into pushing or tears, spring into action. Rather than dissecting the feud or handing out lectures, change the pace by introducing a new activity or showing the children a brightly colored toy. You'll divert their attention from the conflict and restore peace quickly.

Don't call it quits just because the kids aren't playing together. Most toddler play dates feature a combination of parallel play and interactive play. Kids this age simply need a break every once in a while. You shouldn't feel that every minute ought to count in practicing social skills. If one of the children is excessively cranky or clingy, however, it's probably time to break up the party.

> ### PARENT TIP
>
> #### How Play Groups Help <u>You</u>
>
> **P**arenting a toddler is an all-consuming business. And many parents find it harder to run errands, keep up with friends, or just get out of the house with a toddler in tow than they did when the child was an infant. If you're feeling isolated, you may want to check out a play group for your own sake. There you'll meet other mothers or fathers of toddlers who share many of your concerns and preoccupations. And oh yes, your child will have fun, too!

Nip renegade behavior in the bud. Play groups sometimes feature a child who consistently acts up or behaves more aggressively than his peers, disrupting the scene time and again. If this becomes a problem for you, consider a group meeting of all the involved parents, preferably without the children around so that you can put two sentences of meaningful conversation together. Without pointing fingers, try to get to the root of the problem. Is there a temperament mismatch in your group? Is one child much older or much younger than the others, causing clashes? Is the play space too small or the toy assortment inadequate, therefore causing the children to sometimes lash out in frustration?

Discuss discipline. Even if your play group consists of just you and one other mother, it's smart to compare ground rules at the outset. For example, how you will handle biting or hitting? Will each mother deal with her own child, or can either parent intervene in an agreed-upon way? How will you handle house rules? One family may be more strict than another about eating snacks in the living room or running indoors. Usually it's best to let the host enforce her own home's rules, which keeps her sanity and avoids giving her own child mixed signals. Kids are very adaptable and will understand that one set of behavior applies at home but certain variations occur at Peter's house.

Fun Things to Do

Physical Games

Outdoors, you and your child can find an infinite number of ways to explore. Try to catch a squirrel or rabbit, fly like a butterfly, water the plants, play with a garden hose, take a walk in the rain, lie on the grass and watch the clouds float by, make snow angels after a fresh snowfall. Toddlers love bending low to concentrate on ladybugs and other insects. (The ground, after all, is closer to them than the tops of many bushes and flowers.) They also love almost any activity—running, jumping, sliding—that involves moving fast.

The following are active games that can be done outside or in:

Parade. Jazz up your march by wearing hats. Anything will do—consider party hats, winter caps, or costume headgear such as crowns, pirate hats, or cowboy hats. Carry flags or musical instruments. Use pot lids for cymbals, cardboard tubes for horns and flutes, an empty oatmeal container and a wooden spoon for a drum. If there are several children and you are outside, decorate ride-on vehicles, tricycles, and wagons with streamers or flags.

WHAT IF...

My child tries to eat the play dough and paint?

Don't give up, believing that your child is simply "too young" for these activities. Most young toddlers can't resist sampling the materials. It's part of their general approach to exploring and examining all things through their hands and mouths. Use materials that are labeled nontoxic, as most children's art supplies are. Choking is the biggest danger. Keep a watchful eye, and issue reminders: "This is for your hands, not for your mouth." Before long your child will be satisfied that art materials don't taste very good and are more fun to work with than to eat.

Walk this way. For this variation on Follow the Leader, guide your child on a jaunt in which you encourage her to walk as many different ways as you can think of. Try great big steps and tiny tiptoe steps. Walk fast and slow. Hop like a kangaroo and slither like a snake.

Tightrope. This game helps your child practice coordination. Place a long board (about four inches wide) flat on the ground, or use masking tape. Have your child try to walk across it without "falling" off. You can also pretend that the board is a balance beam, a bridge, or a pirate ship plank.

Ball games. Play catch by sitting a few feet away from your child with your legs spread open. Roll the ball back and forth. Gradually increase the distance between you. Eventually you can begin to toss the ball underhand.

Toy wash. Toddlers love to play with water. Give your child a small bucket and a cloth and show him how to scrub his tricycle, wagon, or other washable toys. Or let him help you wash the car. (Always be vigilant when your child is around large buckets of water.) Kids also like to "paint" with water. Provide a brush and water and let him use them to paint small objects indoors. Outside, a larger brush is a great tool for painting the driveway or the side of the house.

Be a beast. Encourage your child to pretend to be different types of animals. Ask her to move and make noises like the animal. Give prompts: "What does a bear sound like?" "Show me how a frog hops." "Can you fly like a bird?"

Nestled in the crook of your legs, your child can enjoy the sensation of "flying."

Pony rides. The thrill of this game, for your child, is being the one in charge for a change. Get down on all fours and let your child clamber aboard your back. Neigh, snort, buck, and trot. Let your child indicate where you should go. He also gets a workout mounting and dismounting and trying to hang on while you rear and try to throw him. A variation for the youngest toddlers: Cross your legs and let your child sit on the foot of the top leg, holding your hands. Gently kick your leg up and down as the child "rides." Here's one old nursery song (it's sexist but a classic; substitute your own nouns, if you like): "This is the way the ladies ride, clippity, clippity clop" (gentle bounces). "This is the way the gentlemen ride, clippity clippity clop" (faster bounces). "And this is the way the cowboys ride—clippity clippity *clop*" (faster bounces, ending in a dismount).

Song and Dance

Depending on the sound and the accompanying activity, music can be used to burn off energy or slow the day's pace. Add these musical games to your repertoire:

CHECKLIST
Ten Favorite Songs

Having trouble thinking up tunes to sing with your tot? The words to these classics ought to come back to you as soon as you hum a few bars:

✔ "Mary Had a Little Lamb"

✔ "Hey Diddle, Diddle, the Cat and the Fiddle"

✔ "I've Been Working on the Railroad"

✔ "Twinkle, Twinkle Little Star"

✔ "Here We Go Round the Mulberry Bush"

✔ "Home, Home on the Range"

✔ "Hush Little Baby"

✔ "Row, Row, Row Your Boat"

✔ "Pop Goes the Weasel"

✔ "The Farmer in the Dell"

The freeze dance. Play a tape or turn on the radio and dance. When the music stops, everyone freezes and holds their position. Then restart the music and dance some more. The freezing action challenges kids to keep their balance, and the dancing channels a wild child's vigor.

Mood dancing. Call out different emotions for your child to act out in a dance: the angry dance, sad dancing, happy dancing, and so on. This game teaches your child about emotions while he's practicing body control and burning off energy. It's even better (but not necessary) if you play different, appropriate musical selections that underscore the point.

Fill-in-the-blank songs. Try this one in the car. Young toddlers who are just learning their nursery rhymes will delight in calling out the missing words or phrases to songs you sing. For example, you sing, "Hickory dickory dock, the mouse ran up the ———." Obviously, you need to use familiar tunes. "Old MacDonald Had a Farm" is a wonderful song with built-in blanks. Let your child choose the different animals for each verse, or look at a book with animal pictures while you sing as prompts for him to name.

Finger play. Your child can practice coordination by imitating you as you accompany these stories and songs with hand motions. Classics include "The Itsy Bitsy Spider," "Patty Cake," and "Where Is Thumbkin?" A variation on the latter that also teaches body parts is to sing "Where is ankle [belly button, nose]" and touch that part of your child when you say "Here I am!" Don't forget "Bingo" ("There was a farmer had a dog, and Bingo was his name-o"; repeat the verses, each time substituting claps for another letter, or spell out your child's name or nickname). Another favorite is "Three Little Ducks": "Three little ducks went out to play [hold up three fingers], over the hills and far away [wiggle fingers to indicate swimming]. Mama Duck said quack, quack, quack, quack [make your hand move like a duck's bill], two little ducks came running back [hold up two fingers]." Repeat verses, counting down until all the ducks disappear, and then make them reappear.

Ring around the rosy. You remember the tune: "Ring around the rosy, a pocket full of posies, ashes, ashes, we all fall *down!*" On the last word, everyone tumbles to the ground. Add a teddy bear to your circle if one parent and one child don't seem like enough bodies for tumbling. Another familiar song with movement is "I'm a Little Teapot."

Rainy Day Play

These fun indoor monotony breakers work great in sunny or in gloomy weather.

I spy. Pick an object in the room. Say, "I spy, with my little eye, something that is... yellow." Start by giving your child lots of clues, such as "something that is yellow and in a bowl on the table" or "something that is on the wall and rings whenever Grandma calls." This game helps toddlers learn to classify objects by color, size, shape, or purpose.

Water play. Water engrosses a toddler longer than almost anything. Set up a safe space where your child can play, under your supervision. Place a dishpan of water on the floor, in the kitchen sink, on the opened door of the dishwasher (where any spills go right into the dishwasher when you close the door). Good water playthings include measuring spoons and cups, sponges, the plastic tops of shaving cream cans and similar canisters, plastic teacups, small plastic squirt bottles, and funnels. Keep plenty of towels on hand to mop up spills.

Cooking. Toddlers love to watch their parents fixing meals as bystanders, but their concentration may be brief. Keep your child involved by giving her simple tasks such as dumping the flour into the mixing bowl or stirring bat-

---

PARENT TIP

Are You Exhausted?

Before many adults have children, they feel self-conscious about playing with kids. It does require a certain degree of surrender to make like a duck in your living room or fly around the front yard with your arms outstretched like an airplane. But there are lots of good reasons to let yourself go. Not only does actively playing with your child let you see what's on his mind and how he thinks, but it's the perfect grown-up stress breaker. Child's play can be both physically and mentally releasing. So pound that play dough! Crawl under that table! And here's the best part: Your child will love you for it.

It's worth the mess to let your child "help" in the kitchen.

ter. Applying decorations—to cut-out cookies or cupcakes—is another surefire, if messy, kitchen treat. Or let your child pretend to be the chef himself. Clear off a space on the counter or table. Put an apron on your child (both to keep him clean and to add to the ambiance). Let him stand on a step stool or sit in a chair, so that he's at a comfortable height. Give him measuring cups and spoons, and a set of bowls for transferring the mix. Foods that work well include cooked rice or uncooked oatmeal (interesting texture, not too messy, okay to taste) or uncooked pasta (which has the added advantage of coming in a variety of interesting shapes, but don't let your child put raw pasta in his mouth—it can be a choking hazard).

Do you like this smell? Toddlers are becoming aware of different smells. Have fun with this development by exposing him to different scents around the kitchen. Try your spice rack, fruits, flowers, teas and coffee. Show your child how to sniff, so the powdery substances don't get into his nose. Name the object being smelled.

Post office. Make a mailbox out of a cardboard shoe box by cutting a wide slit into the top. Give your child old junk mail, postcards, or the subscription cards found in magazines to use as pretend mail. She will love inserting the papers into the box one after another, and then opening the box and beginning again. Send your own postcards to her—she'll love to receive real mail and add them to her mailbox collection. You can also make postcards out of heavyweight paper, cut to postcard size, that she can color and send to relatives.

Keys to the city. Improve your child's hand-eye coordination while allowing him to emulate you. Gather up your old keys, or purchase colorful blanks at a hardware store, and place them on a special key ring for your child. Most toddlers love the jangle of the real thing more than plastic baby toy keys. For one thing, they fit (more or less) into the doors around your house. Your child will love to go from door to door pretending to work the locks.

Indoor picnic. The novelty of this experience is its delight. It's a surefire way to break the monotony of a rainy day. Spread a tablecloth or blanket on the living room floor and fill a basket with lunch goodies. Eat on the floor. And no ants! (Outdoor picnics in your backyard make great unexpected treats on sunny days, too.)

Scrub-a-dub. Fill a basin with sudsy water and let your child wash all her dolls and their clothes. To dry them, hang a string for a clothesline between two lawn chairs in the basement.

Make-Believe

Most toddlers will develop pretend dramas on their own with just the everyday dolls and playthings available to them. Additional ways to spark creative play:

Play telephone. Young toddlers love to have imaginary conversations on a toy telephone. Show them how it's done, including making the phone "ring" and saying hello and goodbye.

Puppet shows. Buy plush puppets or use ordinary dolls or action figures. Or make your own puppets out of paper bags, gloves, or socks that you decorate. Fancy wood puppet theaters are available in toy catalogs, or you can improvise with a cut-out box or by crouching behind a low table or hamper. Help your child get the idea by staging a simple story or two yourself. Something as simple as two puppets meeting, saying hello, and saying goodbye constitutes a fascinating plot for most 1- and 2-year-olds. Then let your child entertain you.

Dress up. Foster more vivid role playing by making costumes available to your child. Invest money in pretend costumes if you like, but you probably already have plenty around the house. A dress-up wardrobe can include old Halloween costumes, ready-made outfits bought at toy stores (such as pirate

---

WHAT IF...

My toddler doesn't want to stick with one activity very long?

It can be disappointing if you've invested a great deal of time and effort into planning an activity and have to watch your child lose interest after just five or ten minutes. But that's the way it goes with toddlers. Forcing your child to soldier on will only make both of you unhappy.

HOW TO
Make Play Clay

Softer than modeling clay, this dough has countless uses. Provide lots of tools to extend its interest. With play dishes and plastic knives, it becomes pretend food. Add toothpicks and macaroni flourishes, and it becomes art. Show your child how to sculpt shapes, roll balls, flatten it with a cup, and use a rolling pin and cookie cutters. (It's not edible, however.) The basic recipe:

1. Mix 1 tablespoon vegetable oil, 1 cup water, and ½ teaspoon food coloring in a saucepan.

2. Add 2 teaspoons cream of tartar, 1 cup flour, and ½ cup salt. Stir until it forms a soft paste.

3. Cook over medium heat, stirring constantly, until the paste begins to come away from the sides of the pan, forming a ball (about five minutes).

4. Cool the dough until you can work it with your hands. Knead until smooth.

5. Store the dough in an airtight container in the refrigerator. It should last for several months.

gear, a ballerina tutu, crowns, cowboy duds), and your own castoff pieces, including jackets, slips, and sweaters. Half the fun is in the details: old shoes and boots, costume jewelry, hats, purses, shawls, vests, ties, gloves, and the like. Keep these things in a special trunk or basket. Don't stage-manage the game. Take your cues from your child. If he wants you to tuck a kitchen towel into his collar for a superhero cape, that's wonderful creativity. Nor should you make light of your child's actions or suggest that there's a better way to do it. For example, avoid pointing out that a real bride wouldn't wear a blanket for a veil and you'll take her to the store to look for something more appropriate. To her eyes, the blanket is the veil, and that's all that matters.

Instant village. Cut apart and flatten a large brown-paper grocery sack so that you have a large piece of paper on which to draw. Tape the ends onto the floor. Ask your child what he'd like to see in the village. With thick markers or crayons, draw roads, buildings, railroad tracks, lakes, and rivers. Cut holes in both ends of a shoe box to make a tunnel, for example. Half the fun is in the making, but your child can also use the scene for his toy cars or farm animals.

My hideaway. Construct a tent by draping a blanket or large sheet over a table. It's best if the ends touch the floor, creating a cozy hiding space. Let your child keep a special blanket and toys there, or some favorite books. Add a sleeping bag, a flashlight, a pair of toy binoculars, a knapsack, and play dishes such as pots, and your child can go camping. Or pretend that the tent is a cave, a fort, a castle, a house, or a bunny hutch.

More play with props. Assemble appropriate items to create an imaginary scenario. Toddler favorites include a grocery store (toy cash register, empty cartons and food boxes, basket or shopping cart), restaurant (low table and chairs, plastic dishes and food), airplane (lined-up chairs), doctor (doctor's bag and tools, such as bandages and a toy stethoscope), and nursery (baby bed and diaper-changing area). A laundry basket makes a marvelous boat, or a large cardboard box can become a car or a train. You don't need to construct an elaborate set or invest much money in such a project. Simply provide a few skeletal props and your child will do the rest.

Arts and Crafts

Many toddlers, often boys, show little interest in projects involving fine-motor skills. Before 18 months, he may not have the manual dexterity to hold a crayon well, let alone draw you a picture. Or his consuming passion may be more physical right now. Give it time. When your child does pursue an art project, let go of your adult expectations; concentrate less on the finished product than on the process.

A few spare blankets can transform a simple table into a fairy tale castle.

Beaded necklaces. Cut a length of string or ribbon, or use a shoelace, which is easy for a toddler to grasp. Tie a fat knot in the end. Provide a bowl of stringable items, such as macaroni (penne and ziti are ideal for chubby fingers), wooden beads, or large buttons. Supervise your child closely if the items pose a choking hazard.

HOW TO

Make Bubbles

Here's the main thing you need to know about kids and bubbles: You will never have enough. Containers inevitably spill or get knocked over. And you'll use bubbles all summer long. (You can even blow bubbles inside, if you're a lenient sort with an easy-to-mop kitchen floor, but be careful about slipping if the floor gets too slick.) Buy a few bottles at the store (so you can use their bubble wands over and over) or make your own:

1. Into a large pot, mix 1 gallon of water, ½ cup dishwashing liquid, and 2 tablespoons of glycerin (available at drugstores). Experiment. Depending on the brand of dish soap, you may not need the glycerin.

2. Let your child stir the pot with a spoon or, for more bubbles, an eggbeater or wire whisk.

3. Use blowers saved from store-bought bubbles to blow them into the air.

Painting sticks and stones. Little artists aren't fussy about the canvases they use. To vary their painting activity, try using sticks, stones, or seashells they've collected. The bigger they are, the easier they'll be to handle. Experiment with watercolors and tempera paints on different surfaces.

Make your own book. Staple together paper trimmed to about four by six inches, or use a small photo album or a multipage plastic wallet insert for pictures and credit cards. Attach to each page photos of people and objects familiar to your child, both snapshots and pictures cut out of magazines (Grandma, Barney, a dog, a banana). You can let an older toddler choose the pictures and make up stories about them.

Make your own puzzle. Have your child draw a picture on a large sheet of construction paper. When he's finished, cut the paper into several pieces (two or three for young toddlers, eight or ten for an older toddler). If you like, cover the paper with clear contact paper before cutting it, which makes it easier to handle. Other good puzzles: a large photograph or color photocopy glued to cardboard, old greeting cards, or a piece of printed cardboard, such as the bright back of a cereal box.

Paper garden. Look through old magazines and have your child find as many different pictures of flowers as she can. An older toddler can cut out the pictures with child-safe scissors, but you'll have to do the cutting for a younger child. Paste the images onto a piece of green construction paper. Or look for pictures of another theme: a puppy farm, a dinner tray, or a family of people.

Field Trips

One of the best gifts you can give a toddler is to expose her to the outside world. Take her along on errands. Places you take for granted—the grocery store, the car wash, the florist—are fascinating new worlds to her. Give your outing extra time. Pause to point out the racks of clothes that go round and round at the touch of a button at the dry cleaner's, for example, or let her drop the mail in the chute at the post office. Make special journeys to places of interest such as these:

Firehouse. Toddlers are enthralled by big machines. And the flashiest of all is the fire truck. On a visit to your neighborhood station, introduce your child to the fire-fighters. Some stations will let you schedule special visits during which you can even sit on the truck.

Construction site. Diggers, cement mixers, men in hard hats, and lots of dirt—what's not to like, from a toddler's point of view? Never let your child run free at such a site, of course, and beware that some kids may be frightened by the noise.

Petting zoo. Many zoos and some open-to-the-public farms feature children's petting areas where young kids can get up close to the animals. Next best thing: a pet store. You won't be able to handle the merchandise, but it's a free way to see a mesmerizing display of fish, exotic birds, guinea pigs, and puppies.

WHAT IF...

I'm not very arts-and-crafts-oriented?

Rest assured that your child won't be deprived. Despite the widespread popularity of craft projects in magazines and books, not everyone has the talent or patience to lead children in these kinds of activities. Fortunately, art to a toddler can be as simple as finger-painting on a piece of white paper. It's the process of creating that's more important than the results. Keep on hand a box of crayons, a tub of play dough, and some of those paint-with-water coloring books (available at dime stores) and you're set. What's more important is that you join your child in activities that you enjoy. He'll get as much out of putting on a puppet show with stuffed animals as he will in actually making the puppets with you, and collecting leaves on a walk is fun whether or not you make leaf rubbings out of them later.

CHECKLIST
Terrific Toddler Videos

What's appropriate entertainment for the very young? Try these ten reliable choices:

✓ *Barney's 1-2-3-4 Seasons* (Barney Home Video). TV episodes on video featuring the big purple dinosaur and lots of lively songs.

✓ *Dumbo* (Walt Disney Home Video). Many Disney cartoons, especially those made in the 1980s and 1990s, are far over the heads of young viewers, but this classic holds 2-year-old appeal.

✓ *Good Night Baby, Good Night* (Company Company Partners). Familiar lullaby music and scenes of children going through bedtime rituals.

✓ *Here Come the Teletubbies* (Warner Bros. Video). First in the gentle series about toddler favorites Tinky Winky, Dipsy, Laa-Laa, and Po.

✓ *Jane Hissey's Old Bear Stories* (Sony Wonder). Stuffed animals come to life in these funny, gentle tales.

✓ Maurice Sendak's *Little Bear Family Tales* (Paramount Home Video). The loving family scenes of Else Holmelund Minarik are beautifully rendered.

✓ *Richard Scarry's Best Sing-Along Mother Goose Video Ever!* (Random House Home Video). Friendly animated animals and familiar nursery songs.

✓ *Sesame Street Kids' Guide to Life: Learning to Share* (Sony Wonder). Starring Muppet favorite Elmo.

✓ *Where's Spot?* (Walt Disney Home Video). Engaging, gentle vignettes starring the dog from Eric Hill's lift-the-flap books.

✓ *Winnie the Pooh and the Blustery Day* (Disney). Academy Award–winning cartoon starring Pooh, Tigger, Piglet, and the gang.

Nature walks. Announce a mission or theme for each walk. For instance, you might spend one walk looking for dandelions, and another counting birds. Bring along a magnifying glass one day, or a basket for collecting pretty rocks and feathers. Another day you could focus on identifying different smells (freshly mown grass, flowers, dirt) or looking for as many different blue things as you can find.

Library. Aside from saving you money, these visits open a wider world of books to your child and provide a gentle introduction to conducting one's self in a public place. Find out if your library has a story hour for young children (but don't expect a toddler to stay still and attentive the entire time).

Airport. Find a good spot for watching the big birds take off and land. At smaller airports, you may be able to watch outdoors or visit a hangar. Take turns guessing what kind of cargo is on board and where the planes are heading.

HOT TOPIC

How Much TV?

There's no doubt that television has the power to entertain, to teach, to inspire, and to influence the way even its youngest viewers think about the world around them. When should TV watching become a part of your child's life, and how much is appropriate? Many toddlers aren't interested in TV until around age 2, when their attention span lengthens. They then become fascinated. Ideally, a child younger than 18 months should be exposed to very little TV, just ten or fifteen minutes a day at most. After 18 months, you can introduce a half-hour program a few times a week, up to about an hour a day for 2-year-olds.

The main reason for such stringent guidelines is that there's simply no need to develop the TV habit so early. Especially during toddlerhood, your child is learning at a rapid pace and establishing many of the lifestyle ground rules that will shape his later years. Heavy TV viewing has been linked with a sedentary lifestyle, childhood obesity, poorer school performance, aggressive behavior, and fewer social interactions.

That said, there's nothing like a half hour of *Teletubbies* to buy you some relief while you put away groceries or make dinner. And television can have educational benefits, broadening a child's horizons or enticing him to read books that feature familiar characters, for example. Fortunately for today's parents, the VCR provides a safe TV haven, a way to guarantee high-quality programs that are suitable for toddlers. It's not a bad idea to invest in a small library of age-appropriate tapes. Your child will watch the ones he loves over and over. Or, record your child's favorite TV show for repeat viewings.

But choose carefully. You can't, for example, assume that just because a show is a cartoon, it's right for a 2-year-old. Some of the best programming for the very young features a friendly host (Big Bird, Mr. Rogers, Steve on *Blue's Clues*), young children that your child can identify with, lots of music, and simple presentations about familiar scenarios.

CHAPTER FOUR

Beginning Discipline

Many parents are shocked the first time they hear themselves shouting a sharp "No!" to their baby. From birth, your child has been cuddly and compliant. Discipline? It hasn't been much of a priority. But in fact you have been shaping your child's behavior practically since birth. She cried; you fed her. She was wet; you changed her. She reached for a dangerous object, and you snatched it away. In this way, you've been teaching your child to develop a set of expectations about the world, which help her learn how to act.

Now that your child is walking, the need to guide her behavior becomes more apparent and more urgent. The way you respond to your child's behavior now shapes her future actions and, indeed, her very personality. Some experts believe that how a child is disciplined during the second year of life has a profound influence on whether she's a delight or a terror by age 3.

Now the rub: How do you teach good behavior to a not-yet-rational, nonverbal young toddler, whose understanding of the finer concepts—such as manners, sharing, and empathy, not to mention personal safety—is primitive to nonexistent? Start with a lot of patience and practice, and the advice in this chapter.

The Basics

Defining Discipline

To most people, the word *discipline* means punishment. Playing cop. Laying down the law. Yet in reality, punitive measures should be only a tiny part of the discipline picture—especially with toddlers. Discipline shouldn't be something that you do *after* your child misbehaves. It ought to be an everyday, ongoing process of correcting undesirable behaviors while promoting desirable ones. Think of discipline not as something bad, but as a force for good. In a sense, it ought to be your overarching attitude toward child rearing, the very backdrop of your family life.

The basic guideline: You are the teacher and your child is your pupil, or disciple. The words *disciple* and *discipline*, in fact, share the Latin root *discipulus*, meaning "one who learns." The only way your child is going to learn standards of behavior, right from wrong, and self-control is through your showing him the way. It doesn't come naturally.

Seem too early for all this? Whether your child is a perfect angel or already demonstrates normal toddler daredevilry, there are plenty of good reasons why thinking about discipline is so essential now. Start with safety. Your child doesn't know that he can't dive willy-nilly off a staircase. He doesn't understand that an open flame will burn him. Yet his natural exuberance and curiosity compel him to experiment in these ways. Discipline for 1- and 2-year-olds is also important because it sets the stage for later social development. Your goal should be to instill *self-discipline*, so that as your child grows he's increasingly able to make his own choices about behavior that's safe, appropriate, proper, moral, and considerate.

The Golden Rules

The specific ways you'll shape your child's behavior will vary in a zillion ways, depending on such factors as the situation, your child's age and temperament, where you are, and even the hour of the day. But the following general guidelines should provide the foundation of your overall approach to loving, effective discipline.

WHAT IF...

My child hits me?

A child resorts to his fists when he's too upset to find the words to express his anger, or when he lacks the word power. Understanding why he hits should make you more empathetic. But it's never wise to excuse or condone antisocial behaviors. Say, "No hitting. Hitting hurts." Let your child know that he can slug a pillow when he's upset—you might designate a special one for that purpose—but never a person. Follow up with an appropriate punishment, such as a time-out. Never hit back.

Accentuate the positive. It's easy to fall into the habit of simply reacting to your child, forever intervening and correcting when something goes amiss. But you'll have better success if you look for opportunities to actively reinforce good behavior. Your child prizes your affection and approval above all else. That's why positive reinforcement makes for a better teacher than more punitive forms of discipline.

Give hugs when your child is behaving well. Praise or compliment her in a specific way, when it's appropriate: "I like how you put your puzzle back on the shelf when you were finished." Provide attention before she starts to whine for it. Pace your child so that she doesn't get overtired or frustrated. When she does show signs of flagging, shift gears for a nap, snack, or different activity before a total meltdown occurs. Above all, show your child respect. Your efforts foster a sense of security and build self-confidence. You'll also reduce the overall need for intervention.

A few hugs and a lot of positive reinforcement go a long way toward guiding your child's behavior.

Prevent problems whenever you can. Toddler-proofing removes most of the no-nos from your child's environment—which means you spend less time chastising. (See Chapter 6, page 224.) It's also wise to avoid situations that you know will cause trouble: trying to run one more errand when it's already past nap time, or wheeling a hungry tyke past the candy-filled checkout counter at the grocery. If you know your child can't sit still in a restaurant, why tempt fate? Order take-out instead. Ward off battles over inappropriate clothing by storing winter things out of reach in summer, and vice versa.

Another way to minimize the odds of a tussle is to offer your child helpful reminders *before* things go awry. Toddlers are just getting used to the idea of having rules, and their memories are short. Before a bath, for example, gently remind your child: "The rule is, if you splash, you have to come out." As you give her an ice pop, say, "Eat this in the kitchen."

Set limits. All kids need limits—clear, consistent, and plentiful limits. In fact, they crave them in order to feel secure. Limits define for your child the boundaries of acceptable and unacceptable behavior. Such boundaries are reassuring. They let your child know that you're in charge, that there are predictable forces at work in his universe. Your child learns limits through your cues, your spoken reminders, and by testing.

At first, defining and enforcing rules may not seem very necessary. What harm is it, you might ask yourself, if your 12-month-old pulls every book off the shelf or your 18-month-old neglects to say "please"? The answer is that your responses shape your child's future actions. If you don't approve of a behavior now—even if your child looks comically cute as he's defying you—you won't like it after you've experienced it a few dozen times, either. This means that you need to decide how you feel about the assorted mischief your toddler will inevitably get into as he begins to push the envelope of his world. He's trying to figure out what's okay and what's not. Your job is to tell him. It's easy to excuse toddler transgressions by saying, "Oh, he's just a lit-

GOOD ADVICE
Foiling Spoiling

"When Kendall, 2, sees a toy she wants, I tell her we can't buy it now but we can put it on her wish list for her birthday. When we get home, we write it down together. She doesn't have a fit at the store because I take the time to listen to her when she wants something."

—*Kristy Isaak, Manhattan Beach, California*

"Sometimes when 14-month-old Katherine acts naughty, I pretend she's not bothering me. Usually she gets bored and moves on to the next thing. If kids get attention every time they want it, they'll think that's how the world works."

—*Cynthia Foote, Annapolis, Maryland*

"I'm good at saying no, but with my daughter, Taylor, who's 2, I always want to say yes. She's Daddy's little girl! I'm tempted to spoil her, but I've learned that when you give in once, like buying a balloon at the grocery store, she'll want one every time she goes there."

—*Doug Dunn, Valley Forge, Pennsylvania*

tle guy" or "He won't understand if I say no." But toddlers are smart. With your help and patience, they're perfectly capable of learning right from wrong.

Don't be afraid to be firm. Some parents err too far on the easygoing side of discipline. Perhaps remembering their own dislike of rules and regulations as a child, they institute few of their own. Or parents may be so focused on having a good time with their child that they hate to spoil it by saying no. It's natural to want your child to enjoy your time together. Dreading playing the heavy is a common predicament for a father or mother who feels insecure about his or her relatively new role as parent, or works long hours, or is divorced without full custody.

Certainly indulgence has its place in parenthood. So does allowing your child a healthy measure of freedom. But these things should exist side by side with clear-cut expectations. Over time, a lack of firmness tends to backfire. If no limits are enforced, you're depriving your child of an understanding of how you expect him to behave. Rather than making him feel liberated, the opposite tends to occur: a lack of controls unnerves a small child. Parents tend to wind up facing more discipline dilemmas rather than fewer. Kids without limits also fail to learn to take responsibility for their actions or to respect others' feelings.

Sure, your toddler's defiance is as comical as it is annoying, but if you want to nip that behavior in the future, it's best to stifle your laugh.

If you're too lenient, your child is also apt to take advantage of you. He'll soon discover which buttons to push to get the response that he (not you) desires. And you can be sure he'll push them again and again. That's how small problems blossom into big ones. Better to make it clear that you run your home, not your child. The sooner you start, the easier it is for everyone.

Of course, being firm doesn't mean that to be an effective disciplinarian, a parent ought to act like the humorless, inflexible director of a junior boot camp. The other extreme is risky, too. It's possible for mothers and fathers to be overly rigid. Not only do such parents set limits that cover every possible aspect of the child's life, but they proceed to enforce each and every one. Authoritarian parents tend to be perfectionists or people accustomed to control. They may lack the patience to understand the unique mind-set of a

WHAT IF...

My child resists so much I can't buckle him into the car seat?

Especially from about 12 to 18 months of age, toddlers hate to be immobilized. That goes for being diapered, getting dressed, or sitting in a high chair when they're not eating. They want to be on the move. Your life will be easier if you accept this fact and keep restraints to a minimum. Of course, for safety's sake, you can't compromise about car seats. Try tickling your child's upper leg. He'll relax just long enough for you to get him in a seated position and buckle the belt. Distractions such as songs or a special toy to hold can further relax him long enough to be strapped in securely.

young child, resorting instead to the because-I-said-so school of discipline. They may also rely on such tactics as fear, intimidation, and nonstop nagging. These parents may have been raised in similar homes themselves. But a too-tough approach to shaping your child's behavior fails on many levels. It sets up an adversarial relationship, which is rarely a useful way to teach anyone anything. Being inflexible with your child inhibits his natural curiosity as well, and may cause him to grow up lacking confidence and self-esteem.

A middle course between leniency and authoritarianism usually works best. Respect your child's individuality and freedom, but help her move with confidence toward a socially adept and well-adjusted future. Combine love and limits.

Hold realistic expectations. You'll set yourself up for failure if you're forever aiming for unrealistic goals regarding your child's behavior. One-year-olds can barely sit still for fifteen minutes, let alone for an hour at the table while the entire family dines. A 2-year-old isn't physically capable of making her bed all by herself. Familiarize yourself with the basics of toddler development so that you have a sense of what's plausible. Do take care, though, to increase your expectations as your child grows. An 18-month-old with a fifty-word vocabulary is capable of learning *please*. Biting should not be condoned at any age.

Aim for consistency. Once you make a rule, enforce it regularly. Inconsistencies confuse a learning child. Why could he have a treat at the supermarket yesterday, but not today? If it was all right to dump sand out of the sandbox yesterday, why are you so mad about it today? Follow through on your rules in a predictable fashion, too. If you say that it will be time to leave the playground after your child goes down the slide two more times, then do so. Don't wait for him to make three more trips, or ten. That may not seem like a big deal, but the next time you're ready to leave after "two more times," you probably won't be taken seriously. And why should you be? You've already proven that you don't really mean what you say. Both parents should present a generally consistent and unified approach as well.

Of course, it's virtually impossible to be 100 percent consistent in all things, all the time. Exceptions are unavoidable and have their place. For example, you might decide to let your child bounce on the sofa cushions—something ordinarily verboten—when she's been trapped inside for several rainy days, or to eat her snack in the living room instead of the kitchen if friends are visiting. Explain why a deviation from the norm is special and just for that day. No need to let your quest for consistency turn you into a total killjoy. Trust your instincts. What's important is that you make the general standards of behavior clear.

Keep your cool. When you're setting limits, a serious demeanor sends the message "This is important." Be somber, yet gentle. Also, being neutral keeps the focus on the behavior rather than the child. Yes, this is easier said than done. It can be a challenge to curb your temper when your 1-year-old has just written with permanent marker on the wall or your 2-year-old has unspooled an entire new roll of toilet paper. Raising one's voice is a natural reaction to anger or disapproval. But yelling is both degrading and poor role modeling. About the only thing it accomplishes is making you feel better (maybe) and inspiring your child to scream as well. Your disciplinary message will have much more impact if you can deliver it in a calm, rational manner. If you're furious, take time to count to ten or run through some Lamaze breathing before you intervene.

A too-timid response, on the other hand, can be just as ineffective as shouting. Sounding too mild or uncertain dilutes your message. Avoid couching commands as questions: "Stop jumping on the sofa, okay, honey?" "Do you want to go to bed now?" Also try not to issue a reprimand even as you're laughing. It can be hard to keep a straight face when your child is up to his

> ## WHAT IF...
>
> ### My child just laughs when I say no?
>
> **T**hink how you'd react if you heard something over and over all day long: You'd tune out. That's what happens to a toddler who hears a constant refrain of no's.
>
> See how many no's you can eliminate by rephrasing. Tell your child what you *do* want. Instead of "No throwing food!" try "Food stays on the tray." Or say yes, as in "Yes, I'll get you out of the high chair after I wash your hands." Quick, urgent phrases often pack the same power as no while delivering a more specific message: "Hot!" "Stop!" "Dirty—don't touch!" Finally, take care to avoid what's called "piggybacking" —that's adding on to a no a long string of extra words that are typically lost on the child in the heat of the moment. For example, don't say something like "No! Don't do that. Give me the book. Why would you tear the pages? See how it's breaking?" Better to take the book away and firmly say, "We don't tear books."

Shaken Baby Syndrome

Don't let the name fool you. Toddlers, too, are susceptible to shaken baby syndrome (SBS), a severe and potentially fatal form of head injury. It's caused by sudden, traumatic motion, such as by being shaken, thrown vigorously into the air, or hit too hard on the back. Children from birth to age 2 are at the greatest risk. Young children's neck muscles aren't fully developed and their brain tissue is very fragile. If a child is shaken, the brain is literally jostled within the skull. This can cause brain swelling and damage, blindness, and even death.

While frightening and practically unthinkable, it's important to remember that the vast majority of SBS cases are caused by deliberate child abuse. Gently bouncing on Grandpa's knee or riding on the back of your bicycle over a gravel road doesn't place a child at grave risk. It's a whiplashlike motion that does the damage. Still, it's important to be aware of the danger. Toddlers *do* cry and whine and drive their parents crazy. It's not always easy, but try to handle your child in an even-tempered manner. If you find yourself enraged beyond control, don't address the situation right away. Place your child safely in a crib or playpen until you've had a chance to calm down.

Never leave your child with someone whom you suspect of having a problem controlling his or her temper. Seek medical care immediately if you believe that your child may have been shaken. Signs of SBS include a stunned, glassy-eyed look; an inability to lift the head; blood pooling in the eyes; dilated pupils that don't constrict in the light; or vomiting in an otherwise healthy infant. A victim may have only one of these symptoms or none at all.

elbows in an upturned chocolate cake. Either laugh it off or issue a reprimand while keeping a straight face. Reactions that send a conflicting message—"I'm serious, sort of"—are counterproductive. If you care enough to intervene about a matter, convey your message with appropriate gravity.

Be brief. Use as few words as possible to get your message across. There's no need, for example, to stray into the medical facts about why sticking dried beans up one's nose is a bad idea. A toddler benefits most from short, to-the-point messages: "Not safe." "We don't do that." "Biting hurts." "Hot." "Walk, don't run."

Take your child's temperament into consideration. "One size fits all" doesn't apply to discipline. Some easygoing children respond well to low-key reminders and a single warning. Others have temperaments that are more persistent and demanding. They may need more stringent limits; if you give in once, they'll take advantage of it later. Be open-minded about good ways to handle various situations. Your child's personality comes into ever-sharper focus during toddlerhood. You'll learn what works best as you go along with your child.

Don't expect miracles. Discipline is an ongoing process. The conversion from untamed baby to model citizen takes a good twenty-one years or more—it won't happen overnight. Be patient. You'll find yourself imparting the same lessons over and over for years to come: "Sit on your bottom." "Say please." "Walk, don't run." It's helpful if you can phrase some of the most common reminders using the same words every time: "If you hit, you sit" (as in sitting down for a time-out). Or in the bathroom, "Pee in a line, everything's fine. Pee on the floor, clean up more." The effect of your repetitive efforts is cumulative. Even when your child is defying you or ignoring you, he's absorbing a lesson. One day he really will say *please* without prompting and pee straight into the toilet bowl.

Set a good example. We've all heard about the mother who slaps her child's hand as she scolds, "No hitting!" Another negative behavior parents unwittingly demonstrate is grabbing. If your child has something you don't want him to have, it's better to calmly ask for it in a no-nonsense tone and hold out your own hand. Or gently unfurl his fingers from his grasp and say something like, "Not safe." Practice what you preach.

Why Toddlers Misbehave

Before you get angry when your child behaves in an undesirable way, take stock of *his* point of view. Why is he acting the way he is? When sizing up a situation, always take into account the circumstances and your child's developmental stage. This doesn't necessarily excuse the behavior, of course, nor mean that you shouldn't respond. But first asking yourself "What was that all about?" helps you shape a more empathic and appropriate response.

> ## WHAT IF...
>
> ### My toddler walks away when I talk to him?
>
> **O**ne-year-olds can be maddeningly oblivious, even in the middle of a scolding. Or your child may be deliberately ignoring you. Don't yell from across a room and expect him to freeze until you've finished. Go over to your child. Get down to his level, with one hand around his waist or gently resting on his shoulder. Be kind but firm. Keep your discussion short and focused. No long lectures. Then let him go on.

Common causes of acting up at this age include:

WHAT IF...

My child deliberately defies me?

She's not being mean-spirited. At this age, willful disobedience is called testing. Your child wants to know what happens if she does something you've just warned her not to do. Unfortunately, it can take countless repetitions for your lesson to sink in. Use words ("Don't touch!") or actions (such as a time-out) to reinforce your message. Persevere, and eventually you'll be rewarded with a child who knows and follows the rules.

Physical discomfort. Take a child on a long morning of errands past nap time, and the tantrum in aisle ten of Wal-Mart isn't about a toy she's spotted. It's her way of saying, "Enough!" Along with fatigue, hunger and sickness can also cause misbehavior.

Curiosity. A 1-year-old who persists in playing with the telephone, or a 2-year-old who can't stop chasing the cat, is fascinated and having fun, rather than being willfully disobedient. Toddlers learn about the world through hands-on exploration. Your child may be intent on discovering how a spoon dropped off a high chair sounds different from a pea. A toddler lacks the self-control to curb this kind of discovery-by-doing, especially in the face of a new and intriguing situation. If there's no real harm being done, it's best to resist intervening.

Testing. Even the best-behaved children go through a contrary phase around 14 to 22 months, which can last for six months or longer. This is when a child grows increasingly aware of his personal power. Intoxicated by the discovery, it's as if your child is asking himself, "Just what am I capable of, and how much can I get away with?" He tries to wield this newfound power at every opportunity. This impulse to push the envelope is compounded by a high degree of willful determination, a low tolerance for frustration, and poor communication skills. Contrariness is intensified if the child is asked to make a major behavioral change during this phase, such as getting rid of the pacifier or beginning toilet training.

A desire for attention. A child might be bored, lonely, or just thrilled with the agitated response he's learned to create by playing with the buttons on the TV set. So boundless is a child's craving for attention that he may find it more appealing to face the consequences of a misdeed than to be ignored.

Frustration. Toddlerhood is fraught with limitations, both physical (such as an inability to stack blocks perfectly) and imposed (such as having to hold your hand when crossing a street). What's more, a toddler lacks the verbal skills that enable an older child to make his wishes known or to let off steam. As a result, frustration mounts quickly. It's often vented as aggression, anger, and other forms of anti-social behavior. The swiftness and fierceness of these outbursts can startle you. Remember that although your child may appear far more coordinated and capable than he was just six months earlier, he still has a lot of maturing to do. It's not always developmentally possible for him to control his temper.

When Parents Disagree

Probably because it's such an important and relentless task, disciplining children ranks right up there with money as a top zone of contention in a marriage. Differences of opinion between parents on the subject first tend to surface during toddlerhood. The reason: This is when the need to become active disciplinarians accelerates. Often such disputes come as a great surprise to couples who thought they knew everything about each other.

But conflict is inevitable. After all, no two people agree on everything. Where discipline is concerned, relationships, family backgrounds, and personality all come into play to shape expectations and responses. What should you do if you think a time-out is in order when your child pours his milk on the floor because he doesn't like the color of the cup, but your partner thinks her behavior is a hoot? Or what if the disagreement is more serious, such as pro and con views on spanking? Some general guidelines to help you avoid child-rearing wars:

Present a united front. Foremost, don't argue about discipline in front of your child. Witnessing a parental quarrel always makes a child uneasy. Even a 1-year-old can tune into discord. Especially when it concerns discipline,

---

WHAT IF...

I work? I hate playing the heavy at night when I haven't seen my child all day.

It's no fun to spoil precious time with your child by nagging and yelling. But neither is it fun, in the long run, to have a child who runs amok. All children need rules. Enforcing them won't cast a long shadow over your time together. One reprimand doesn't cancel out ten laughs and hugs.

Kids do tend to act up more at the reunion hour. They may have been on good behavior all day with a sitter and now feel comfortable enough in your presence to let it all hang out, emotionally. They're also excited to see you and can quickly become overly worked up. You're tired, too. It's often easier to look the other way when your child breaks a rule, or to snap when she's testing your patience.

Try to make the mental transition from work to home during your commute, so it doesn't happen so suddenly as you cross the threshold of your home. Some parents buy a ready-made or microwavable dinner on a really rushed day. Or pop a children's tape into the VCR to allow both you and your child thirty minutes to decompress.

True Toddler Tales

"Firmness Really Works"

Mollie Coffey's parents had rules for everything. She knew that she didn't want to impose so much rigidity on her own children, yet she realized the importance of providing some sense of structure. Mollie and her husband, Paul, had seen relatives' unruly children sass their parents and act rudely. "If they don't learn when they're young, they may not be very pleasant adults," says Mollie, who lives in Spokane, Washington.

With their daughter, Hayley, the Coffeys try to ignore small transgressions such as spilled juice. "We try not to get too worked up over everything she does," Mollie says. "But we have clear rules about safety, and about behavior toward others." Playing with electrical cords or hitting, for example, are met with a firm warning. "I'll say, 'Stop that by the time I count to five or such-and-such will happen,' " she says. If the behavior persists, Hayley usually gets a time-out for a few minutes. "The time-out doesn't start until she has calmed down," Mollie says.

Mollie and Paul's advice on disciplining a toddler:

- **Compare notes.** "Discuss discipline with your partner. It's too confusing if Mom does one thing but Dad does another."
- **Think of consistency as a benefit, not a burden.** "I think it provides security. Children like knowing what will happen, and it teaches them what you expect of them."
- **Move on.** "It's not useful to dwell on things."
- **Keep it age-appropriate.** "I try not to expect too much, and to tailor my discipline to her current stage of development. She's too young to understand a lecture, for example."
- **Start early.** "Life will be a lot easier if you teach your child to follow house rules when she's young."

your child will sense that it's about her, and deduce that therefore she's to blame for your unhappiness. A child naturally wants to please both parents, and a fight over discipline makes her feel that she's somehow displeasing one of you. Open discord also undermines any attempt at handling the situation. When a child senses a weakness in your collective response, he's more apt to try to circumvent the rules the same way another time. Let the parent who has begun to handle a situation follow through. Wait until after your child's bedtime to hash out your differences.

Acknowledge your individual parenting styles. Some parents are more strict or more lenient than their partners. How you were disciplined as a child plays a tremendous role in influencing your attitudes as a parent, experts say—especially regarding mealtimes and punishment. Talk about each other's philosophy. Look for compromises. Recognize that on some things you may always differ. While both parents play an important role in discipline, the one who spends more time with the child should set the general tone, to avoid confusing the child. Exception: when that parent's actions are becoming physically or emotionally abusive.

Persuade, don't attack. Nothing puts a parent on the defensive faster than hearing a partner criticize or belittle the way a situation has been handled. In dealing with your spouse, frame your differences in a positive light: "This is what I do in that situation, and here's why it seems to work." Recognize, however, that there's almost always more than one right way to do things. Don't imply that yours is the *only* right way, especially if you're the one who does most of the caregiving. Ask yourself why you feel that your tactic is best. Do both parents' approaches have the best interest of the child at heart, or do you feel threatened personally by seeing a different approach at work? Often both parents have an effective solution; they're not arguing over discipline as much as they are locked into their own power struggle.

Search for the cause. Another way to move from a personal attack to a pragmatic solution is to pinpoint why you disagree. Maybe a mother is quicker to respond to a cry for any reason than her partner is. Many differences of opinion between parents can be traced to unrealistic expectations. For example, the father thinks that 18-month-olds shouldn't have a bottle, but the mother doesn't mind the habit. Try to delve beyond the immediate disagreement to explore why each parent feels the way he or she does.

Be specific. It's far more constructive to limit your discussion to a specific issue ("You let Sarah watch too much TV") than to generalize ("You always undermine my authority").

> ## PARENT TIP
>
> ### Set Your Child Up for Success
>
> **M**any toddler discipline scenarios can be averted before they happen. Childproofing is the key. Remove most of the perils that cause you to keep saying no—sharp objects, breakables, enticing plants, and so forth. A positive environment is one in which your child can explore freely without dangerous temptations or frustrations.

Agree to disagree. Despite your best efforts, two parents aren't likely to see eye to eye on every single issue regarding their children's upbringing. Nor should they. Even young toddlers are flexible enough to understand that Daddy makes them eat their snack on a plate but Mom puts it right on the high chair, or that one parent can be wheedled into an extra bedtime story at night but the other will be unyielding. Small differences of opinion aren't going to confuse your child. In fact, they're educational, showing your child that individual personalities react to situations in different ways. Just be sure that you're supportive and respectful of each other in front of your child.

When it comes to big issues, however—methods of punishment for hitting or biting, for example—there should be just one rule that both parents have hammered out together. What's most important is that there are clear, consistent standards of general behavior in your home—and that your child sees how abundantly you both love him.

Approaches That Work

Selective Ignoring

You'll drive yourself berserk trying to respond to your child's every uncivil act. There are just too many. When dealing with a toddler, not all undesirable behaviors merit the same weight. Concentrate only on the things that really matter and on the fights you can win.

Before you react to a misdeed, ask yourself if the transgression is a big deal or a small one. Small deals are the childish annoyances that drive grown-ups crazy but don't really hurt anyone. Examples: whining, dawdling, removing a hat, wearing mismatched clothes, singing at the dinner table, or dumping out a basket of toys for the umpteenth time that day. A bad mood can be ignored. So can a refusal to eat supper. Even temper tantrums—provided that no one is getting physically hurt—usually fall into this category. Meddle with them and the result is apt to be an out-of-nowhere tantrum or power struggle over something that makes no real difference in the larger scheme of things.

Save your energy for the truly destructive habits, as well as those that can set dangerous precedents—and there will be enough of those to keep you busy. Examples: hitting, biting, pulling a pet's tail, throwing food, standing up in a shopping cart, or handling dangerous objects (such as electrical outlets, coins that could choke, or anything breakable). And then there are the obvious nonnegotiables that you must enforce, such as those that keep your child safe: yes, he must get his shots at the doctor's; no, he may not run in the street without adult supervision. Remember that making your child's environment as safe as possible will relieve you of much of the job of hovering behind him and saying no all day. This includes removing temptations such as glass vases or planters full of dirt. Yes, you *could* train your child just to leave such things alone, but that's a long row to hoe. It's easier on you both to remove such items while your child is very small and lacks much self-control.

Unfortunately, many would-be battles seem to fall into a gray zone. It's not always easy to decide whether you should take action or look the other way. Should you stop a 14-month-old from putting his arm down your shirt (harmless but irritating)? Or let an 18-month-old sit on your lap during dinner (cozy the first time but intrusive thereafter)? Consider whether the action is one that will worsen over time. It's not hurting anyone for your child to eat on your lap, for example, but if you'd rather that his future meals take place in the high chair, then it's best to gently intervene. One rule of thumb: If you're in doubt about whether to let a behavior proceed, take action. Better to err on the side of firmness than leniency.

WHAT IF...

My mother spanks my child when he misbehaves? She says that's what she did with me and I turned out okay—but my husband and I don't believe in spanking.

Children are able to respond to differing types of intervention from different adults. The use of corporal punishment, however, is one area where it's best for all the key adults in a child's life share the same outlook—and it's the parents, of course, who should establish their preference. Enlighten your mother, for example, about the research indicating that the frequent use of spanking is rarely effective in the long run. If she's still not persuaded, you'll need to weigh how much of a problem this is. It may be, for example, that you differ in principle, but in reality your mom rarely spanks your child. If, on the other hand, your mom is a full-time caregiver for your child and spanks more often than you'd like, you may want to reassess your child care arrangement.

Redirection

Distraction works wonders with toddlers. With an attention span the size and speed of a hummingbird, a 1-year-old is as easily diverted from a danger as he is attracted to it. That's why this technique is your disciplinary secret weapon. It can easily prevent mishaps or pull your child from the brink of trouble. Best of all, it can be done with a minimum of fuss on both sides.

Any fresh sight or sound helps a young toddler shift gears. When he's about to get into something he shouldn't, engage him in a song or hand him a different toy to examine. Or you can pick him up and physically remove

CHECKLIST
What Doesn't Work

Scratch these disciplinary tactics from your arsenal—not only are they rarely effective, but most of them backfire. Rather than teaching self-control, such approaches teach bad habits or, worse, erode self-esteem.

✔ Yelling

✔ Cajoling

✔ Shaming

✔ Guilt

✔ Bribery

✔ Lecturing

✔ Deal-making

✔ Corporal punishment
(See "Hot Topic: Spanking," page 154.)

him from a situation. Two-year-olds are slightly more tenacious than 1-year-olds and may return to an inappropriate behavior repeatedly. For them, you may need to make the distraction a bit more enticing; try an object they've never seen before, such as a new toy or a metal pie pan from your kitchen cupboard. A change of scenery often does the trick, such as going outside to run around if you've been indoors all morning.

Bring a supply of distractions when you take your toddler out in public. Stash one or two objects in your diaper bag for emergencies. Pack more things if you're going on a longer excursion, such as on a plane ride or out to dinner. From 12 to 18 months, your child will look at a book for a few minutes or may explore an unusual toy, such as a finger puppet or a shape sorter. Such distractions tend to be short-lived, though. You may also need to resort to bouncing her on your knee or taking short walks, if she's to be confined in one space very long (such as at a restaurant).

From 18 to 24 months, attention span increases to ten minutes or more at a stretch. Bring toys that allow your child to use her imagination: a doll that can be dressed and undressed; Colorforms; a boxed puzzle; a book of nursery rhymes; crayons and

WHAT IF...

Discipline is handled differently at home than at child care?

Kids have a remarkable ability to understand that distinct sets of rules can apply in different circumstances. For example, at day care your child may be required to eat his snack seated at a table with friends, but at home you let him wander about with a cracker in hand. Or Grandma may allow him to climb on her sofa, which is forbidden at home. Discuss your preferences about discipline with your caregiver. If your child is in a group setting, find out how discipline is handled and be sure you are comfortable with it.

GOOD ADVICE

Correcting Misbehavior

"I don't believe in physical punishment. When Eli, 19 months, is doing something like using a toy to hit things, I say, 'Stop or we'll have to take it away.' If he continues, I clap my hands once forcefully. I say, 'I don't want to scare you, but when Papa claps his hands we have to stop.' He's learned to understand what clapping my hands means."

—*Bret Sidler, Lebanon, Pennsylvania*

"I didn't start using time-outs until Julian was 18 months old, when he could understand what I was saying. I use them only for serious infractions, like hitting or throwing things at other people. He sits on the floor between two bookshelves for about two minutes. I kneel in front of him and briefly explain why this is happening and then I go into another room, so that he doesn't associate time-outs with attention from Mom. Once the time-out is over, I never reprimand him again for the behavior that sent him there. I also make sure I'm clear about which behaviors warrant a time-out."

—*Naomi Williams, San Francisco, California*

"I use redirection when Brandon, 14 months, does something he's not supposed to. I don't make positive or negative remarks about what he's done. I just focus his attention on something else. If he's climbing on the stove, I'll interest him in a book."

—*Kelly Raby, Washougal, Washington*

paper. A 2-year-old can be kept busy for fifteen minutes or longer with a surprise package. Fill a bag with several different amusements, such as coloring books, play dough, party favors, or small plastic animals. Let her include one of her own choices in the bag before you leave home. Don't forget snacks. When you're out and about, a treat is often the best distraction of all for a hungry toddler of any age.

Verbal Discipline

A 1- or 2-year-old may not speak very eloquently yet, but she can certainly understand most of what you have to say. Often using the right words is sufficient to prevent or to stop a problem. You don't have to do anything more. Forms of verbal discipline include:

Positive reinforcement. Catch your child when she's acting nice rather than naughty. Praise appropriate behavior in very specific terms: "It was so nice of you to kiss Grandpa when we walked in the door." "I like how you're sitting the right way [or "on your bottom"] in the chair." When your child has been helpful, be sure to thank her: "Thanks for hanging your coat on the peg. Now Mommy won't have to pick it up off the floor."

Reminders and warnings. To steer your child to meet your expectations, issue reasonable reminders in dicey situations. Say "Drink your juice at the table" as you hand her the juice cup, or "Remember, no splashing on Mommy" as bathtime begins. Another strategy, when your child does misbehave, is to give fair warning before advancing straight to the penalty phase: "Michaela, get down from the table." This reminds her of the rule and is often enough to end the incident. Toddlers have notoriously short memories. In their curiosity or excitement, a young child often simply forgets what's acceptable. She'll also be better able to link her action with the consequence if you first warn her what will happen: "Get down now or you'll have to take a time-out."

Reprimands. An effective reprimand has four parts: (1) a command to end the behavior; (2) an explanation of why it's wrong; (3) a reminder of the consequences; and (4) a suggestion of an alternative. Sound like a lot of words? It doesn't have to be. For a toddler who is shoving a playmate over a favorite toy, this might translate to: "Connor, stop shoving. Shoving hurts. If you do it again, you'll have to sit in the corner."

Reprimands are most effective when they're not shouted across a room in the general direction of your child. Go to him and address him at his eye level. To get him to look at you, you can say something like "Let me see your eyes." Speak in an even but firm tone. Wind up your talk with a smile or a hug. But if your child goes right back to the misbehavior, follow through on the penalty that you outlined.

Cooperation and reasoning. This technique works best with older toddlers who are more verbal, but even younger ones can begin to grasp the idea. In simple terms, explain *why* certain things aren't done: "You can't tip over the water glass. It will make your food and your clothes all wet." Or "Louisa is sad because she was reading the book that you took away. How can we make her feel better?" This kind of collaborative reasoning helps a child

IT'S HOW YOU SAY IT

Building your child's sense of self-worth is an essential part of discipline. Take care to avoid "psychological spankings"—hurtful words that can humiliate a child and erode his self-esteem.

Don't say this	Say this	Here's why
"Bad girl!"	"Throwing blocks isn't nice."	It's the behavior that's bad, not the child.
"Don't be so selfish!"	"When you're finished, you can give it to Will."	Toddlers can't yet understand sharing.
"No one will like you if you act like that."	"That's not polite."	You don't want to imply that your child is inferior to others.
"Don't be so lazy."	"You must be tired."	Avoid negative labels about your child's character.
"What's your problem?"	"That's hard, isn't it? Let me help."	Be empathetic and constructive, rather than insulting.
"I said, pick up your cars. We're late!"	"When you pick up your cars, then we can go to the party."	When/then phrasings inspire better cooperation than nagging.
"If you don't stop throwing trucks, I'll throw them all in the trash."	"We don't throw toys. Let me help you keep them safe in the toy box."	Never make idle threats, or your child quickly learns not to take you seriously.
"Hurry up already!"	"The bathwater will get cold if you don't get in now."	Simple reasoning teaches; blanket chastising merely annoys.

HOT TOPIC

Spanking

It takes a rare amount of self-control to be a parent who never pops her child's hand or swats a bottom. Even moms and dads who abhor physical punishment succumb to the slap in the heat of the moment. Spanking may seem to send an I-mean-business message. Or it may be an impulsive last resort born of frustration. The problem is that either way, it's not terribly effective.

Numerous studies have shown that hitting a child is a weak deterrent to misbehavior. Although in the short term you may quickly end an undesirable behavior, you also introduce longer-lasting problems. A child who is spanked is likely to remember your physical force far longer than what he did wrong. Therefore hitting a child imparts no lasting lesson about the right way to behave, only that it's best not be caught in a misdeed. Worst, corporal punishment reinforces the idea that might makes right, that bigger people can control smaller ones by force. And because hitting is a learned behavior, kids who are struck tend to strike out at others.

For all these compelling reasons, many authorities and parents believe that spanking should never be used under any circumstances. Others, however, believe that a swift swat on the rear imparts a strong message when a child does something particularly dangerous, such as run into a street. The latest thinking is that an occasional spank—the kind given only rarely, and always with an open hand and on a clothed bottom—isn't going to damage your child mentally or physically. It certainly isn't likely to lead to serious behavioral problems down the road, as has sometimes been reported.

Overall, spanking is best used judiciously, if at all, especially with toddlers. It's easy for a habit of spanking, begun early in a child's life, to escalate into too much, too hard. Build a disciplinary repertoire with other tried-and-true tactics you can turn to first, such as redirection and time-outs. For safety's sake, it's generally recommended that children under age 2 never be spanked.

begin to consider others' feelings and needs. She begins to understand the bigger picture. Reasoning is far more instructive than simply saying no or "because I said so." Keep your tone gentle rather than sharp. A child as young as 12 months can begin developing this awareness.

Time-Out

Time-out has become one of the most popular discipline methods. It's non-violent. It's portable. It's applicable to a number of circumstances. It relieves stress for both child and parent. And when done properly, it's very effective.

That last point is the rub, of course, because many parents don't use time-out in the best way. Basically, a time-out involves removing your child from a scene or activity in which he's misbehaving and substituting a brief period of forced boredom. This provides a break in the action, usually enough for a child to forget the unacceptable behavior or understand why he ought to stop it.

Be quick and consistent about handling behaviors that are hurtful or destructive.

Time-out is often thought of in terms of punishment, which, in a sense, it is. But its beauty lies in its ability to teach children self-control by giving them an opportunity to regroup and change their behavioral course. Not all parents have success with the method, often because they begin when a child is too young or because they fail to enforce time-outs consistently enough. Some parents find little need to use this device because their children have temperaments that respond most readily to methods such as redirection. But scores of parents of older toddlers find the method useful enough to continue on with it into adolescence. To use time-out (also called "think time" or "taking a break") to your best advantage:

Don't start time-outs before your child is old enough. Development plays a key role in what kind of results you can expect. Time-outs are futile before a child can control her impulses or connect her actions with your responses. Around 18 months, you can introduce the idea by firmly holding your child in your arms for a few seconds. But limit even this abbreviated time-out to such antisocial behaviors as hitting or biting. Under age 2, child-proofing and redirecting are much more effective.

Don't use time-outs for every little thing. Yes, firmness is important. But if you invoke a time-out for every minor infraction, you'll soon have an escalating battle of wills on your hands. The focus shifts from the child's mis-

Caught in the act: Offer an enticing distraction to a toddler who's getting into mischief.

deeds to how "mean" you are. Time-outs should only be a small tool in your overall approach to discipline. It's not the be-all and end-all every time something goes amiss. Reserve time-out for aggressive or antisocial acts, or extremely wild behavior that borders on the dangerous.

Pick the right place. Some parents designate a special chair or spot on the floor where their child must sit. Don't choose the child's room, since there are too many entertaining distractions there. (Also, bedtime ought to be associated with pleasant things, not punishment.) Be sure that the time-out spot isn't frightening, either. It's often effective to do a time-out with a toddler right where she is at the moment. She could put her head down on the floor for a count of twenty, or long enough for you (or, eventually, her) to recite the ABCs.

Keep it brief. Ignore the old one-minute-per-year rule for determining how long the time-out should last. Keep them under 2 minutes for a two-year-old, otherwise your child will forget why he's sitting there. All you really need to accomplish is interrupting the inappropriate behavior. Some parents don't time their time-outs; they simply release the child once he appears calm and ready. If your child won't sit still to even begin the time-out, however, keep putting him back in place and sit with him. In such cases, warn that you won't even begin the time-out until he calms down, which means he's going to have to sit still even longer.

Use time-out consistently. Because the method takes a certain amount of energy—announcing the penalty, making sure your child sits still, counting down the time—many parents apply it in a raggedy or halfhearted fashion.

It's only fair to make clear ahead of time (when everyone's happy) what constitutes a time-out infraction. (Obviously toddlers learn as they go, but you can provide gentle warnings, in a neutral way, to help your child learn right from wrong.) Enforce rules consistently. Don't call a time-out for pushing today, then ignore the same behavior tomorrow. When misbehavior occurs, intervene with a warning the first time it happens. Don't wait for the fifth.

Never let 'em see you sweat. Most actions that lead parents to issue a time-out fall on the extremely irritating or infuriating end of the emotional scale. Yet how you play it is everything. Keep your reaction brief and bland: "We don't hit in this house. You need a time-out to calm down." Don't argue. Don't harangue. Above all, don't lose your composure. Time-out works only when it's a very banal process—the dullness is what makes it unpleasant for your child. When your child complains "I didn't do it" or says "I hate you," don't take the bait. Often toddlers make you chase them into the designated penalty box. To your child, your anger packs as much entertainment as a playful chase would. Resist the chase ploy; instead, make her sit right where she is. For the same reason, there should be no toys and no television—no, not even the beloved blankie—during a time-out.

The bottom line is to be engaging when your child is good and boring when she's naughty.

When you give a reprimand, crouch down to your child's height to better make your point.

Don't show remorse. It's natural to take pity on a repentant rule breaker. A parent's impulse is to soften the blow: "I wish I didn't have to put you in time-out, but hitting is bad, so let's not do it anymore, okay?" Or the parent hugs the child or pats her back consolingly during the time-out. The catch: In effect, you're providing positive feedback in response to a negative action. Better to stay mum and keep your hands off. When the time-out is over, simply tell your child that time's up and she can go back to play. No further explanations, apologies, hugs, or kisses are recommended. Some experts advocate a terse reminder for toddlers: "Remember, no hitting." But skip the lecture.

Make sure your child is ready to rejoin. Obviously, a child who's still crying or kicking when the time is up still needs to chill a bit longer. Some parents ask an older toddler, at the end of a time-out, whether the child feels ready to resume play or not. Some kids may feel they need to break a bit longer. You're also helping your child learn to make choices.

Common Problems

Temper Tantrums

Why they happen: Beginning at around 15 to 18 months (sometimes earlier), tantrums flare like so many Fourth of July fireworks. The basic reason is developmental. Your child realizes that things aren't the way they used to be. He still wants to be nurtured and coddled like a baby, but he also craves the autonomy of an older child. Along with this sense of push-pull comes a host of other influences that can drive him to the brink in the blink of an eye. Each day brings a million new skills to begin mastering, from pulling off a sweater to finger painting. His speech isn't adequate to explain what he means or needs. And he faces many new expectations as well, from potty training to behaving well in a restaurant. Emotions change as quickly as the images on a computer screen saver. Fatigue or hunger intensify a sense of overload.

Little ones have lots to be frustrated about—you can't prevent every single tantrum.

A tantrum is your child's way of saying, "Enough! Help!" She's expressing her frustration in the only way she knows how: with screams, flailing limbs, dramatic contortions, or collapsing in a heap. Tantrums are perfectly normal. You're not likely to make it through toddlerhood without experiencing one. Or maybe a hundred.

Tantrums peak around age 2. They taper off as your child approaches 3, as her verbal skills and physical control increase and she learns more appropriate ways to channel her displeasure and outrage (though they can persist right up to kindergarten).

Prevention advice: The simpler and more pressure-free your toddler's days are, the more calmly they will unfold. Look for ways to streamline the morning rush, for example, such as letting your child go to sleep in fresh play clothes the night before. Keep your expectations realistic, too. Never mind if her shirt isn't tucked in or her hair isn't combed. Don't try to haul her around on six different errands on Saturday morning. Also helpful: increasing your tolerance. Ask yourself if an irksome behavior (or uncombed hair) really makes a difference. If it's not hurting anything and doesn't set a dangerous precedent, let your child have her way. But don't abandon all restrictions in a misguided effort to circumvent tantrums. It's believed that persistent tantrums are especially common in the homes of parents who are overly permissive. Firmness lets a child know what the limits are so he doesn't have to test you as much.

Your best response: What to do once Mount Toddlersuvius erupts? The sights and sounds of a full-scale tantrum can be absolutely frightening. Your child is completely out of control and cannot be reasoned with. Most parents wish desperately that they could make it stop immediately. Unfortunately, you can't. Your best strategy is to be neutral and supportive. The calmer you are, the quicker the tantrum is likely to pass.

Sometimes it helps to intervene. You may be able to distract a young toddler, for example, and squelch the cries quickly. Some children respond to hugs or caresses. Soothing works because your child has lost control of herself, which is frightening for her. She feels free to yell and work through her frustration in the relative safety and comfort of your arms. *Don't* try to reason with your child. Long-winded explanations about why she feels the way she does, or why she can't have something she wants, will fall on deaf ears. They may simply further enrage your child. Generally, the less you say—during and after the tantrum—the better. Nor should you give in if she's throwing a fit because she wants to do or have something you've already nixed. Giving in only teaches her that a tantrum is a good way to get what she wants.

WHAT IF...

My child just won't cooperate?

Two-year-olds, especially, have a strong renegade streak. Because they're almost entirely self-focused, they have a hard time understanding your point of view even if you think you're making yourself perfectly clear ("Let's get dressed" or "Lie still while I change this diaper"). The other problem is that when grown-ups say, "Why can't you cooperate?" they really mean, "Why can't you do it my way, right now?" Toddlers are notoriously resistant to commands because they like to be their own bosses.

Praise your child when she does comply with a request. Sometimes, though, it's best to simply take action. Rather than asking your child to get dressed on a morning when she's being particularly resistant, for example, do it for her.

WHAT IF...

Someone criticizes me or begins to chastise my child when she's in the middle of a tantrum?

Embarrassment undermines the most confident parent. Frowns and unhelpful comments make you more critical of yourself and, in turn, your child. Do your best to tune out all onlookers. If you can stay calm and unflustered, you're better able to focus on the person who needs you most: your child. Remind yourself that, anyway, most of the people in earshot aren't thinking, "What a bad mother!" They've probably been there themselves and are fully sympathetic.

Often it's best to do nothing. Remain nearby, a reassuring presence. But let the tantrum burn itself out. Chronic tantrum throwers are often surprised to be ignored. Within a few minutes, they may calm themselves and move on to something else.

Public Tantrums

Why they happen: In addition to the same factors that fuel a tantrum in the middle of your living room, a few other things may cause those that explode in public. Social pressure, such as when you bring your child to a party, can push a child over the edge, for example. Parents, too, feel added pressure in some social situations (a baptism, visiting a new school) when they sense, rightly or wrongly, many judgmental eyes are upon them. Or you may want so badly for your darling to act sweetly in front of Grandma that you unconsciously telegraph your anxiety to your child—maybe you fuss about his clothing or dirty face more than usual, or cluck a few too many warnings ahead of time. Kids also act up in public just to get your goat. They know that you respond more quickly or feel less sure of yourself when there's an audience—meaning they may have a better chance of winning their way.

Prevention advice: Prep your child before you go somewhere so that the experience is not unnervingly alien. If you're going to a friend's house for dinner, for example, let your child know who will be there and what sorts of things he'll be able to eat. Before you enter a toy store where you must pick up another child's birthday present—always a dangerous mission—remind your child that you won't be buying him a toy that day. Say, "It's Susie's birthday. We're buying Susie a toy. You'll see lots of things that you'd like to have, but you can't this time. I'll need your help finding something Susie will like. But if you start to cry or scream, we'll have to leave the store." Be fully prepared to follow through on this warning.

In outlining your expectations, be as specific as possible. A toddler doesn't know what "Please be good" means. You might remind him to use his quieter indoor voice, for example. Time outings around naps and mealtimes to help ensure your child's good humor. If your toddler is finicky, tote along your own food and drinks.

Once you arrive at your destination, make your child feel comfortable. In a toy store, for example, you could bring one of his own toys inside to hold while you shop. You shouldn't buy him a toy just to bribe him to cooperate. Keep him feeling involved by describing what you're doing and thinking. Let him help you make choices—even nominal ones, like which way to turn the cart. At a party, pay him special attention to warm him up before you go off and mingle with the other grown-ups. Carry him, bring his favorite blanket, and pack some age-appropriate entertainment, such as favorite toys.

WHAT IF...

My child begs for candy in the checkout line? Is it okay to give in sometimes?

If you give in to pleadings once, you can be pretty sure that your child will whine for candy *every* time you go through the checkout line. You won't spoil him if you give him something reasonable and nutritious instead—either at the start of your shopping trip or as an alternative to the candy. If you choose to buy candy as a treat before your child asks for it, that's one thing. But never say, "If you stop crying, I'll give you some candy."

CHECKLIST
Tantrum Triggers

You can avoid some tantrums by minimizing the situations that set a toddler off. These include:

✔ Extreme fatigue (skipped nap, late nights)

✔ Not getting what she wants fast enough

✔ Being unable to verbalize desires

✔ Hunger

✔ Sickness

✔ Physical inability to do something

✔ Having too much expected of her for her age or developmental stage

✔ Big life changes (new sibling, new sitter)

✔ Little life changes (popped balloon, time to leave playground)

✔ Too much to do (too many errands, classes, playdates)

Your best response: What if, in spite of your careful planning, a tantrum happens anyway? Do your best to tune out everyone but your child. You may imagine that they're recoiling in horror, but chances are good that anyone paying attention is full of empathy. If ignoring the tantrum for a few minutes doesn't work, take your child to a private place (a corner of the store, your car). Remain neutral and let her regain self-control. You may be more anxious yourself than usual because you want to finish your errand or your dinner or return to your party. But don't rush or chastise your child. Once she's calm, go back to your activity as if nothing ever happened. There's no need to rehash the incident. She barely understands it herself, and a reminder of the trigger may start the cycle all over again. If she's having a very difficult time and has simply melted down, be prepared to abandon your activity. Chalk it up to life with a toddler.

Whining

Why it happens: Whining—a.k.a. whimpering, bellyaching, fussing, moaning 'n' groaning—is a natural developmental step midway between crying and being able to speak well. Babies have no choice but to cry in order to get you to feed or change them. Toddlers rely on this same plaintive sound, mixed with their growing vocabulary, to express their discontent and to signal their wants. And, as with temper tantrums, their relative lack of control over their world means that they can find plenty to be unhappy about. What starts out legitimately enough, however, quickly becomes a bad habit if left

NOT TO WORRY
"Bad" Words

Parents of verbal children are thrilled when they begin to string together their first sentences. But pride swiftly turns to mortification when words such as *poop, doo-doo, stupid*—and worse—escape those angelic lips. Kids age 2 and under are parrots. They repeat most anything, especially when the words are funny-sounding alliterations *(wee-wee, poo-poo)*. Ignore such talk without comment. At this age, it's your reaction, whether amused or angry, that inspires toddlers to persist in using juvenile swearwords.

unchecked—one that can take years to outgrow. (Guess what most whiny adults were like as children.)

Kids whine because it works. It's a classic catch-22: Parents give in to whining because when they respond, the annoying sound stops. Alas, kids then keep on whining on future occasions because they see that it yields great results. The parents' and the child's behaviors reinforce each other. All kids whine—at least sometimes, and at least until they're taught better alternatives. Handling this behavior the right way early in life can nip more problems later.

Prevention advice: You can't anticipate every one of your toddler's needs, of course. She's going to whine, at least a little. The more her basic needs are met—being fed and rested, getting plenty of your attention—the less of a problem whining is apt to be. Some children simply need a lot of attention. You may find that if you stop what you're doing and indulge your child in play or read her a book for just a short while, she'll be more likely to play by herself afterward. Another tip: Say no to your child's requests only when you really mean it. Parents often deny simple, reasonable requests—to read another book, to play outside—because they're preoccupied or tired. But if you become a habitual naysayer, you're more likely to have a child who whines.

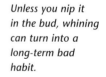

Unless you nip it in the bud, whining can turn into a long-term bad habit.

Your best response: A whine is, admittedly, a formidable opponent. It's grating. It sounds like fingernails on a chalkboard. And it goes on and on. Instead of getting cross, try to think of your child's whining as a warning siren. Consider these possible causes and address them accordingly (note that many of these situations can also lead to temper tantrums, which, like whining, stem from an inability to express oneself):

- *Illness.* Behavior is often the first sign that something is amiss. If your child is unusually whiny, check her physical condition.

To head off a tantrum when making a transition, give your child notice well before it's time to go home.

- *Neediness.* Five minutes is like a lifetime to a toddler, especially if he's waiting to have a physical need met (such as thirst or getting his coat zipped). Your job is to teach your child a more acceptable way of phrasing his request. Label his attempt, so he understands why you're annoyed: "I hear whining." Then redirect: "As soon as you can ask me calmly, I'll get what you want." If your child isn't using many words yet, you might help him with a simpler redirection: "You want juice? Say, 'Juice, please.'" Even if your child can't enunciate the words well, ask him to calm down (or, if possible, to try to say the word); then, when he makes the effort, quickly reward him with praise and the juice. Give a funny demonstration to teach your child the difference between what a whine and a normal tone of voice sound like.

- *The gotta-have-it syndrome.* Faced with the countless temptations of a toy store, for example, a child's notion of what constitutes his immediate needs skyrockets to include everything in sight. New sights and sounds entrance toddlers. They often reach out and beg to investigate. When you don't plan to give in, the best tactic is to flat-out ignore this kind of whine. Don't say anything. The more you address the behavior with comments like "I won't speak to you until you stop" or "Stop whining or else," the more your child will persist in trying to get a rise out of you.

- *A desire for attention.* Funny how your child's needs suddenly escalate the minute you're on the phone or in the midst of some other task that diverts your attention from her. The hour before dinner is another common whine time. Your child is bidding for your attention. It's best to ignore her, however, until she can use an ordinary tone of voice or act calmer.

- *Fatigue.* Crabbiness picks up when kids are tired. Flare-up times for whining: morning rushes, missed or late naps, bedtime, or the months during which your child is outgrowing a nap but still occasionally needs it. View sleepy whines more empathetically than you might at other times. Say,

"You sound worn out" or "I know how that feels." Look at the overall situation to see if you can make any improvements: Does your child go to bed early enough? Would he benefit from quiet time in lieu of a dropped nap?

- *Your failure to follow through on a promise.* What parent hasn't responded to some urgent request with the words "I'll be there in a minute"? Or "Let's do that later." Or "Eat your dinner first and then you can have cake." Aside

BEST AND WORST WHINE STOPPERS

Responses That Don't Work

- *Threats.* — "Quit that or I'll really give you something to whine about!"

- *Commands.* — "Stop it right now!"

- *Giving in.* — "All right already! You can have it."

- *Making vague promises.* — "Maybe later."

- *Promising but not following through.* — "I'll be there in a second."

- *Punishment as an immediate response.* — "Enough! Time-out for you."

- *Whining yourself.* — "Pleeeze stop! Why do you have to whine all the time? It drives me craaazy!"

Responses That Do Work

- *Redirecting.* — "If you can say that in a normal voice, we can talk about it."

- *Ignoring.* — "I don't pay attention to whines." (Or say nothing.)

- *Humor.* — "Did you say something? I don't understand Whinese."

- *Labeling the whine.* — "That's a whine, not a good way to ask for something. Here's a better way to say it."

- *Praising.* — "I like how you asked me that. You're much more fun to be around when you're not making that sound."

- *Empathy.* — "You sound very unhappy. Why don't you sit there and think about why you're sad, and when you're calmer, I'll help you."

- *Admiring good behavior.* — "I haven't heard you cry all morning, and that makes me very happy. Let's have a snack!"

from a young child's difficulty in grasping time, a problem can develop when parents don't follow through. The child was told one thing, but something else happened. It doesn't matter if you've forgotten or been distracted. The effect is to perpetuate your child's insistence. This can become a habit if your child begins to feel that nagging is the only way it will get done. A child who knows that promises will invariably be carried out, on the other hand, learns to develop trust and the ability to wait patiently. If you say, "I'll be there in a minute," be sure that you can follow through that swiftly, or don't make the promise.

Biting

Why it happens: Whether your child is the biter or the bitten, it's small comfort to know that sinking little teeth into the soft flesh of a friend is very common toddler behavior. Because it's so primitive and painful, however, most parents worry. Rest assured that biting doesn't mean your child is anti-social or a Dracula in the making. Children begin to bite people soon after their first teeth appear. The behavior is most common among 1- and 2-year-olds. Sensitive children who are impulsive or easily upset are especially prone to biting. The practice is usually outgrown during the preschool years, as children learn more socially acceptable ways of expressing themselves.

The first bites may be accidental. Babies often gnaw to relieve teething pain. They also use their mouth to explore the world. If you breast-fed, you

CHECKLIST
Minimizing Day Care Bites

Toddlers in child care often resort to their teeth to settle some arguments. Check whether your care provider uses the following tactics to reduce biting:

✔ Age-appropriate activities (to minimize frustration)

✔ Small play areas for different activities (to reduce conflicts)

✔ Abundant toys (including duplicates of popular items)

✔ Enough teachers (one teacher to six toddlers is ideal)

✔ Plenty of play time (alternating physical activity with sedentary play)

✔ A clear disciplinary policy (find out what steps your center takes regarding biting)

may remember the shock of your baby biting your breast when her new teeth came in. And she, in turn, probably noted your response, whether it was an exclamation of pain or a surprised "Hey!" Early biting persists when children discover they can use the behavior to get a rise out of their parents. It's fun. One-year-olds often bite out of excitement, such as when they get too worked up during wild play. As with a baby's first curious nips, biting can escalate as a child learns that it inspires an instant reaction, and often a ruckus when another child is involved. Remember that negative attention appeals to a toddler just as much as positive.

Older toddlers bite others out of frustration. Lacking language skills or social skills, they resort to their teeth to say "Stop!" or "Enough!" The typical target is a playmate of similar age. Biting acts as a kind of defense mechanism, too. A friend may have crowded a child into a corner, for example, in a tussle over a toy. Feeling threatened but unable to summon the right words or another form of physical force, the cornered lad lashes out with his handiest weapon, his teeth. Rarely premeditated in young toddlers, biting takes the perpetrator by surprise almost as much as the victim.

Stress may intensify the impulse to bite. For example, a child may be in a new care situation or tired by an overscheduled day. Some experts believe that biting is on the rise among toddlers because they are under increased amounts of stress from long days at child care, sometimes without adequate stimulation or guidance.

WHAT IF...

My child keeps getting bitten by playmates?

It's rare for toddlers to single out one child to pick on. More likely, the general situation (whether a play group or day care) is in need of better supervision. Parents and teachers need to work together to understand what's behind the behavior. Are there enough similar toys, which minimizes turf battles? Is the age mix good? Is the caregiver-to-child ratio appropriate? Sometimes it's not that the child who is bitten is especially meek, but rather that he's too exuberant—in his enthusiasm, he may unwittingly be invading the space of a child who feels threatened, triggering a defensive bite. Be sure that your play group or child care center has a clear policy on biting so that no one is caught unawares. Sometimes mini-epidemics occur in a classroom as playmates learn biting from one child and then test it out on each other. If your child is persistently bitten and you don't feel satisfied with steps taken to control the problem, you may want to consider an alternative care situation.

PARENT TIP

Locked in a Power Struggle?

You say black, your child says white. You say, "Give me the toothpaste tube" (which your child has squeezed all over the bathroom counter), and your child shouts, "No!" Your child says, "I want another video now," and *you* say, "No!" Disagreements over a behavior can soar as high, as hot, and as often as Old Faithful.

Remember that it takes two to tango. If you sense yourself locked in a power struggle with your toddler, just stop. Disengage. Continuing to dig in your heels won't get you anywhere, because a toddler has a will of iron (at least as strong as your own). A power struggle is a sign that it's best to shift gears and tactics. That's not the same as giving in, however. Acknowledge your child's feelings. Let her know that you disapprove of the behavior and that she has alternatives. But stay calm and unaffected yourself. Let her shouting and name-calling pass without comment. When she sees that you're not going to play her game, she'll slink off or burn out—or change her own tactics and try something more civil.

Prevention advice: You can't entirely prevent bites, but you can reduce their frequency. Avoid sending your child mixed messages by nibbling his fingers or toes in play. Roughhousing in general is not a good idea for a child going through a biting spell. Try to minimize the odds of your child feeling overwhelmed, for example, by providing age-appropriate toys and keeping an eye on things when he's with a playmate. (See the checklist "Minimizing Day Care Bites," page 166.) If your child becomes a chronic biter, take a step back to consider his overall day. Is he spending more hours in child care than you think is optimal for him? If he's in a large center, would he thrive better in a family-oriented care situation where he might get more individual attention? Are there extenuating circumstances, such as a new baby or the death of a pet, that are putting him under stress, and if so, can you and your caregiver think of ways to provide extra TLC? Give your child ample attention when he's being good. On occasions when you notice that he's channeled feelings of anger or frustration in more socially acceptable ways, be sure to comment and congratulate him. The long-term goal is to teach your child self-control, so that he's able to resist the urge to lash out by biting.

Your best response: React to a biting incident immediately but calmly. Pull your child aside (if another child is involved) and say, in a firm voice, "No biting. Biting hurts people." You could point out the other child's reaction: "See how sad Adam feels?" If you can figure out the cause of the bite (anger? frustration? a toy showdown?), help your child see alternative ways he might have responded. For example, you could say, "If you were angry that Adam got to go first, you could have used your words to say, 'I'm so mad!' Or you could jump up and down to get the madness out." A very brief time-out (say, thirty seconds) is more effective than other punishments in reinforcing your message that biting isn't appropriate. Don't overscold or overreact. The child who's been bitten should get the lion's share of the attention (from you as well as from his own mother), not the biter. When your child regains control, simply underscore, "Remember, no biting," and send him back to play.

What not to do: Never bite a child back "to show you what it feels like." This only sends the child a confusing message: "Is biting okay, then, if Daddy does it?" Nor is it effective to use such old-fashioned remedies as making the child taste hot-pepper sauce. Even with patience and persistence, reforming a biter can take a while. But you'll begin to see longer periods elapse between incidents.

Screaming

Why it happens: All toddlers scream sometimes. The first high-volume howls are usually accidental as your child discovers all the different things that her voice and lungs can do. She may learn quickly

Some children bite because it gets a rise out of adults, so respond firmly but calmly.

GOOD ADVICE
Taking a Toddler Out in Public

"We prepare Daniel before we go out by playacting at home, so he knows what's expected of him. If we're going to church, we talk about sitting still and being quiet. Then when he's in that situation, we can refer back to the role playing and say, 'Remember the quiet voice that we used?' "

—Rebecca Prewett, Santa Maria, California

"When we go out, I always have water and something like Cheerios for Michael, 2, and his sister, Anna, 4. And I've found that with two small kids, a double stroller is invaluable."

—Mary Walker, College Station, Texas

that a good holler can be even more effective than a whine to capture grown-ups' attention and make her wishes known (and, more important, heeded). To a power-loving toddler, the throw-back-your-head-and-shriek method may simply feel better, too. When it's responded to over time, screaming becomes a chronic habit.

Prevention advice: You can't really stop an occasional scream, but you can take steps to keep a child from shrieking all the time. A scream can be so ear-splitting that it's tempting to say, "Hush already! Here's your toy [or book, or cookie]." But you should never give in to a screamer, no matter how irritating the sound. Nor should you scream back. Yelling simply communicates that it's okay to raise the decibel level.

Best response: Stay calm. Tell your child that you can't understand what she wants when she's screaming: "It hurts my ears when you talk so loud. When you're quieter, I can listen." Ignore her until she calms down. Teach your child other effective ways to use her voice. See if she can mimic you whispering or singing instead. Explain the concept of using an indoor voice (normal speaking tones) and an outdoor voice (which can be louder). Later, you can simply warn, "Inside voice, please," rather than the more negative "No yelling!"

Interrupting

Why it happens: In a nutshell, persistent interrupting is a bid for attention. Something else—the newspaper, the telephone, your partner—has your focus, which annoys your ever-loving egocentric child, even if she seemed to be happily engaged in a book only seconds earlier, before you picked up the paper, dialed the phone, or asked your spouse a question. Because a toddler has a rudimentary sense of time, "just a minute" seems like an eternity. If you say, "Don't interrupt," the problem only gets worse

Prevention advice: Ideally, try to schedule concentration-heavy tasks such as balancing the checkbook or reading a novel for when your child is asleep. At minimum, make sure that your child is engaged—with an absorbing toy or a lift-the-flap book, for example—before you embark on something during which you'd rather not be interrupted. Save particularly engrossing toys, such as a simple puzzle or a toy farm set, for such moments. Make sure your child isn't too hungry or tired, either. Don't disappear. As you work, preemptively give your child attention with pats on the head or an occasional comment ("I like the way you're lining up those cows") so that he's less covetous of you. But be realistic. You might be able to manage a five-minute business phone call with a toddler underfoot, but not a half-hour one.

Your best move: With a young toddler, interruptions are inevitable. It's best simply to stop what you're doing for a moment and quickly respond to your child. But by the time your child hits 24 months, he's ready to learn what the word *interrupt* means. He probably has no idea what he's doing that upsets you so much. In simple terms, explain that "interrupting is when I am talking to someone else and you ask a question." Or put it on his terms: "It would be interrupting if you were watching TV and I turned the TV set off in the middle of *Blue's Clues* without telling you first." Tell your child that he should say "Excuse me" or tug once on your shirt when he needs to interrupt. But when he does so, respond immediately. Praise him for his politeness. If you can't fulfill his request right away, let him know when you can.

Be consistent about the way you handle interruptions. If you give in to them sometimes, your child will learn that he doesn't need to be polite. "If I nag enough," he'll reason, "eventually I'll get my way." Of course, you shouldn't expect too much patience of a 1-year-old. And no emergency or basic need (such as a dirty diaper) should ever be considered an interruption.

Supermarket Squalls

Why they happen: As a baby, your child was a fine shopping companion, content to sit placidly in the little seat at the front of the shopping cart and receive the compliments of his fellow shoppers. As a toddler, however, he has a harder time sitting still. Everywhere bright packages and produce call out to be seen and felt. He recognizes his favorite foods and sees countless new temptations. He may smell doughnuts in the bakery section or spy a display of bright plastic toys in the middle of the cereal aisle. This cornucopia of temptations is simply too great to ignore. Being belted into a seat compounds your child's itchiness. What's more, you get to touch everything and steer the cart, so why can't he?

Prevention advice: Few parents can escape grocery shopping with a toddler in tow. You may be able to minimize such trips, however, by trading off child care with your partner or a friend so that the other can shop solo. When you can't escape bringing along a toddler, however, you can still have a pleasant, productive outing. The trick: Keep him engaged, involved, and happy. Set yourself up for success by timing a shopping trip when your child is rested. Early Saturday morning, for example, is better than five-thirty on a weekday on your way home from work and day care. (The store will be less crowded then, too.) Resist the impulse to march through the aisles as quickly and effi- ciently as possible. If you focus more on the food than on your child, you'll only wind up ignoring him and aggravating him. Instead, take a few extra minutes to give extra attention. It will save you time in the long run.

Keep up a running narrative of your excursion. "Let's see, what's next? We need bread. With bread we can make sandwiches and French toast. What's your favorite sandwich?" Find ways your child can help you, too. Let him hold the shopping list or coupons. Hand nonfragile items to him so that he can deposit them in the back of the cart. Ask him to help you search for items. "Can you find a can of corn?" (This can be done from his seat. No need to let your child out of the cart to run free unless you're buying only a few items.) Most toddlers are eager assistants.

Schedule grocery outings when your child is rested. Snack time is a good choice, because while you shop you can let him eat something, maybe bread or animal crackers (ideally, an item stocked in the first few aisles). Remind your child of the mission: "We are here to buy the food on Mommy's list so we can have good things to eat for dinner. We can't buy everything that you see or want. But if you cry or whine, we'll go home without anything." Some parents allow their child to make certain coveted choices during the excursion, such as which type of cereal or snack cracker you'll buy. Others let the child select one special treat in the store, such as a fresh cookie from the bakery.

When it's time to pay, keep your child in the cart, if possible. Let him leaf through one of the small, digest-sized magazines there, or bring along a special toy or book for use during checkout. You can also divert his attention from the candy zone by letting him sit up on the edge of the checkout counter while you hold him, watching the goods roll past on the conveyor. Praise your child for his good behavior on successful outings. Use specific terms: "I sure liked how you put the things in the cart and ate your snack quietly. And you used such a calm inside voice. You were a real helper."

When your child loses it in public, try to tune out the spectators.

Your best response: What if, despite your best efforts, the grocery store gremlins get your child? The main transgressions include tantrums (especially the gimme-gimme variety), tossing items out of the cart, and trying to escape the cart. Keep your cool, to avoid escalating the tension. Sometimes a positive spin helps: "If you stop yelling [stop throwing, sit still], then we can keep shopping and look for the kind of cereal that you like." Distraction helps, such as offering a snack. Or engage the child: "Look, apples! Can you find the biggest red ones?" Be prepared to cut your losses, however. If your child has a total meltdown, it's best to leave. You'll both be disappointed, but the lesson is apt to linger with your child the next time you enter a store. Never give in to requests for candy or toys just so you can hush your child and finish the shopping.

Another no-no: Never allow your child to stand up in a shopping cart—not the seat or the rear basket. The safest place for her is securely strapped in the front seat. Remember that toddlers are lightning quick, so don't turn your back for long, or walk down the aisle away from the cart. The number of children injured by shopping carts is on the rise, mostly because parents are in too great a rush to strap toddlers in.

CHAPTER FIVE

Big Transitions

As much as a toddler craves consistency and routine, major changes are an unavoidable part of life. These changes can be exciting or unnerving—or, more typically, a little of both. How smoothly your little one weathers the transitions that are a natural part of growing up depends on many factors. One is timing (not always something you can control). Another influence on your child's adaptability is how he is prepared for the change. And that's where your efforts can definitely make a difference.

This chapter focuses on several of the biggest transitions that tend to fall during toddlerhood: learning to use the toilet, attending day care or having a baby-sitter, enrolling in preschool, and becoming a big brother or big sister.

Toilet Training

When to Start

The task of potty training looms large for most parents. Relatives ask about it ("What, still in diapers?"). Friends and doctors offer advice about it. Some day care centers and nursery schools make it a prerequisite for enrollment. Not least, a potty-ready child is a welcome labor-saver. Parents pile added pressure on themselves by viewing this milestone as something that they (rather than their child) need to accomplish, as if it's a reflection on their parenting skill. Some have the added incentive of wanting to get their firstborn out of diapers before a new sibling is born. It's little wonder that most parents of toddlers have anxieties about when to start the process and exactly how they're supposed to go about it.

Before you do anything, though, memorize these three realities: (1) every healthy, normal child gets potty-trained eventually—60 percent of them by age 3, and 98 percent by age 4, according to one large study; (2) no child can be taught this skill until *he* or *she* is ready to learn it; and (3) there's no "right" way to go about toilet training, because "right" is whatever works.

Most experts agree that children do need some help learning to master the toilet, just as they need help learning to walk or to feed themselves. And toddlerhood is the best time to initiate that help. There seems to be a window of opportunity when toddlers are most open to trying, usually between ages 2½ and 3. But behavior is a far better guide than the calendar. (See checklist, page 179.)

According to one major study, just 4 percent of toddlers are toilet-trained by age 2. Boys often take longer than girls, with nearly half not being trained until after age 3, compared with roughly a third of girls waiting that long. It may be that boys tend to be more active than girls, and find it harder to sit still; a child may become so preoccupied with what he's doing that he forgets to take potty breaks. Other theories include slower neuromuscular development in boys, difficulty identifying with Mom (who's usually

Few children are ready to start potty training before 18 to 24 months of age.

the teacher), or even "castration anxiety"—fear of the penis falling off and disappearing into the toilet the way their BMs do. Whatever the cause, the overall timing difference between boys and girls is relatively slight and shouldn't influence either when or how parents handle training. Boys take especially longer when it comes to achieving nighttime dryness. Opinions are divided as to whether the age at which a child is potty-trained is related to whether he has older siblings or attends day care. Mostly, toilet-training readiness is highly individual.

You can cause far more unnecessary frustrations by starting too early than by giving it time. Around 18 to 24 months—when your child shows several signs of readiness—is a good time to introduce your child to a potty. If you start too soon, your child will not be developmentally ready to put all the pieces together. A couple of generations ago, mothers prided themselves on training babies as early as 9 to 12 months. But in reality, it's more likely that the mother had trained *herself* to time and catch eliminations, via the potty; a child that age is too young to understand the big picture. Control of the sphincter muscles doesn't become voluntary until about 18 months of age. Also bear in mind that a toddler's natural drive toward willfulness and a desire not to be directed peaks around 15 to 18 months, which can make this phase counterproductive to toilet training. A child who starts prematurely may also wind up feeling bored or pressured, thus setting your efforts back further.

Other times to postpone training: When there's a major change in your child's life, such as a new sibling, a move, or a new day care situation. Similarly, try to avoid the distractions of the holiday season. You want to present the toilet transition as the relaxed, everyday process it should be.

Relapses are perfectly normal and to be expected. Some toddlers become intrigued by the newness of the potty, or simply comply with your requests to pee in it because they want so very much to please you. Despite these encouraging first steps, however, their interest gradually fades. If this is the case, then your child just isn't ready. Escalating your efforts will only backfire into a power struggle. Keep the potty in view in the bathroom, but don't make any

---

WHAT IF...

My child seems afraid of the toilet?

To you, it's an everyday implement. But to a small child, a toilet has many unnerving features. It's big, it contains water and a drain, and it makes loud noises. The seat may feel cold against bare skin. Some kids worry about falling in or even being sucked in if they get too close. Never mind that none of these fears is rational. To a child they are real, and that's all that matters. Be nonchalant. Explain in simple words what the toilet does, and reassure her that it can't hurt her. Try to identify exactly what your child dislikes. If it's the flushing, for example, you can simply wait until she leaves the room to do so.

mention of it for a few weeks. Wait until you notice more signs of readiness, and gradually try again. Don't make any mention of the previous attempt.

Ask yourself, too, if there have been any stresses in your child's life. Anything out of the ordinary, such as a big vacation, a new sibling, or moving into a new house, can cause relapses. Be low-key about disinterest even if your child was completely trained for a period of time before the regression. Return without much fuss to training pants. (But do make things somewhat easier on yourself by not going all the way back to diapers if you can help it.)

What To Do

Exactly how you go about encouraging your child's potty training depends on many things. Possible factors include your parenting style, whether you have a deadline in mind, the tricks you read about or hear from others, and your general energy level toward the task. Whatever system you use, you must feel comfortable with it. The following basic approaches have many permutations, limited only by parental creativity.

The at-their-own-pace method. This is the training route favored by most pediatricians. It could also be called the take-it-slow approach. The idea is to let potty training be the *child's* success, accomplished almost entirely on his own schedule.

When your child shows signs of readiness, introduce a child's potty in a casual way. Let him play with it so that he develops a sense of ownership: "It's *my* potty." After a week or two, show him how it works. Have him sit on it clothed; then, a week or two later, unclothed. Tell him that, as he gets bigger, it's the place his urine and BMs will go, instead of his diaper. Some parents illustrate this point by emptying a dirty diaper into the toilet, while their child watches, explaining that someday his BMs will go right from his body into the potty.

Your goal should be to make your child feel in

CHECKLIST

Signs of Potty-Training Readiness

✔ *Dry spells.* Is your child able to stay dry for one to two hours during the day? Does she wake up dry from a nap, or occasionally after sleeping all night?

✔ *Regularity.* Does your child have bowel movements (BMs) at about the same time every day? (Most, but not all, do.)

✔ *Awareness of the process.* Does your child pause during play to squat and grunt when having a BM? (Some kids even steal away to a private spot.) Does she tell you about it afterward, or insist on being changed? These are signs that your child is gaining an awareness of her body and how it works.

✔ *Good dexterity.* Can your child walk to the potty, pull down her pants, and pull them back up again?

✔ *Curiosity about body functions.* Does your child follow you into the bathroom and ask what you're doing? Is flushing the toilet her idea of fun? (Some children are afraid of the noise and may need reassurance that people can't be sucked in.)

✔ *Potty communication skills.* Can your child follow simple directions such as "Let's go to the bathroom," and does she understand the concepts of wet and dry? Can she let you know that she needs to go, even if it's simply tugging on your shirt and saying, "Wee-wee"?

✔ *Monkey-see, monkey-do behavior.* Does your child shuffle around in your shoes or insist on pouring her own juice? Has she asked for big-kid underwear like those seen on a friend or a sibling?

✔ *Diaper rebellion.* Does she wriggle away at diaper-changing time? Does she remove the diaper herself or refuse to wear one?

✔ *A strong interest in cleanliness and orderliness.* Does your child complain when her hands, clothes, or toys get dirty? Does she enjoy washing her hands? Has she developed a sudden aversion to messy activities such as finger painting, or shown a new finickiness about what things go where? This is a natural phase of toddlerhood that can coincide ideally with toilet teaching.

✔ *General agreeableness.* Has your child been in a reasonably accommodating mood lately? That's not to say that she never has tantrums or says no. But many toddlers go through a natural cycle of contrary behavior as they try to establish their independence, generally between 15 and 24 months. If you wait until the peak of this phase passes, you'll be less likely to encounter strong resistance to toilet training.

When your child shows a dislike of diapers, it may be your perfect opportunity to introduce the potty.

My child shows interest but has lots of accidents?

Accidents are inevitable. If your child voluntarily makes his way to the potty much of the time, maybe the problem is that he gets too involved in his play and the need to go just "sneaks up" on him. Try issuing gentle reminders. If your child is enthused about abandoning diapers but resists using the potty, he may not really be ready. Don't abandon all efforts, but a switch to more absorbent disposable training pants, rather than underwear, may keep him encouraged while lessening the mess. Frequent accidents can shake a child's confidence.

charge, conveying that the potty is something to be used at his discretion, not yours. Once he's grasped the basic concept of what it's for, you can leave his diaper off for brief intervals, especially around the times he usually has a BM. Don't force him to sit; offhandedly remind him that the potty is there to use whenever he feels the need to go.

At first, your child may use the potty because it's novel. Even if she pees there three days in a row, however, it doesn't necessarily mean that you'll be pitching her diapers within a week. Learning is often very stop-and-start. For many kids, using the potty is something of a game, and that's okay. Let her take it apart (if it's clean, of course) and reassemble it, or sit for ten seconds and run off, if she likes.

Expect accidents. Clean them up nonjudgmentally. Rather than chastising, show a little empathy and encouragement: "I'm sorry you have to change the pants you liked. Soon you'll be able to get to your potty right on time." Keep diapers on at night, however, until your child wakes up dry at least two mornings out of three. During the day, it's easy for a child to remember about the potty because you are there to remind him and he can see it. Many children don't develop nighttime bladder control until age 4 or 5.

NOT TO WORRY
Zero Potty Interest

Some children—make that many children—take a leisurely route to toilet training. Even if they show many of the signs of readiness, they're still not ready or willing. It's best to give a recalcitrant learner some slack. Sure, it may mean longer diaper duty for you if your child is creeping up on his third—or fourth—birthday with little interest in what bathrooms are for. But a child who pursues his own pace in the matter is doing no harm—in fact, it's healthier mentally. Try to separate your own competitive urges, or the criticisms of friends and family, from what's best for your child. Rest assured that whether your child learns to use the toilet early or late is no reflection on his intelligence—or your parenting prowess. Besides, by the time he hits kindergarten, no one will know whether he was an early learner or a latecomer in this department.

The sit-'em-on-the-pot method. This approach is similar to the first, but with one significant difference: Instead of waiting for your child to initiate use of the toilet, you schedule the visits. Bring your child to the potty about six times a day for the first week or two of training, at the times when he's likely to actually use it. Sit together for a few minutes. Read a book to him or talk about using the toilet. If he wants to get off without producing anything, let him go. What's important is that he begins to make the connection between what comes out of his body and the potty chair. Regular repetitions reinforce that idea.

Eventually your child will begin to make progress. And once he begins to use the potty of his own accord—which may take days, weeks, or longer—you can cut back to gentle reminders.

An alternative version of this method is to wait for signals that your child is ready to go to the bathroom (such as stopping play, crouching, clutching the diaper), then promptly usher him to the toilet. Some parents find it useful to track BMs on a chart to give them an idea of likely times to do the escorting.

MILESTONE

DRY BY DAY AND NIGHT (3-4 years)

Keep your expectations about toilet training realistic. While some children master total dryness by the end of toddlerhood, most do not. Your child may need to wear disposable training pants or diapers for six months or more after achieving daytime dryness. It's physically and mentally difficult for a toddler to keep dry all night. Help your child by minimizing before-bed drinks. To encourage a child who is being toilet-trained, make a potty stop part of her bedtime ritual.

Some parents choose to wake their child for one last trip to the bathroom before they turn in themselves. For some children, this approach works well. Others may not weather such disruption as easily and may have a hard time falling back to sleep afterward. Gradually the bladder learns all by itself to hold urine through the night. While it's possible for a child as young as 2 or 3 to stay dry all night, complete nighttime dryness may not be achieved until age 7 or later.

The all-in-one-day way. You may also hear about another alluring but controversial method, the twenty-four-hour approach. Originally developed by a psychologist for several mentally disabled adults, it has been adapted for nondisabled children. It's a rather complicated plan involving a carefully graduated series of steps and positive reinforcement.

Some parents like the over-and-done-with aspect of such an approach. They make a gala event of the training event, such as calling it Bye-Bye to

CHECKLIST
How to Prime a Young Toddler for Toilet Training

Your 12- to 20-month-old may not be ready for actual toilet training, but you
can lay some useful groundwork now.
You should:

✓ Change diapers as soon as they're soiled or wet (so your child gets used to
that nice dry feeling)

✓ Narrate diaper changes, saying, "Good, you're still dry" or "Let's get this
wet diaper off so you feel better" (to seed your message)

✓ Use the lingo you'll echo during training (to get your child accustomed to
what the words such as *wee* or *poop* mean)

✓ Refrain from negative comments, such as referring to feces as "stinky" or
"disgusting" (so that your child doesn't associate BMs with shame)

✓ Let your child accompany you to the bathroom to watch, flush the toilet
for you, wash hands, and so on (to help make the place and process
become familiar)

✓ Encourage self-dressing (which is a big part of using the bathroom all
alone)

✓ Teach her to follow simple instructions, such as "Bring me the book"
(so she'll be used to following your directives during toilet learning)

Diapers Day, or taking a similar fun approach. It can work, if your child is very
ready to be trained and of a compliant, agreeable temperament. But many
experts question the rush of such an intensive approach. Pressure is not generally considered an effective way to get a child to do anything, particularly
learning a rather complex skill.

Details, Details

Whatever your overall toilet-training strategy, you'll need to make some deci-
sions about equipment and style.

Big potty or small? Most experts recommend starting out with a child-sized
potty rather than an adapter seat on a toilet. Your child will feel more secure
if his feet can touch the ground and the opening where he sits is not so large

that he feels like he's about to be swallowed up. Select one with a sturdy base that won't tip over. A potty with a removable plastic bowl makes clean-up easier. Fancy models that play music and are shaped like dinosaurs make the job more fun but can be distracting. Many kids respond best to a potty that looks most like the real thing.

A potty is not only less intimidating than the toilet, it's also portable. If you live in a two-story house, consider having a potty on each floor to help your child get there in time. Some people stash a spare in the trunk of their car to use when they're out and about. Parents of twins tend to find that two potties side by side speed training along. Most parents locate the potty in the bathroom, since that's where, ultimately, you'll want your child to do his business. Another line of thinking goes that it should be placed wherever the child is most often, such as the playroom, the backyard, or even the kitchen.

If you'd rather have your child start on the big toilet (which lets you skip the step of cleaning out the potty after each use), you'll need a step stool or an adapter seat with a stepladder. Adapter seats come in molded plastic or softer cushioned vinyl. Some kids like to sit backward so they won't feel like they're falling in. A container of pop-up wipes in the bathroom can make hygiene easier for little hands than toilet paper, though wipes usually can't be flushed. (Don't forget to show girls how to wipe using a front-to-back motion to prevent infections.)

Wee-wee or urine? What terms should you use? Most pediatricians and child psychologists prefer teaching children the correct anatomical terms for body parts. To describe what comes out, however, you might choose something less precise—*pee, wee, poop, doody, kaka,* or *BM,* for instance. That's because while the grown-up world refers to penises and vaginas by their rightful names, very few of us ever say, "Excuse me, I need to defecate." Some parents find it useful to use the same terms that their child's day care center uses; if you have an in-home provider, compare notes so that you're all speaking the same potty language.

Diapers, training pants, or underwear? You need to decide what, if anything, to put on your child's bottom during training. Removing the diapers is the usual first step. Unfortunately, this switch leaves you to face a messy in-between stage when your child is learning but having inevitable accidents. One option is to substitute cloth or disposable training pants, which are very

True Toddler Tales

"I Tried Too Hard"

Cariann Linehan started potty-training her twins, MacKenzie and Connor, during the summer after they turned 2. They had begun to show signs that they were ready: They had begun to mention that they didn't like being wet anymore and that dirty diapers were "yucky." They took great interest in other people's bathroom use. The twins could also stay dry for two hours at a stretch.

Cariann, who lives in Solvay, New York, took the twins to a store to select their potties (one apiece). She made a big deal about the purchase. "They thought it was the greatest thing at the store," she recalls, "but when we brought the potties home, they showed no interest." When the weather warmed up, she let them play outside naked and brought a potty along. In this setting, they excitedly used it a few times, but the novelty wore off quickly.

"They were just being curious two-year-olds," Cariann says. "They would say things like, 'I'm a baby, I don't want a potty' or 'I want a diaper.' "

Reluctantly, she let it drop. Six months later, she began to gradually introduce a video and some books on toilet training. Soon after, the twins began announcing to Cariann when they had to "go pee-pee." Training went slowly but steadily after that. She posted their names on a piece of paper tacked to the fridge, and gave them stars whenever they sat on the potty (whether or not they produced).

"They had accidents, but now they were both so much more mature. I don't know why I tried so hard before," she says. By the time the twins were 3, they achieved daytime dryness.

Cariann's tips on potty training:

- **Squelch your competitive-parent instincts.** "Every child is different. Don't think that because your friend's child was potty-trained by a certain age that yours will be, too."
- **Don't force it.** "If you push, they might rebel. Then the whole thing becomes a negative experience for both of you. Wait for them to show you that they're ready."
- **Be supportive through setbacks and accidents.** "Show encouragement at every stage, good and bad." Accidents are simply part of the process and should be expected.
- **Give rewards.** "Sometimes I'd say, 'Let's go pick out a special present just for you.' Toilet learning is a big step for a child, and kids love to be patted on the back for their accomplishments."

absorbent, as an intermediary step on the way to regular underwear. Say, "Diapers are for babies. You are so big that you are ready to wear pants." Stepping into training pants gives the child a feeling of mastery and helps him understand that this is a new experience. On the other hand, disposable training pants cost more than diapers. Also, they sometimes work *too* well, feeling so comfortable and absorbent that the child refuses to either move on to regular underpants or revert back to diapers. Also, the cloth kind can get tiresome to clean if training goes on for months.

A third alternative is to continue using diapers but fasten them loosely, showing your child how to pull them down before he uses the bathroom. (This can also be done with pull-up-style disposable training pants.)

Yet another option is to move directly from diapers to underwear. You can make the switch cold turkey, or use underwear only in certain situations, such as during the day, and revert to diapers for naps, at preschool, or while in the car. Like cloth training pants (only more so), underwear has the advantage of helping a child feel the difference between being wet and being dry. They also come in snazzy designs, often featuring favorite cartoon or TV characters, and more closely resemble grown-ups', which may appeal to your child. Again, however, you'll have to contend with the mess of accidents.

Whatever you choose, the baggier the better, so that pants can be pulled up and down easily. Buy a size too big, or make a snip in the waistband to loosen the elastic. Some parents favor boys' underpants for their daughters at first because they tend to be more durably constructed, with a wider waistband that helps a child figure out how to put them on. Rethink your child's wardrobe for toilet-training ease, too. Leave the overalls or one-piece rompers in your child's closet for the time being. Zip-front flies also slow down a child who needs to get to the toilet fast. Choose easy-on, easy-off elastic-waist styles.

Should you teach by example? When most parents of toddlers use the bathroom, they have a hard time keeping the child out. The loss of privacy can be irritating, but it's a real boon when it comes to toilet training. Even a very young toddler learns a lot from straightforward modeling. A child under age 3 is too young to need to be shielded from these normal body functions for reasons of privacy. Older siblings and friends make great role models, too.

For some children, mimicking potty behavior with a doll is a good way to gain confidence. A doll allows a child to practice over and over until she feels in control of the process. Any doll or teddy bear will do; you don't have to invest in a special model that drinks and wets. Some stores do sell training dolls with miniature potties to match, or you can fashion your own from a small box or downsized juice can. Books can reinforce your message, too. Most bookstores carry a number of relevant titles, geared to toddlers.

For boys: Standing or sitting? A toddler's inclination to imitate makes some parents wonder whether they should teach their son to urinate while standing or sitting. Most experts recommend starting a boy sitting, to minimize sprays and dribbles on the walls and floor. This makes it easier on him, too, since he may not be sure at first if he needs to wee or poop. Sitting also keeps a boy grounded—less likely to get distracted and walk away. Fathers who are actively training their sons might want to let the child observe them urinate while sitting, just to help them get the idea. While he's seated, teach a boy to point his penis down into the potty or to lean forward as he sits, which naturally accomplishes the same thing. (Detach the urine-deflector cup that comes with many models; it's too easily, and uncomfortably, bumped into.)

To minimize spraying, it may be easier to start teaching a boy to sit when he urinates.

Eventually, however, boys want to stand to "be like Daddy." Give them practice learning to aim. You can buy special so-called "tinkle targets" in stores, or use bits of toilet paper or Cheerios, or even paint a spot on the back of the toilet bowl.

Wild applause or a quiet pat on the back? Whether or not you leap like a cheerleader when your child shows you her first BM depends on your style and on how your child tends to respond to praise in general. Supportive nonchalance works for most parents, since making a fuss over successes can make them seem too important.

GOOD ADVICE

How We Did It

"The easiest time to potty-train is summer, when kids are running around without clothes on. It makes it easier if you don't have to fuss with clothes."

—*Melissa McLeod, Portsmouth, New Hampshire*

"I was folding laundry with Lily when she picked up her older sister's underwear and said, 'I want to wear panties!' She was only 19 months old. I told her she would need to pee in the potty. We practiced, to reinforce what she'd need to do. Practicing helps you find out if the child has a problem pulling down her pants or something. We rehearsed getting to the potty ten times from different areas of the house."

—*Heidi Bingham, North Charleston, South Carolina*

"Ryker would run around without a diaper after his bath and start to urinate anywhere. So we'd lift him up and set him on the potty. I had heard that if you poured lukewarm water on a boy's genitals, he'd pee, so I tried that and it worked. We made a game of it and he learned to go there. Now when he has to go, he says, 'Pee-pee. Potty!'"

—*Tami Pelles, Pendleton, Oregon*

Likewise, your child could come to like the attention she gets if you cluck or fret over accidents. Keep the focus on the act ("Good job!"), not the child ("Good boy!"). Convey that the purpose of learning to use the potty is for your child's benefit, not yours or Grandma's or the day care center's. Hovering or nagging only turns this everyday occurrence into a battle of wills.

Some parents dangle bribes as incentives. Every time your child goes, for example, you might offer a small edible treat (like a raisin or animal cracker) or let your child put a sticker on a special potty calendar. Some parents choose a set of toys with many parts—such as small cars or farm animals—doling out one for every day their child stays dry. Incentives are somewhat controversial. Some experts believe that the child should learn to use the potty out of self-pride, not because of some external prompt. Others think that a reward can be a useful incentive when a child is learning a new physical skill. But it's best if the object is small and given immediately so that the child doesn't forget why he's being rewarded.

Day Care and Baby-Sitters

Keys to a Better Partnership

Having a child broadens your social world in unexpected ways. The people who care for your child in your absence, for example, become a huge part of *your* life, as well as your child's. Whether your child is just beginning to have a regular baby-sitter or is a child care veteran, take care to nurture this important relationship.

WHAT IF...

My caregiver doesn't seem as well suited to a toddler as she did to a baby?

A good caregiver ought to be able to adapt and grow right along with her charges. It's not unusual, though, for some women to prefer babies. Or toddlers may place physical demands that are too great. If leaving is her preference, there's not much you can do.

What if the concerns are yours alone? Above all, you must feel good about the care that your child is receiving. If you genuinely like the person but are concerned about the ways she responds to your toddler or entertains her, you might be able to make simple suggestions to remedy the situation. For example, perhaps your care provider could attend a music or dance class with your toddler, to enrich the child's day in a way that she doesn't feel comfortable or creative enough to do on her own. You can also make age-appropriate toys available. But if you just don't feel that things are working out, make a switch. Yes, it's hard—both to confront your sitter and to locate a replacement. But you and your child will both feel better in the long run.

Respect your caregiver as a professional. Despite their relatively low pay and low status in society, most child care workers view their work as a profession. Many are indeed experts in caring for a child, though not all. Be sure that you have a good understanding of what your caregiver knows about child rearing. If you can justifiably think of your caregiver as an expert in the art of looking after a child, as opposed to being "just a baby-sitter," you'll immediately infuse your relationship with better rapport. Remember, too, that you're entrusting her with your most cherished possession. This is no minor-league responsibility. Don't take her for granted.

Take a team approach. Sometimes parents feel the nagging sensation that they're competitors with the caregiver for their child's affection, especially if they work. Of course, you're not. Instead, consider your caregiver to be your collaborator. Make time at the beginning and end of her shift to compare notes, rather than either one of you handing off the child and rushing out. If the caregiver changes from morning to afternoon (such as at a day care center), ask for a written record so that you know what your child ate and did throughout the day. Keep your caregiver informed about your child's health and moods, her eating habits, and situational changes that might affect her behavior, such as a parent's business trip or a family death. Ask questions about what goes on during her day, too. Don't be afraid to speak up about any concerns or gripes that you may have.

Play by the rules. Establish clear parameters about hours, duties, and pay. Have a written agreement that covers both your expectations and your nanny's. If your child attends care away from home, the center will be sure you know its regulations. Picking your child up late once in an emergency is one thing; having the same thing happen once a week is a problem. Know the regulations about illness, and keep your child home if he meets one of the facility's criteria. Don't forget to stock the diapers and clothing that your child needs.

Be reasonable. Think twice before you make any unusual requests. In a group setting, it may not be possible for your child to stay indoors during outside time because you don't want him to get too much sun. Nor is it practical to send your child to day care in a party dress and ask that she not get messy.

Similarly, you may be expecting too much if you want your nanny to do all of the cooking and cleaning and shopping while also tending a toddler. Try to put yourself in your caregiver's shoes before you voice a special request. It's not fair to ask her to clean house because you're having a party, if that's not her usual responsibility (unless she's willing and is compensated accordingly), or to tell her on Friday that she's not needed next week because you're taking an impromptu vacation.

Show your appreciation. Thank your caregiver. Send her birthday and Christmas cards. Better still, provide a concrete thanks in the form of a small gift or a bonus. Even a center that frowns on gifts will welcome such tokens as flowers or food for the staff. Whatever form of care you use, pay promptly.

WHAT IF...

The house is always a wreck when the baby-sitter leaves?

If your arrangement with the sitter is that she's responsible for cleanup and she's ignoring her part of the bargain, you need to address the issue. But do so out of your child's earshot. You don't want to undermine her relationship with your child as a trusted, loved authority figure. Restate your agreement in a neutral but firm tone. Many families who use a regular baby-sitter find a written job description that outlines expectations (such as picking up toys) to be helpful for both parties.

Be reasonable, however. A certain amount of toy-and-book clutter is a good sign that your sitter was busy entertaining your child. Ask yourself whether you'd really rather have a pristine house or a happy, well-tended child.

NOT TO WORRY

The Velcro Farewell

Your child clings like a koala when you part at day care. "Don't go, Mommy!" he begs. The teacher helps you peel him off and engages him in another activity. You kiss him goodbye and reassure him you'll be back soon. You can still hear his wails as the door closes behind you. Then, minutes later, everything's fine. No more tears.

Short-lived separation angst is very common. In fact, it should make you feel good, not bad. A clingy goodbye is evidence that your child is securely and lovingly attached to you. Help your child make the transition easily by keeping your farewell short and sweet. Don't act hesitant about parting. Be upbeat and reassuring: "It's time for me to go, but I will see you after snack time. Give me a big hug." Stay as long as you need to for your child to grow comfortable, but don't linger once he's engrossed in play. Never sneak out. This only makes the next parting more difficult; your child clings all the more tightly because he's afraid that if he lets you out of his sight, you'll vanish without warning.

Adjusting to New Care

A toddler might experience a new care situation for many different reasons: Your nanny quits. You move and must enroll your child in a new day care center. Or maybe you're returning to work and your child will be experiencing outside care for the first time. Here are some ways to make the transition easier:

Prepare your child in advance. Help your child get comfortable with a new situation by warming up to it gradually. If he will be attending a new child care facility, make several visits together before his actual first day. Play on the playground, have a picnic, tour the building, and meet the teacher.

Imbue the place with happy Mommy (or Daddy) associations, so it will seem less intimidating once your child goes it alone.

Tell your child about the change a few weeks in advance. Talk up the positive points: that there will be lots of children to play with, that there's a tire swing and a slide, and so on. Don't extol the praises of the forthcoming change too much, however. Your child may grow suspicious that you're feeling anxious, and begin to have such feelings himself.

Overlap the old and new care situations, if possible. If you're switching nannies, for example, arrange for them to work together for a few days before the old one leaves and the new one takes over. In addition to helping your child get used to the replacement, she can observe firsthand how naps, feedings, and other

Plenty of preparation will help make your child eager to greet a new day care center.

GOOD ADVICE

Saying Good-bye

"Before I left for work, I would practice with Jamie Junior, who's 19 months. I would tell him I'd be back, then leave out the door for two minutes, and then come back. We worked up to a long time. He used to cry until he'd throw up, but within three days, it worked. Now I say, 'Daddy's going to work.' He'll say, 'Be back?' and I say, 'Yes, be back.' I give him a kiss and there's no problem with my leaving."

—*James McDaniel, Sunnyvale, California*

"Twenty-one-month-old Amelia is in day care four days a week. When I drop her off, I give her a hug and a kiss, I tell her to have fun and that I love her, and I reassure her that I'll see her soon. By saying this every morning, she's learned what to expect. She now goes through the same routine with her dolls when she plays with them."

—*Maryann Esh, Minnetonka, Minnesota*

True Toddler Tales

"Our First Trip Away from Home—Alone"

*L*eigh and Mark Primeau waited until their daughter, Julia, was almost a year old before they went away on a solo vacation. They live in Yarmouth, Maine, and Mark's brother was getting married in Colorado.

Before the trip, Leigh was a nervous wreck. Planning ahead for the sitter was her salvation. She wrote down everything about her and Julia's day, from where she sat when giving Julia her bottle and what they did before nap time to which stuffed animals were her favorites. "I do things a certain way with her," Leigh explains. "I wanted her to maintain our routine when I was away."

Leigh's mom came to watch her granddaughter. "I knew my mom would throw herself in front of a bus before anything happened to Julia, and that she would probably be even more cautious than me," Leigh says. "But I felt so guilty about leaving her. What if something happened to my husband and me? Our child would never know us." The couple drew up wills before the trip. Leigh also handed her mom a book on CPR, just in case.

From Colorado, Leigh checked in every few hours. She had even packed a cell phone so she'd be accessible at all times, only to discover that reception was nonexistent in the mountains. And her bed-and-breakfast stopped answering its phone after eleven at night. "I panicked, calling to tell my mom I was unreachable. But she reassured me that she'd call the local police if she needed me," Leigh recalls sheepishly. Finally, resolved to relax, she and Mark ended up having a wonderful time, both at the wedding and being alone together. "I had been itching to get away," Leigh says. I really missed her and was ready to get home, but I'd like to do it again."

Leigh's and Mark's tips for traveling without your toddler:

- **Trust your sitter.** "It's much easier on your mind if you leave your child with someone you feel very comfortable with, like a family member."
- **Make lots of lists.** "I felt better knowing that I'd prepared everyone well without leaving any loose ends."
- **Remember that couples need time alone.** "When you're at home, you do spend time together, of course, but you're always so tired. It was healthy to just think about one another for a bit."
- **Enjoy yourselves.** "I loved having time to myself for the first time since my daughter was born. I read a lot just because I had the opportunity to do it. Call home if you need to, but go out and forget about home for a while, too."

transitions are handled. If you're changing child care facilities, try to spend a few half days at the new facility while winding down at the one you're leaving. Even if it means that you must drive across town or take added time off work, it's worth the effort to help your child grow more comfortable with the change more quickly. A phased-in transition also works well if your child is being cared for outside his home (or by an in-home provider) for the first time. Arrange half days at first, or stay home during the nanny's first few days. Overlapping should last a week or less. You don't need to draw it out. Play it by ear; some kids adapt easily within a single day.

Make it fun. Give your child added TLC on the big day. Be more forgiving than usual about dawdling, poutiness, tantrums, or demands. Remember, any change is stressful. Some parents find it useful for a new one-on-one caregiver to greet the child with a gift, such as a favorite type of toy or a stuffed animal to hug (that the parents have purchased in advance).

Give it time. If at day's end your child declares that he "hates" the new nanny or school, don't assume that the day was a disaster. He may have had a terrific time during the day, but the rush of emotions upon being reunited with you led him to overstate his feelings. Ask the care provider for a detailed report about how the day went. Ask specific questions of your child, too, rather than open-ended ones. ("Did you sing any songs?" and "Did you play outside?" are likely to elicit more information than "How was school?") If negative comments persist after the first two weeks or so but your child is unable to articulate what he doesn't like, spend some time observing first-hand. Be encouraging when you see things going well, praising your child for art projects, for example, or chatting up a new friend. Consider inviting classmates over for play dates to help your child grow even more comfortable.

WHAT IF...

My child suddenly has a hard time separating from me at child care, even though he never did before?

This is a common development. Many parents take it to mean that something is wrong at child care. This certainly could be a possible explanation—perhaps your child is being bullied by another youngster or was frightened by something that happened, such as having had water poured over his head at the water table one day. Your child's caregiver ought to be able to report any unusual circumstances of this nature to you. More likely, though, your child is responding to another kind of stress in his life. Have you or your husband been working later hours than usual or traveled overnight, for instance? Have you or your child been ill?

Discuss the separation problem with your caregiver, as well as ways to handle it. You'll both need to be sensitive to your toddler's special needs during this transition. You may need to spend extra time saying goodbye, for example. If the problem seems to have arisen because of something that's happening at child care, go over potential solutions with the caregiver and be clear about how she's going to proceed.

Starting Preschool

Is Preschool Necessary?

It used to be that parents never gave much thought to school until it was time to march their child into kindergarten. But nowadays, because of the swelling ranks of young children cared for outside the home and a cultural shift toward giving kids a smart start in life, many parents of toddlers begin to wonder whether home care or day care is enough. Should your 2- to 5-year-old attend a preschool program?

Before you decide, it's important to understand what preschool is *not*. Preschool isn't academically oriented preparation for "real" school. You don't send your child to preschool so that he will learn to read or write or begin basic math. Nor is a child who does not attend a preschool doomed to fall behind his peers educationally in kindergarten. (And if he does lag, the difference is usually made up within a year or two.)

Still, the benefits of early education are numerous. A recent Carnegie Foundation study, for example, found that children who attend preschool achieve better in real school later, and that there is a lasting positive effect. A preschooler learns basic concepts (such as colors or practice in fine-motor skills) that are the building blocks for primary-grade skills such as reading and math. Moreover, he learns these things at an age when his brain is most ripe for learning them. He also learns how to be part of a group, including sharing, negotiating, turn taking, and helping others.

A good preschool (also known as nursery school, play school, or pre-kindergarten) is a safe, stimulating environment in which young kids can enjoy themselves and express their zest for learning and life, while rehearsing the social skills they'll need as they grow. Preschools tend to have a more formalized educational philosophy than straight child care, and they emphasize social interactions more than baby-sitters do. Preschools also expose young children to age-appropriate materials, toys, and learning concepts, all under the guidance of professionals experienced in child development and early education.

Many child care centers are also preschools as well. The advantage to this situation is that more hours of care may be provided. (Some preschools offer only all-morning or all-afternoon sessions and don't provide extended day care beforehand or afterward, which working parents need to arrange separately.) If your toddler is already in a child care center, you'll want to evaluate the type of preschool program offered to determine whether you should continue your present arrangement or make a switch.

Because of preschool's many benefits, it's worth looking into, at least for a year before your child enters kindergarten. If you don't plan on sending your child to preschool, consider the kinds of things that these facilities emphasize and try to make them a part of your child's everyday world. For example, you'll eventually want your child to spend time with other children, through play groups or informal get-togethers. Broaden your child's horizons with outings to places such as the airport or the fire station, or consider an exercise or music class for enrichment. Make a wide variety of play materials available. Some parents choose to start their child in a preschool program part-time, for just a day or two per week. An abbreviated introduction enables a child to sample the larger world of preschool in a more manageable way, which may be better suited to his needs. Be aware, though, that attending infrequently can make separations harder on some children.

Many parents hear the word *school* and think only about ABCs and 123s. You can be sure that your child will learn amazing new things during his preschool days. But not necessarily traditional academics. By attending preschool, for example, your child will be able to:

- Practice separating from you
- Interact with other children and develop such social skills as sharing, turn taking, and cooperation
- Learn about friendships and peer interactions
- Learn to practice self-control and appropriate behavior in various circumstances
- Empathize with others
- Boost his self-confidence and self-esteem
- Practice increasingly sophisticated language skills
- Gain exposure to basic skills (such as colors, size and category matching, counting, fine-motor skill practice, letters and their sounds)
- Gain a broader sense of the world (how things work, nature, animals, and so on)

PARENT TIP

It's Never Too Soon to Look

Don't wait until your child turns 3 to begin investigating preschools. The ideal time to start thinking about the preschool option is when your child is 12 to 24 months old. Hard to picture your diaper-wagging tyke sitting in a circle singing finger-play songs? Actually, starting to make preschool plans early is for your own benefit. It can take a long time to sort through the various options in your community. You'll want to talk to other parents, make calls to get basic information from the prospective schools, and spend time visiting them. Even if you're not inclined to be so thorough and have your choice narrowed down to one or two possibilities, some schools may have long waiting lists. You may need to apply early to reserve a space. Having a good head start will spare you later panic.

When to Start

There's no optimal time for a child to begin preschool. Age 3 is the typical entry point, but children (and programs) are far too individual for this to be an automatic start date for such an important transition. Some children are gregarious, are comfortable with transitions much sooner, and thrive in such programs during toddlerhood; others take more time.

Look at a variety of factors in deciding whether your child is ready for preschool. How well does she handle separations from you, for example? Is she terribly upset when she's left with a baby-sitter, or does she calm down soon after the initial separation anxiety? Has she had much exposure to other adults (such as a baby-sitter, child care workers, Sunday school teachers, Grandma)? Is she comfortable talking to them, and can they understand her without your interpretation? Consider, too, whether your child can handle the physical tasks that preschool requires, such as carrying a lunchbox, putting one's coat on and off, and following directions. Some programs require children to be toilet-trained before they can attend. In general, children who thrive in care outside the home make an easy transition to preschool programs because they are accustomed to alternative caregivers as well as lots of other children and activities.

Types of Programs

At first glance, preschool programs may appear fairly similar. They all seem to have pint-size furniture, and in all of them kids sing songs and create art. All are committed to the care and growth of young children; all want children to be safe, happy, and enriched. The differences lie in how a given school goes about achieving those aims. No two preschool programs are identical. Even within a particular genre, such as Montessori, you'll find a dramatic range of structures, materials, and philosophies. Here's a quick introduction to the most common types of preschools and what they entail (listed in alphabetical order). Most preschools are an amalgam of these basic types, combining various elements of the different approaches.

Academic. Some preschool classes are set up like junior versions of elementary school. The day revolves around designated periods for reading and language skills, math, foreign languages, and other lessons, such as computer work. They may feature rows of desks or workspaces. Lessons tend to be teacher-led, often with the entire group participating in the same activity at one time.

CHECKLIST

What to Ask the Preschool Director

✓ What are the school's hours? Are there full-day and half-day plans? Full-time (five days a week) and part-time (two or three days a week) enrollments? What is the tuition for each plan?

✓ What's the school's educational philosophy?

✓ Is potty training required?

✓ What's a typical day like? Is there a set routine? Ask about snacks, naps, lunch, and outdoor playtime.

✓ What is the student-teacher ratio? (The National Association for the Education of Young Children—NAEYC—recommends that 2–2½-year-olds be in a group of twelve or fewer, with two adult supervisors; 2½–3-year-olds, a group of no more than fourteen, with two adult supervisors. And for 3–4-year-olds, the ratio is one adult to ten children, with two caregivers.)

✓ What are the teachers' credentials? (Look for backgrounds in early childhood education and some teaching experience.) Is turnover high or low? (Long teacher tenures indicate satisfaction all around, but of course some changes are inevitable.)

✓ What are the director's credentials?

✓ What kind of parental involvement do you prefer? Can parents visit classrooms at will? Are they required to spend a certain number of hours in the class? (An open-door policy is ideal. How much time you can or would like to spend in a class is an individual matter, but you should be aware of the school's expectations.)

✓ How do teachers interact with parents about student progress?

✓ How does the school handle transitions? Can your child bring a comfort toy or blanket to school, for example? Are parents welcome to stay as long as needed to help a child settle in?

✓ What is the school's philosophy about discipline? How are transgressions such as biting handled?

✓ What are the policies regarding illness and how accidents are handled?

✓ Does the school or the parent provide snacks and lunch?

✓ Is anyone on site trained in first aid and CPR?

✓ What is the application deadline?

✓ What is the vacation schedule?

✓ Are there additional fees for registration or supplies?

✓ Is the school licensed or accredited by NAEYC or another group? NAEYC schools have voluntarily met rigorous requirements to qualify.

✓ How is security handled? Does someone man a front desk at all times? How are visitors identified? Are the grounds locked? Is there an emergency fire plan?

✓ Is extended day care available before or after school hours (if you work full-time and need this)? If so, does the child switch to a different room, and do the teachers change? What is the cost for this service?

WHAT IF...

My child has special needs?

Be up front about your situation during an interview with the school's director. Often children with severe allergies, certain physical disabilities, or a chronic illness (such as diabetes) can be seamlessly integrated into the classroom. You and the teacher may need to work through specific situations and how they would be handled. Some schools would rather not deal with exceptions that are significantly beyond the norm. You won't know until you ask.

Such programs are somewhat controversial for young children. There's little evidence that teaching a 3-year-old to read or write puts her at any advantage. By the time her peers master those skills, she isn't likely to be well ahead of the pack, and if she is, she probably won't maintain that lead. The vast majority of child-development experts maintain that early learning comes through play and fun.

Cooperative. Co-ops rely heavily on parental involvement. Typically, a professional director runs the program and an experienced teacher leads each class, although some cooperatives are strictly parent-led and -run. The nature of the program depends on those who run it, so you'll find an enormous range, from the very structured to the loose and casual. Co-ops may pattern themselves after the various other types of preschools described here.

A potential negative for working parents is the amount of parental involvement that is generally required. Parents are usually asked to commit a certain amount of time helping the school, usually in the classroom or possibly with administrative and maintenance work. Because of the comparatively high parental input, co-ops tend to be less expensive than other private preschools.

Developmental. One of the dominant kinds of preschools, this type also goes by the terms "whole-child curriculum" or "Piaget school" (the latter in reference to the Swiss psychologist who identified distinct stages of a young child's mental development). Some developmental-style schools use none of these monikers to describe themselves. Essentially, the general developmental level of the age group is the centerpiece for the way everything is taught—so for preschoolers, lessons are all play-based and integrated with one another. Classes tend to be age-segregated (all 2-year-olds, for example, or all 3-year-olds).

At the same time, developmental curricula tend to cater to each individual's pace and abilities (physical, mental, and emotional). Periods of free play are typically interspersed with some organized group activities, such as teacher-led singing, art activities, or circle time. A teacher may let some children work independently while assisting only those who need special help at the time.

HOT TOPIC

Computers in the Classroom

Computers have come to be associated with all that is new, fast, and far-reaching. And for education, the reasoning goes, that can only mean one thing: a keyboard for every child! Certainly school systems are finding many innovative, wonderful uses for computers in the classroom. But it would be premature to automatically extend the more-computers-are-better thinking downward to preschool. The reason? Three- and 4-year-olds don't

All children will eventually be introduced to computers, but they aren't essential for toddlers.

need Internet access and CD-ROMs in order to learn; in fact, they have many far more important activities to engage in during classroom time, such as interacting with peers. And since no child born in the 1990s or later need ever worry about being computer-illiterate (computers being frankly unavoidable in their lives), there are no real advantages to starting so young. (See "Hot Topic: Computers," page 39.)

Nor, on the other hand, are there disadvantages for 3- and 4-year olds. If a school you're considering has computers in the classroom, that's fine. Ask about how they're employed, how often they're available, and what software is installed. But neither should you mark down a school for a lack of hardware. Ask the director about it; there may be solid educational reasons the school has decided against computers for its youngest pupils.

Foreign-language. More prevalent in large urban areas or places where there are significant ethnic populations, these schools immerse a child in the language and culture of another land. In some programs, only the foreign language—Spanish, German, Japanese, French, Korean—is spoken. Others teach the second tongue but conduct most of the day in English. You may be interested in such a program if your child is of a particular heritage, or simply because you'd like him to learn another language. Kids ages 1 to 3 are particularly adept at doing so.

Montessori. Montessori preschools are widespread. In many ways, they overlap with the schools that follow a developmental curriculum. But there is usually a greater focus on supporting each individual child's unique development. Created at the turn of the century by Dr. Maria Montessori, an Italian educator, this approach to learning emphasizes multiage classes (say, a mix of 3- to 5-year-olds), free choice among activities for large blocks of time, an emphasis on chores (such as cleaning up one's own spills), and specially prepared sensory-based materials. Special wooden beads and blocks, for example, are used to help children learn quantity concepts in a tactile, visible way. Children are encouraged to learn at their own pace.

Beware, however, that *Montessori* is one of those terms heavily bandied about but interpreted in widely different ways, in the same way that the term *Lamaze* doesn't refer to a single, predictable kind of childbirth education. A school that describes itself as a strict or traditional Montessori program will most closely resemble the above description. Some schools embrace many of the traditional Montessori learning materials and philosophical approaches but broaden their classrooms to include many other play materials and activities, such as dress-up clothes, computers, and art projects. The best way to see where a particular school falls on the spectrum is by direct observation. Also ask if the school belongs to the American Montessori Society; credentialed programs require teachers to have a college degree and follow a Montessori training program.

Religious. Faith-based preschools tend to be affiliated with a particular church or synagogue. (Sometimes preschool programs use church buildings but have no religious agenda.) Inquire how religion is woven into the daily routine and overall curriculum. There may be daily Bible study and singing hymns, or merely a more heartfelt observance of religious holidays than you'd find at other schools. Families who prefer religious preschools tend to like the way they complement or underscore their own values. For couples whose entree into parenthood has inspired a religious reawakening, a religious school can be a comfortable reintroduction into that part of their life. Look beyond the spiritual aspect of the school, however, to also evaluate such things as the teacher's background, the class size, and the curriculum. You may also want to balance the program's benefits to your child against the lack of diversity that such a school may represent. Often parents like the specifics of a program so well that this becomes more important than its spiritual focus. Some church preschools welcome children from other faiths.

Waldorf. These schools root their lessons in the arts and the natural world. They tend to incorporate the outdoors into their day (such as nature walks and gardening), emphasize music and seasonal celebrations, highlight fantasy and play, and encourage the use of many simple, natural materials. Many teach foreign languages as well. As with any school, you'll want to evaluate a specific program and teachers.

How to Pick a Program

Which setting is right for your child? You'll need to take many factors into account. Practical considerations, such as the convenience of the location and cost, are usually paramount. You may

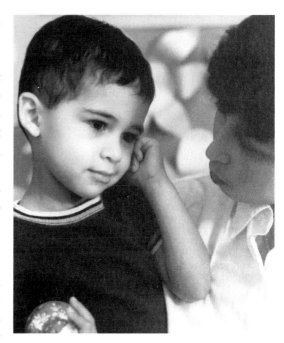

A good preschool teacher will help a child learn to take turns, share, and be part of a group.

want a school whose hours mesh with your work schedule, for example. But don't let the nuts and bolts be your only concerns. Take the following into account as you begin your preschool search.

Start out with an open mind. Develop a thorough list of your options. Look in the phone book and local parenting magazines and newsletters. Ask community child care referral agencies, play group leaders, and others who work with young kids. Go on-line to post inquiries with local parenting chat groups.

Word of mouth is often the best way to map your options. Talk to other parents in your neighborhood, at your pediatrician's, or at work. Probe them for frank details: What did they like best about the program, and why? What was less than ideal? What was a typical day like there? You'll be able to pick up subtle details from a parental perspective that might not be so obvious from a visit or an interview, such as how persnickety the school is about sugar-free snacks and how much individual attention teachers are able to give students.

As you gather opinions, keep in mind that families' priorities differ. Kids do, too; what was right for your next-door neighbor's child may not be as suitable for your own child.

FINDING THE RIGHT PROGRAM FOR YOUR CHILD'S NEEDS

If your child is:	Look for a program that:
High-energy, always on the go	Provides opportunity for free movement
Reserved	Has smaller groups or a smaller child-adult ratio
Slow to warm up to new situations	Encourages a gradual introductory period and parental involvement
Quiet, easily overstimulated	Provides a lesser number of activity choices and private areas to read or be alone

Consider your child's temperament and learning style. A key element of a successful match is the fit between the child's personality and the nature of the preschool. Think about how your child responds in other types of situations. Is he rambunctious or reserved? Quick to join in the fray or more likely to hang back and warm up slowly? Give thought to the types of activities that your child enjoys, both indoors and out. This type of assessment will help you realize his strengths and his needs so that you have a sense of what you're looking for in a school setting for him.

Ideally, a preschool will take an individual child's needs into account and bend around them. But this isn't always the case, and some types of programs have less inherent flexibility.

Take your parenting philosophy into account. You might never have given much thought to your personal parenting style. But it's useful to factor this into your school equation. Some questions to consider: Do you plan to play an active role in your child's school day? Are religious or cultural influences especially important to you? Do you lean toward a very structured day or prefer to take things as they happen? (While program philosophies vary, all parents should look for evidence that a school has some degree of structure built into its toddler program, although the extent will vary.)

Spend some time at prospective schools. For efficiency's sake, you'll want to prescreen by telephone. (See Checklist, "What to Ask the Preschool

Director," page 197.) But nothing will give you as clear a picture of a preschool as direct observation. Don't enroll your child in a preschool until you've seen it for yourself. Spend one or two mornings watching a class in action. Visit alone at first, so that you can focus on the classroom rather than your child. (Some schools insist on this.)

Look around the physical space. Make note of what you see on the walls and worktables. Is the art highly individualized, or is each picture exactly the same? (This provides a clue to the school's approach to creativity.) Examine the materials available for play. Do they seem varied, interesting, and age-appropriate? Ask how often they are rotated, so that there is always something new and interesting for the children. Optimally, a preschool environment should offer a mix of hard spaces (such as wooden floors) and soft ones (pillows or mats); active and still areas; places to congregate and places to be alone.

Consider the daily pace, too. To watch how the day unfolds, stay for as much of an entire session as possible. Is there a balance between group and individual work? Between quiet and noisy activities? Indoor and outdoor play? Teacher-directed activities and child-directed (self-selected) play? Are the children led in activities or free to choose their own? Does there seem to be enough to do to keep everyone engaged, or do many of the children wind up wandering restlessly?

Observe the teacher. How does she treat the children—with respect, patience, imagination, and gentle control? Does she listen to them? How does she handle squabbles or tears? Does she grit her teeth, or does she turn to humor to help set the overall classroom tone? Watch for how she defuses tense situations, too. Can she sense trouble before it erupts and redirect children before problems occur?

Remember that toddlers and preschoolers thrive on routine. Is the classroom's organization consistent with the kids' needs? Ask, for example, how snacks and use of the toilet are built into the day. Make note of the way diapering and hand washing are handled—if corners are cut while you're watching, what's it like when you're not there? Is the place clean, yet not so compulsively immaculate that you can't tell young children are at play here?

Finally, trust your instincts: Do the children seem enthusiastic and content? Does this feel like a place where you would want to spend *your* days if you were 3 years old?

Before you leave, be sure to tour the entire premises, including the playground and the other classes. Introduce yourself to some of the parents you encounter and ask how they found out about the school and what they think of it.

Trust your intuition. The bottom line is that you've got to feel comfortable with your choice. Ask yourself, "Do I feel good dropping my child off in the morning? Does my child seem to enjoy herself?" Never mind if all your friends rave about the "best" place in town or if a hot new school has arrived on your local scene. If you've taken the time and trouble to search out the best option for your child and are happy with your choice, that's all that matters.

The First Day

A bit of preparation and patience will help make the big transition easier. Some suggestions to ease the way:

Make sure that the first official day of attendance is not the first time your child has ever seen the place. Well in advance of the first day, bring your child to the school. Many schools encourage such visits and allow your child to stay and play awhile. Don't limit your visits to classroom hours. Spend time on the playground together, have a picnic on the front lawn, and tour the empty classrooms at the end of the day. The more you can do to familiarize your child with the place before you leave him alone there, the more confident he'll feel without you. Some schools also have a gradual introduction plan, in which kids first come for just an hour or two, then a half day, and so on.

Give your child practice around other kids. If this is the first time your child will be in a group setting, it's especially helpful to broaden his social horizons before he steps into a classroom. Well in advance of the start of preschool, encourage regular play dates with a neighborhood friend, start a play group, or enroll in a Mommy-and-me class.

Talk about what your child can expect. Walk him through a typical day. Who will bring him to school? What does he do first? Will he have a special locker or cubby for his things? Can he bring his stuffed rabbit along? Describe the daily routines; use his teacher's name. Be upbeat when you talk, but take care not to oversell the place. Anticipate his fears: "Sometimes kids miss their mommies when they're at school. And mommies miss their children. That's normal. But there will be so many neat things for you to do, the time goes by fast." Weeks before the actual start date, you can prepare your child for school in a generic sense, by reading children's books on the topic.

Let her call the shots on the big day. Help build your child's confidence and excitement by letting her decide what she'll wear and what

At preschool or day care, be sure to say "See you later!" before you slip out the door.

she'd like inside her lunchbox. Squelch your grown-up drive to want to make good first impressions with a darling smocked dress or a color-coordinated playsuit. Your child won't be the only one who shows up in mismatched plaids or a beloved tutu. What's important is that she feels good about herself—and that you avoid getting ensnared in a power struggle on this special day.

Don't just drop him at the door. For as long as several weeks, you may need to help your child warm up to the classroom. Depending on your child's temperament and the general circumstances, this might take anywhere from an extra ten minutes to a couple of hours. Help him get settled in. Tell him that you will stay until he feels comfortable and ready to play with the things in the class or the other children. He might never actually say, "Okay, you can go now," so you'll have to watch for an opportune moment.

Always say goodbye. It's tempting to dash for the door once you see your child engrossed in the water table. But your child will panic when he realizes that you've sneaked out—and he will feel betrayed. It's much better to be straightforward. In a chipper but firm way, tell your child that you're going now but that you'll see him soon. Put it in a time frame he can understand: "After you have circle time and a snack and you play outside, it will be time for Mommy to come back." Once you've determined that it's time to go, make your farewells short and sweet. Your child may pick up on your ambivalence or guilt if you gush too heavily: "One more kiss, okay? I'll miss you! One more hug, now..."

Some kids find a parting ritual to be helpful. Perhaps your child's teacher takes him over to the window and you blow kisses from the parking lot. Or you kiss his hand and leave a lipstick print that acts as his happy talisman throughout the day.

Provide extra TLC. Big transitions can be as unnerving as they are exhilarating. Be sensitive to the hugeness of this change in your child's life. Even big preschoolers need to be rocked and cuddled sometimes—especially at a time like this. Indulge minor regressions, such as thumb sucking or the rediscovery of an abandoned blankie. Remember that your child isn't quite as big as he looks yet.

Reassure yourself. Parents are often just as distressed as their child about the first day of school—sometimes more. It can be tough to put on a cheery, confident front when inside you're privately mourning your little one's advancement into the bigger world. Focus on the good things that a wonderful preschool program will do for your child: the opportunities for learning and friendship and personal growth.

Birthdays

Turning 1 and 2

A first-birthday celebration is for the parents, not the child. Your 12-month-old will sail rather obliviously through the occasion. She'll enjoy (or ignore) the cake and presents, but she's not likely to realize that she's the center of attention. That's not to say you shouldn't celebrate. The 1-year mark is a major milestone, the official transition between babydom and toddlerhood. You've all made it through an amazing, wonderful year of adjustments and change. Observe the day with a large party or a small one; just don't expect your child to remain graceful, or even awake, throughout. Too much fuss and too many people can be overstimulating, even unnerving. Preserve your child's nap and snack schedules, for everybody's benefit. Whatever you do, don't forget to take a picture of this memorable event.

When your child turns 2, you may witness a bit more excitement. Don't pump up the big day too far in advance—weeks are interminable to a toddler.

It's best to let her know that her birthday is near just a day or two ahead of time. You may be itching to launch into full party mode, perhaps dreaming of the circus clowns and pony rides that you were denied in your own childhood. After all, your child can now walk and talk somewhat, she may have a small circle of friends, and she has a rudimentary understanding of what a birthday party is all about—so why not go all out?

The problem is that while 2-year-olds love birthdays, they're easily overwhelmed by too much of anything. That includes too many people, too much excitement, too many costumes or balloons or activities. The best parties for a child turning 2 are small, simple affairs. Serve a cake decorated with candles after dinner, wear party hats, and let your child open a few gifts. A larger gathering may work fine, too, but take care not to invest so much of yourself in the preparations that you expect more from your child than she's ready for. She may be content to watch the other children play games, for example, but decline to join in herself. A chance comment from a kindly aunt may ignite a temper tantrum. The clown may frighten her. With young toddlers, you just never know what kind of behavior to expect.

Turning 3

It's during the preschool years that birthday party fun really begins. A toddler turning 3 is old enough to realize that it's his special day. He'll also have his own opinions about how to celebrate. Your child may know exactly what kind of cake and ice cream he wishes to be served, for example. Many kids turning 3 can articulate the party theme they'd prefer, too: dinosaurs, pirates, ballerinas, Barney, swimming, and so on. A small family-only gathering still satisfies, or you may choose to invite your child's friends and get your feet wet as a children's party planner.

By a child's third birthday, she knows it's a special occasion.

What makes a 3-year-old's celebration a hit? (These tips apply to 2-year-olds' parties, too, if you're so inclined.)

Keep the scale manageable. Some parents use the formula of inviting one guest for each year (that is, three children to a 3-year-old's party), or one guest per year plus one (four children to a 3-year-old's party). A slightly bigger group (say, two kids for each year of age) usually works fine, too, provided most of the parents stick around to help, which they generally do with kids this age. You'll want to verify beforehand that you'll have enough grown-ups. Just resist the impulse to go way overboard with a guest list in the double digits.

Keep it short. One to two hours is plenty of time. Let the children warm up and play for the first twenty minutes or so, while guests arrive; orchestrate some planned activities and free play for another twenty to thirty minutes; then bring on the birthday cake.

Time it right. Since most of your guests (and perhaps your honoree) will still be taking an afternoon nap, schedule accordingly. Two- and 3-year-olds generally do best in the morning. Plan a late-morning party and you can end the fest with a light lunch and birthday cake.

Pick the right setting. A child-safe, easy-to-clean space is best. Perfect at this age: your backyard or a local park. It's familiar and stress-free, provided the weather cooperates. Another beauty of having a small group for a 3-year-old's party is that the festivities can easily be moved indoors to a playroom or a few contained rooms in your house. For a larger gathering, you may be able to use or rent a large empty space in a church or community hall. Many locations cater children's birthday parties, but how well your child and her friends will do at such a site depends on the facility, the size of the group, and your child's temperament. Again, the smaller the number of children at an away-from-home party, the better the celebration will be. Possibilities: kid-oriented chain restaurants, kids' play spaces (such as Discovery Zone), the zoo, a pottery-painting studio, a gymnastics center, a local pool, or a children's museum.

Decorate simply but festively. You needn't expend much effort to wow these guests. What impresses toddlers: a balloon tied to each guest's chair and taken home after the party; pointy party hats and blowers; a cake that makes up for what it lacks in candlepower with toy figurines or edible decorations.

Plan a few simple activities. When guests first arrive, let them warm up by playing with a few toys you've set out. Or get an activity going that can be done individually or as a group, such as blowing bubbles. At this age, you don't need a three-ring circus for featured entertainment. Three-year-olds will be happy just running around together and participating in one or two planned activities. Many parents like to hire a clown, magician, or puppeteer to be the main attraction. Prescreen your entertainer to ensure that such performances are geared to toddlers' brief attention spans. Classic childhood games (Duck Duck Goose, Musical Chairs) don't go over well for 3-year-olds because the children may not understand the rules. They also respond poorly to scenarios featuring a winner and a loser. Better: noncompetitive activities (see checklist).

CHECKLIST
Birthday Activities

Instead of competitive games, consider these pastimes:

- ✓ Draw with crayons on a large white paper tablecloth
- ✓ String macaroni necklaces (large pasta)
- ✓ Make and decorate construction-paper crowns
- ✓ Sculpt with play dough
- ✓ Play in a sandbox

- ✓ Hunt for toys hidden in a sandbox
- ✓ Have a parade
- ✓ Decorate cupcakes
- ✓ Ride on trikes and riding toys (each child brings his own)
- ✓ Open a piñata
- ✓ Play Ring Around the Rosy

NOT TO WORRY
Party Poopers

It's one of those adages about birthday parties that there will be tears—most of them shed by the honoree. Birthday boys and girls often collapse at their own fetes under the weight of too much excitement. There's been the anticipation, the treats, the gifts, the friends, the activity, the attention. Even the most even-tempered child can feel overwhelmed in the spotlight. Placate your child as best you can. Suspend the house rules that say guests go first and let the birthday celebrant have that honor during games and when you cut the cake. When he acts up, you may feel a little embarrassed ("This is his shining moment! Why can't he act like the delightful boy I know he is?"). Shrug it off. You'll be the parent watching someone else's child fall apart at the next party.

Plan when to open gifts. Parental opinion is sharply divided about the tradition of opening gifts at a birthday party. Some believe that the unwrapping is the main event and ought not to be denied the birthday boy or girl. On the other hand, 3-year-olds have a hard time understanding why only one child gets to open all the presents, and an even harder time sitting by idly and watching. You're liable to wind up with a group melee, each child tearing into a different package. If there are just a few gifts to open, this might be less of a problem than if you're expecting ten children to sit patiently while ten gifts are unwrapped. Divert the crowd with an activity immediately afterward to remove the temptation to play with the new toys (and possibly break them). Some parents provide an at-table activity for the other children, such as coloring, while gifts are opened. No one will be offended if you choose not to open gifts at the party, as kids this age don't fully understand this ritual anyway.

Remember the grown-ups. Unless you're an ambitious host, skip trying to host an elegant adult spread alongside the kiddy one—keep the focus on the children's fun. Since parents usually hang around during

True Toddler Tales

"Too Much Birthday!"

Jennifer and Richard Rice wanted their daughter Ryleigh's second-birthday party to be something special. The Knoxville, Tennessee, couple had forty invitations printed for family and friends. They rented a moonwalk tent and set it up the day before the party. Jennifer ordered a six-foot-long submarine sandwich and two Winnie the Pooh cakes, one in the bear's shape and another decorated with the character and his friends. She even planned gift bags for the guests, varying them according to age.

On the morning of the party, Ryleigh's excited parents were still tending to details. They had to pick up the helium balloons and hang the streamers and birthday banners. They made vegetable, fruit, and cheese trays and set out candies and chips. "Ryleigh was right in the middle of it, wanting to play with everything that we were putting up," Jennifer recalls.

In all, thirty-five adults, many with kids, showed up. "We weren't expecting a full house," Jennifer says. "But there were people sitting on the floor and the stairs." Neighborhood children saw the moonwalk tent and came over uninvited, adding to the chaos.

Ryleigh weathered the gala with grace, spending most of the party inside the moonwalk tent. Gift opening was less successful. "She wanted to play with what she had already opened and just quit opening them halfway through," Jennifer reports. "We had to finish opening them that night and the next morning."

Would she do it again? "Next time I'll just invite family and close friends, or have the party somewhere like Chuck E. Cheese's so they can handle the mess," Jennifer says.

Her tips on keeping toddler birthdays under control:

- **Keep it small.** "Your friends and relatives won't be upset if they're not invited to a 2-year-old's birthday party."
- **Move it outside.** "If I'd had more activities outdoors, the guests—and the mess—wouldn't have congregated inside."
- **Give yourself a chance to have a good time, too.** "I couldn't enjoy the party because I was too busy refilling trays and worrying about all the guests."
- **Remember that you've got plenty of time for parties in the future.** "Ryleigh won't remember any of it except by video. For that reason, especially, it's better to wait until your child is old enough to enjoy and remember a party before you throw a big bash."

My child's birthday falls very near a major holiday?

Even if your child was born on Christmas Day, it will eventually become important to celebrate the two occasions separately. You don't want your child to feel shortchanged in terms of attention or presents. For the first birthday, your child won't care, of course. (He's too young to understand Christmas or Hanukkah, much less his birthday.) Even for the second birthday, a special cake with candles alongside the Yule log and gingerbread men might suffice. But by the time he turns 3, he'll demand—and deserve—his due. Some parents shift to a big gala on the child's half birthday (4½, 5½) once their child grows old enough to understand this concept.

a toddler party, do offer beverages and snacks to them. Also be sure there's ample seating.

Ease up on expectations. A party isn't necessarily the best place for a toddler to practice party manners. There's too much excitement under way. Coach your child ahead of time about saying hello when guests arrive and saying thank you for the presents. Beyond that, you don't want to spoil the event by nagging about the fine points of etiquette.

Plan a finite ending. It's best not to let the party drag on too long, lest you see too many fights and tears. Designate an ending time in advance. As that hour approaches, begin passing out treat bags to the guests as a signal to the parents that it's time to go. Inexpensive and identical are the hallmarks of sure-fire treat bags. Include simple pleasures such as crayons, play dough, play jewelry, sunglasses, balls, bubbles, or other small but toddler-safe plastic toys, as well as edible treats such as animal crackers.

GOOD ADVICE
Best Birthday Traditions

"We have a box that we started when Rachel was born. Every year around her birthday, I put into a manila envelope a picture of her, significant birthday cards, clippings from newspapers, and a picture that she's drawn. It's sort of like a time capsule. I date the envelope and put it into the birthday box. I plan to give it to her when she gets married."

—*Martha Grail, Hagerstown, Maryland*

"We got a special birthday plate when Nicholas turned 1, and I let him choose what he wanted to eat—as best he could for a 1-year-old. I plan to continue that birthday dinner tradition."

—*Tina Bird, King George, Virginia*

New Brother or Sister

Before the Arrival

You're expecting another baby—congratulations! When and how do you share your happy news with your firstborn? Most experts recommend waiting until after your first trimester. Your odds of miscarriage will have decreased, you'll begin to show (giving you a conversational starting point), and you and your partner will have had some chance to adjust to the news as well. If your child is under 18 months, he won't have much grasp of what a new sibling will mean to his life almost until after the baby comes home. An older 2-year-old can share some of the anticipation. You might tell your child during the second trimester that he will be a big brother (or sister) to a new baby, but don't talk it up much until the eighth or ninth month. Some parents don't begin preparing their child until the last trimester. If you build up the baby's arrival too soon, it will seem to take forever to your child, and might stir up more extreme worries about just what this mysterious event is going to mean for him.

Wait until your third trimester to prepare your toddler for the baby; before then, it's just too abstract.

If you tell friends and family earlier than the second trimester, however, be sure that no one else informs your child. Whatever his age, he should receive the news from you first.

To smooth the path to siblinghood:

Expose your child to other babies. Visit friends or relatives who have a newborn. Perhaps your child's day care center has a room of infants where you can spend some time. Peek into the nursery at the hospital where you'll deliver. (Many hospitals offer sibling-preparation classes, although they're not usually geared to toddlers.) Even exposure to puppies and kittens helps a toddler understand why it's important to be gentle with small, new life.

Talk about what life with a baby is like. Explain that little babies cannot walk or talk. Describe how they eat and sleep a lot. Reassure your child

My child is insistent that we bring home only a brother from the hospital?

Toddlers often express such opinions because they are flush with a new awareness of the difference between boys and girls, and they know to which gender they belong. Toddlers also happen to love declaring their opinions. If your child places an order, so to speak, be honest. Tell him that you don't know which sex the baby will be (unless you *do* know through prenatal testing). Most kids forget their insistence once the baby is born. A newborn looks to them like neither a boy or a girl, but a doll.

that while the baby will need to be held a great deal, your arms are big enough arms to hold him, too (but not always at the same time). Underscore the fact that nothing will change in terms of how much you love your child. Reading books about siblings can reinforce your message. Some books show simple drawings of the fetus growing in the mother's womb, which may help your child visualize what's happening.

Watch for signals that you're going overboard. Your child needs to know about the baby—but he doesn't need to know too much. Cues that your child has heard enough on the topic: changing the subject or asking an unrelated question, running away, pushing away books or movies about babies.

Let her feel your belly. An older toddler will be thrilled to feel the baby move. This makes the baby-to-be seem more real to her.

Reminisce about when your firstborn was a baby. Get out his baby pictures and baby book. Show him what he once looked like. When you unpack his old layette for the new baby, let your child handle the tiny clothes to get a visual sense of how small he was—and how small the new baby will be.

Explain your impending absence. Most toddlers focus more on their mother's disappearance than on meeting the baby. Near your due date, tell your child where you will be going and why. Explain that you might have to leave in the middle of the night before you get a chance to say goodbye, but that if this happens, you'll talk to her soon afterward. Make it clear who will look after your child in your absence, and that her father (or other designated familiar grown-up) will bring her to see you and the new baby just as soon as it's possible. Let your child help you pack your overnight bag. Emphasize that you're not sick, you're just going to a special place where babies are born. If your child will be staying overnight at a friend's or relative's house, you might even practice leaving her there without you for a couple of short visits in the weeks before the birth.

Stay in touch. As soon as you're able, whether before the delivery or after, talk to your child by phone from the hospital. Just hearing your voice will be reassuring. Let him visit you in the hospital if at all possible, and especially if you will be staying more than one night.

After the Arrival

When you bring your baby home, give your toddler the lion's share of your attention. Why? Your newborn won't know the difference, but your older child desperately needs your love and reassurance. The first time your child sees you after childbirth, for example, make sure that you're not holding the baby. Keep your lap and your arms free for a big welcoming hug. Let your child hold the baby himself while in your lap. Take a picture of the two of them together—even better, use an instant camera, so your child can keep the snapshot.

Actually, the first meeting and your homecoming are likely to go more smoothly than you anticipate. At first the baby is like a new toy to the older child, a curiosity to inspect and enjoy. Your child may lavish hugs and kisses on the new sibling in a genuine display of affection; he's also indirectly seeking to please you, since he's aware that this is a special day and that his effusive greetings are expected.

A day or a week (or a month) later, however, you may find yourself in a different script. It becomes apparent to your firstborn that the baby is here to stay. What's more, the baby can't wrestle or play chase. Instead, she spends a lot of time in your arms—formerly your child's exclusive province—or asleep. "Quiet!" or "Gentle!" are the responses your firstborn comes to dread. Don't be surprised to hear your child ask, "When is the baby going back?" or even "Let's give her away." *You* may be growing more accustomed to your newest addition, but your firstborn is not.

Rather than expecting your child to get over his initial feelings, be aware that they are likely to linger for up to six months or longer. In fact, sibling rivalry

> ## PARENT TIP
>
> ### Get Help and Set Priorities
>
> **N**ow that you're the new mother of two children, you'll want, naturally, to be all things to both of them. You can't. Not all the time, and certainly not at the same time. Especially during the postpartum phase, rely on as many helpers as you can muster. Let the housework go (yes, even the inevitable toddler clutter), order take-out, and if you should be lucky enough to have both children napping at the same time, go ahead and snooze yourself. Try to arrange as much time as possible, at first, to be with your toddler. Maybe a grandparent could mind the baby while she naps, or give her a bottle of expressed breast milk. Your baby has physical needs that must be met, but your toddler has important emotional ones right now.

I need to tend to both children at the same time. How do I choose?

Obviously you should handle a true emergency first. But if both children are crying because they are hungry, say, find a way to help them both without slighting your toddler's feelings. Invite your older child to come with you to pick up the baby first: "Help me get Cassie and then we'll make your snack." Grab something quick, like a graham cracker, to tide your older child over while you nurse the baby, then return to your firstborn afterward. Tending two children can feel a little like you're playing Ping-Pong single-handedly, but the juggling will grow more natural over time.

often flares initially and then subsides (or doesn't really appear at all), only to reignite once the younger child learns to crawl and walk, making herself more of an unignorable pest and threat to the firstborn. It's easy to lose your temper over your firstborn's pouts, pokes, and prods—especially when you're sleep-deprived. That's why help (from your spouse, your parents, your friends, or your neighbors) is so important now. Unfortunately, it's often the case that people offer less assistance to second-time mothers because they figure you now know it all; but in fact,

NOT TO WORRY
Post-Sibling Regression

You've been enjoying your first diaper-free month, or your child gave up the bottle long ago. But now, after a new baby's arrival, your toilet-trained firstborn has begun to have accidents, or he begs for his long-abandoned ba-ba. What should you do? Regression is very common in the months after a sibling's birth. Your toddler is wishing that he could be a baby again, too. He's not sure how he feels about his displacement, and regression is a way of expressing those confused feelings, since his language skills aren't sophisticated enough to analyze all this with you.

Be compassionate. Aim for a middle ground between indulging the request and overindulging it. Wordlessly allowing your child to lapse back into diapers is one thing, because it's fairly harmless and toilet training will be relearned when your child is ready. But avoid permitting unreasonable requests that will morph into hard-to-break bad habits, such as letting your child sleep with you in bed every night or carry a juice bottle to bed. Consider regression a tiny call for help. Give extra love and attention to your child and help him find new ways to channel his strong, confusing feelings of love and hate for her new sibling.

CHECKLIST
Ways to Channel Sibling Love

Keep enthusiastic hugs from turning into headlocks with a little gentle guidance:

✓ Teach your child affectionate alternatives to hugs, such as blowing kisses, tickling baby's toes, or high fives.

✓ Suggest that your child sing to the baby or play a music box.

✓ Help your child color a picture for the baby or paint a plain wood picture frame into which you can put a photograph of the siblings.

✓ Let the child hold the baby while sitting in your lap, or in a special oversize chair (or corner of the sofa) where there's room for all of you to sit together.

✓ Encourage your child to care for a baby doll in the same way you look after the baby. Bring a doll high chair into the kitchen and place a doll bed near the real baby's bassinet.

Let your firstborn take an active role in sibling care— with your constant supervision, of course.

mothers of two find assistance especially useful. The more that others can help you with the newborn or with household tasks, the more time you can spend with your jealous older child. You'll need lots of patience and love to be your guides through these months.

More ways to get the sibling bond off on the right foot:

Remember, your toddler is still a baby, too. Suddenly your little cherub will look so big compared with the seeming fragility of a newborn. Appearances aside, a toddler or preschooler is still a little guy. Resist the impulse to assign him expectations that you didn't have for him just a few weeks ago just because he's not your only baby anymore.

CHECKLIST

Great Gifts for Big Sibs

Bestow something special on your firstborn when he meets the new baby. Some parents call this a gift "from the baby," while others use it to celebrate the older child's new status as a big brother or a big sister. Encourage visitors to remember your older child, too. You might even keep a stash of small gifts, such as balls or coloring books, on hand for when your toddler feels left out of the new-baby fuss.

Another gift twist: Have someone (such as Grandma) take your child on a special shopping outing to pick out a gift from the toddler to the new baby. This is a great activity for the caregiver and your child to pass the time while you're at the hospital.

Some suggestions for the gift to your firstborn:

✔ Books, especially about babies (such as *Spot's Baby Sister*, by Eric Hill, a lift-the-flap book; *I'm a Big Brother / I'm a Big Sister*, by Joanna Cole; and *Our New Baby*, by Pleasant T. Rowland, which incorporates hands-on activities, including a zipper to zip and a musical lullaby to play)

✔ A baby doll

✔ Baby-doll accessories (stroller, diaper bag, bottles)

✔ A stuffed animal (especially a favorite familiar character)

✔ A shirt that says "I'm the Big Brother" or "I Love My Baby Sister" (buy a matching onesie for the newborn that says something like "I'm the Little Brother" or "I Love My Big Sister")

✔ A tape player and children's cassettes

✔ Simple wooden puzzles or Colorforms

✔ A big-boy or big-girl toy, such as a riding vehicle

Avoid sending "hands off" signals. Toddlers love to explore, and you can bet yours will want to touch and inspect this new mysterious creature. Put aside your nervousness or fear of germs (unless your child is clearly contagious, of course). Encourage hugs and loving. *Always* supervise, since toddler affection can take a rough turn—on purpose or by accident—lightning fast. Designate a special spot where the older child can safely kiss the newborn, such as the feet or the very top of the head.

True Toddler Tales

"How We Handled the Arrival of a Rival"

Knowledge is power, figured Susan and Ricky Hood. The Chesapeake, Virginia, couple thought that the more they talked about Dylan's new sibling, the better prepared he'd be. Dylan would turn three the same month his sister, Karlie, was born. So early on, they told him that "a baby is growing in Mommy's tummy." They read books about babies and explored a pregnancy CD-ROM. "He seemed excited, but a lot of the time he was indifferent," recalls Susan.

At the hospital, Dylan couldn't care less about meeting his new sister. He was too busy exploring the new environment. "I noticed a new distance between us," Susan says. "He was in his own world." An active child used to being the central focus, Dylan in the following weeks began to do anything to get attention, whether positive or negative. More than usual, he began to show off, talk loudly, run around the house, make messes, and get into things he wasn't supposed to. "He'd say, 'Mommy never plays with me anymore.' " He'd also ignore her when she tried to reach out, as if to take revenge for not playing with him, she says.

Dylan also took a few steps backward. He abandoned his potty training to ask for diapers "like baby Karlie." He also wanted his pacifier back, asked for a bottle, and once asked to nurse. Patience, indulgence, and attention have been Susan's mainstays. Not that the situation has entirely eased. Now that Karlie, 8 months old, is more mobile, she can grab Dylan's belongings and take his food, both of which upset him. "I read to him while I'm breast-feeding Karlie. I also make sure to get down on the floor and spend one-on-one time with Dylan while Karlie crawls about," says Susan. "I involve him in things that I'm doing, like cooking, so that he feels like my special helper."

More ways to ease new-sibling rivalry:

- **Don't expect instant affection.** "It seems hard at first, but everyone has to go through a period of adjustment. Karlie is almost a year old and Dylan is just now beginning to be fully comfortable with her presence."
- **Accept help.** "Others can take care of your newborn while you spend time with your firstborn alone. Go to the park or just take a walk around the block."
- **Listen.** "Sometimes it's best to take a few minutes just to do what your older child wants to do."
- **Put this transition in perspective.** "Try not to make a big deal about every minute you can't be with your older child. Save yourself for the really big issues of raising kids. And remember, you've given your child something positive, too—the gift of a sibling relationship."

GOOD ADVICE
What Helped Us Most

"We tried to make a big deal about Caitlin when her sister Laurel was born. I did whatever Caitlin asked to when the baby was asleep. Sometimes she wanted to be held and rocked like the baby. Sometimes she wanted to read or play outside. I made sure that she received the attention she demanded and needed."

—*Patricia Curran, Phoenix, Arizona*

"We really involved Mariah during my entire pregnancy. She was 2 then, and we talked to her a lot, brought her with us to my ultrasound, and gave her little gifts in the hospital. I also think that maintaining her schedule is important so that she has some stability. I wanted her to know that she's just sharing the center of our universe, not being kicked out of it."

—*Nicole Bell, Natick, Massachusetts*

"As I became bigger during my pregnancy, I couldn't lift Teddy as much and wanted him to get used to spending less time with me. So he started doing more with his dad. Then it was less of a shock later when I was less available."

—*Sharon McKenna, Alexandria, Virginia*

"The last four of our five children enjoyed the tradition of having the newborn buy a present for the older ones, something small that we bought beforehand. We gave each child his present in the hospital and took pictures of him and his present, and him and the baby. Then we gave him a small photo album, so when visitors come and want to see the baby pictures, they can also see the toddler's pictures."

—*Joanne Gough, Hudson, Ohio*

Spend as much one-on-one time with your older child as you can.
Cradling a newborn is certainly a wonderful feeling, but he or she won't know how much time Mommy is around. Your toddler will. Plan activities—even restful ones like reading books—that you can do with your older child without the baby on your lap.

Enlist your little helper's assistance. Let your child hand you diapers and wipes, run a washcloth over the baby's feet in the tub, help you hold a bottle, or push the stroller with you. Or designate a special job that's hers alone, such as selecting the baby's socks or receiving blanket every day.

Help your child label her emotions. Reassure her that it's possible to feel love and anger for someone at the same time: "Sometimes big sisters feel like kissing their baby brother, and sometimes they get tired of their mommies having to feed and hold the baby so much, which makes sisters not like babies as much. It's okay to feel both ways. I love you no matter what." Expect your child's confused blend of feelings to linger for some time; don't rush her to "get used to it already."

Respect your child's physical space. Even a 1-year-old can be taught that some things are hers alone and some are the baby's. If the two share a bedroom, allow a certain corner to be just for the firstborn's things. Don't force her to share every toy.

Remind your child that being older has special benefits. Point out, when your child is engaged in an activity that she loves, that babies cannot dance or play dress-up or feed goats at a petting zoo. Nor are babies allowed to eat ice pops, wear big-girl panties, or ride in front-facing car seats.

WHAT IF...

I have a miscarriage? How do I explain it to a toddler?

Much depends on your child's age. A young toddler may be completely oblivious. But even a 1-year-old can pick up on your sadness. It's not necessary to hide your feelings from your child. Instead, you can describe to your firstborn what sadness is and why you're feeling that way. Use simple language: "Mommy was growing a baby in her tummy but it was very sick and now it's gone." Tell your child that you will try to grow another one, if this is the case. Answer questions as directly but simply as you can. For an older child, you might use books about how babies grow. Be prepared for questions, and perhaps some anxiety, for a long time from your child, even after you've put the experience behind you.

CHAPTER SIX

Safety and Health

Your child has grown and changed plenty since infancy. So, too, should your considerations about her safety and health evolve. Ages 1 and 2 are the most vulnerable time in a child's life for such killers as accidental poisonings and drownings. Yet the majority of such incidents are entirely preventable.

The types of illnesses toddlers contract, and how to handle them, can also differ from babyhood. Ear infections, for example, are especially common during the second and third years of life. And while a baby might suck down her antibiotic as willingly as she takes her bottle, a 2-year-old may not always be so obliging.

Yes, health and safety advice may seem somewhat familiar. And certainly such topics aren't half as fun as learning new games to play, and not nearly as urgent to your everyday life as information about discipline or sleep. But these pages are too important to skip. After all, if your child isn't safe and well, nothing else really matters.

Toddler-proofing

A Toddler's Special Needs

"Wait a minute," you're thinking. "I already childproofed the house back when my child started crawling." Indeed, long ago you may have taken many of the vital steps necessary to keep your child safe. But your child's physical prowess is changing every day. So are her curiosity and perseverance. Toddlers taste, touch, and test everything in their paths. A house that was safe for a baby's explorations may be no match for an agile, inquisitive 1-year-old.

Better to think of childproofing not as a one-time proposition but an evolving responsibility. You'll need to reevaluate your home continually as your child grows. Get down on your hands and knees and crawl around a room or two in your home for a few minutes. You'll be about your toddler's height. It's a revealing exercise, giving you a child's-eye view of such dangers as sharp table corners, loose cords or wires that can trip, and alluring table-cloths to yank—things that might have posed no threat to a younger baby.

Nor should you let up on your efforts as your child grows. When he's 2 and steady on his feet, for example, you may no longer need a protective bumper on a stone fireplace hearth. But by then he'll be able to reach up and grab objects, so you'll need to exercise extra vigilance with things such as fireplace tools or pot handles on the stove. Toddler-proofing never really ends, it only changes.

Need a few more reminders why childproofing is so critical?

PARENT TIP

Learn Lifesaving Techniques

Seconds count when a child is starved for oxygen. Safety experts agree that one of the most important thing mothers *and* fathers can do is to learn first aid and CPR (cardiopulmonary resuscitation). Look for classes through the American Red Cross or a local YMCA. Be sure that your child's caregiver also learns these lifesaving skills; offer to pay for her training if necessary. Don't put this off.

The biggest threats to your child's life are right in your home. Today's parents have been made hyperaware of the dangers of the outside world. You hold your child's hand while crossing the street and don't let him play alone in the front yard. When he gets older, you probably plan to talk to him about stranger danger and not walking off with people he doesn't know. For kids ages 1 to 4, however, there's a higher risk of death from fire, burns, drowning, choking, poisoning, or falls than from violence committed by a stranger. And an astonishing 90 percent of these tragedies that happen at home could be prevented, authorities estimate.

You can't watch your child every second. Some parents believe they don't need to toddler-proof because they'll keep an eye on their child. But this plan just isn't practical. Parents have to use the bathroom, cook dinner, answer the telephone, and tend to assorted other details throughout the day. Meanwhile, toddlers can get into the darndest things and places in the blink of an eye.

You'll be creating a positive atmosphere for learning and growth. To develop confidently, your child needs a big environment to explore. At the same time, he doesn't need a grown-up constantly hovering behind him shouting, "No! Don't touch that! Don't do that!" The best way to accomplish both these goals is to remove as many of the dangers as possible. Better to create an environment full of yeses than no-nos.

Beware of everything under the kitchen sink.

There's no good reason not to try an ounce of prevention. It's never been easier to childproof your home. Devices such as doorknob covers and drawer latches are available everywhere, from mail-order catalogs to discount stores (usually in the baby-care aisles). Some local services, for a fee, even conduct household safety inspections and make recommendations or install child-safety devices for you. No matter how many such gadgets you have, however, don't let them lull you into a false sense of security. Childproofing is not a substitute for supervising a child.

All Around the House

Every room should be evaluated and childproofed according to its unique risks, but some precautions apply throughout the house:

Electrical safety. Use safety covers to plug all unused electrical outlets. Place lamp and appliance cords behind heavy furniture or use a cord shortener. Unplug small appliances such as blenders or humidifiers when they're not in use, and replug the outlet with a safety cover.

WHAT IF...

I think my child has swallowed something suspicious?

Immediately call your local poison control center. Bring the packaging or container to the phone with you to help in describing it or so you can read its listed ingredients. You'll be told what first-aid steps to take. (Never administer syrup of ipecac, activated charcoal, or any home remedy without being told to do so first.) If you're advised to get to a hospital, bring the substance swallowed (or its packaging) with you, to help doctors.

Fire safety. Install a smoke detector near the kitchen, outside of bedrooms, and on each level of the house. Check them monthly to be sure they're working. Change batteries twice a year—do so when you change your clocks for Daylight Saving Time shifts as a handy way to remember. Keep a fire extinguisher where the risk of fire is greatest, such as in the kitchen and near the fireplace. Ask your local fire department which type of extinguisher is best for your home.

Safety with furnishings. Secure tall bookcases to the wall with L-brackets. Attach cushioned protectors to the sharp corners and edges of furniture (such as glass tabletops) and raised hearths. For a couple of

CHECKLIST
20 Ordinary Household Poisons

Toddlers are undiscriminating samplers. Below are just a few of the common household items that can be dangerous, even fatal, if a young child ingests them—sometimes even a trace amount.

- Iron pills
- Caffeine pills
- Mouthwash that contains alcohol
- Alcoholic beverages
- Some arts-and-crafts supplies (such as epoxy glues)
- Some spices (such as nutmeg) and flavor extracts
- Meat tenderizer
- Cooking wine or vinegar
- Miniature batteries
- Fertilizers
- Insecticide
- Bleach
- Tobacco
- Nail polish remover
- Hair spray
- Perfume
- Skin creams
- Topical medications (such as Ben-Gay, which contains aspirin)
- Bubble bath
- Shaving cream

years, suspend your aesthetic taste about displaying art objects; move any breakable or heavy pieces out of reach.

Window safety. Keep casement windows locked or opened from the top. Low windows should be raised no more than five inches. Use colorful stickers to make large windows and sliding glass doors more visible. Tie the cords of drapes and blinds up and out of reach, since they're a strangulation hazard.

Kitchen

Most families spend a great deal of time in the kitchen. To keep harm out of your child's way:

Keep glasses, sharp knives, and heavy dishes out of reach. Use safety latches on drawers or cupboards. If your child figures out how to unhook a safety latch, move all dangerous items to out-of-reach storage areas. Consider keeping one or two lower drawers stocked with safe items, such as Tupperware or toys, to help distract your child from investigating elsewhere. Change the contents every so often to keep them intriguing.

If objects are dangerous, such as knives and other kitchen utensils, be sure they're out of reach—and keep an eye on your child.

Use back burners on the stove if possible. When using front burners, turn pot handles toward the back. If your stove is the type with the control knobs at the front, or if you simply want to keep small hands away from the burners, consider attaching a plastic stove guard.

Skip the tablecloths and place mats. A child can pull them, and what's atop them, down on himself. Always keep hot food and beverages, as well as glassware and knives, away from the edges of counters and table-tops.

Bathroom

A toddler should never be in a bathroom unsupervised. Even once you begin toilet training, you'll need to monitor his time there. There are simply too many dangerous temptations. Keep a bathroom off-limits to a young toddler by installing a hook-and-eye lock on the outside of the door, or use a childproof doorknob guard or a gate. More things you can do:

Install toilet locks. The danger is that a child can lean into a toilet bowl, lose his balance, and fall forward. If you don't use a door latch, doorknob covers, or a gate to keep your child out of the bathroom, toilet locks will prevent the toilet bowl lid from being lifted by a young child.

Beware electrical appliances and sharp objects. Keep hair dryers, scissors, razors, and other such items in locked drawers or high cabinets.

Safeguard all medications and toiletries. Store these products—including cosmetics, vitamins, and over-the-counter medications such as antacids—out of reach in a locked cabinet.

Better to keep the grown-up dishes in the cupboards: Non-breakable, lidded cups are safer bets with toddlers.

Set the hot-water heater no higher than 120 degrees Fahrenheit. It takes just three seconds for a child to sustain a third-degree burn from 140-degree water. No matter how high or low you set the temperature, always give the tub water a check with your wrist before placing your child in it.

Drain the tub as soon as your child steps out. Make it a habit. A standing tub of water—especially with a few bright toys still bobbing around—is an invitation to disaster.

Use a nonslip mat for tubs and showers. Teach your child to swing her leg completely over the rim of the tub, never to use the rim as a step, and never to enter or exit the bathtub or shower unless an adult is present. (Of course, you should never leave your toddler unattended during a bath or shower—even if you're expecting an urgent phone call.) Make sure that bathroom rugs have liners or rubberized bottoms so that they remain securely in place; a towel tossed on the floor makes a risky bath mat because it's liable to slip on wet tile.

Use plastic cups and soap holders. China or glass may look nicer, but they can cut your child if they're dropped and broken.

Around Water

Where there's water, there's danger. It may seem incredible, but a toddler can drown in just an inch or two of water. Complicating the danger is the fact that young kids are drawn to water like magnets to refrigerator doors. Now that your child is mobile, be supervigilant when he's around any water source. This includes wading pools, toilets, and the buckets you use to wash the family car. The majority of children involved in drownings or near-drownings are between ages 1 and 3; in fact, it's the leading cause of death among 1-year-olds.

Pool safety. If you have a pool, it should be enclosed on all sides by a securely locking four-foot fence. (In some areas, this is the law.) Ditto for your neighbors' pools. Don't be shy about complaining if a neighbor has an unsecured pool. Your child's life is at stake. Almost all drownings involving toddlers take place in residential swimming pools.

> ### WHAT IF...
>
> #### We're being pressured to teach our toddler to swim?
>
> **S**wim programs for toddlers are widely available. They're a great way to acclimate your child to water. And if your child seems to enjoy it, a swim class can provide fun together time. However, toddler swim programs have some inherent drawbacks. For example, it's unlikely that a 1- or 2-year-old will actually learn to swim, much less learn to conduct himself safely around water. Sometimes parents become overly complacent in water after their toddler takes such a course, figuring she'll manage well enough.
>
> Also, if your child is apprehensive or fearful at such a class, it's better not to force the issue. Discontinue swim sessions until he's 3 or 4. If you push too early with a child who's just not ready, he may wind up scared of water.

Typically, a parent is present during toddler drownings. Hard to believe? Consider how fast and fearless your toddler is. Often a child falls into a pool when no one is paying close attention, such as while socializing and drinking at a party. When young children fall into a pool, they tend not to flail their arms and legs and scream for help. Instead, they fall straight down, often with no splashing whatsoever, their lungs filling rapidly. Suffocation and brain damage can occur within four to six minutes.

The best prevention is constant vigilance. Don't try to read a book or entrust your toddler to an older child's care while poolside. In the presence of a group, designate a specific adult to monitor each child. In the water, use Coast Guard–approved personal flotation devices. But again, never use swimming aids as a substitute for a watchful parental eye. Learn CPR and rescue breathing if you have a pool. Keep a cordless phone by the pool for emergencies.

True Toddler Tales

"My Child Nearly Drowned"

Like most parents, Wendy Wright never thought she'd run the risk of losing a child to drowning. Then it nearly happened to her daughter—twice. The first time, Noelle was about a year old. She was at her grandmother's house for a holiday. Everything was hectic. Not realizing that the sliding glass door was open, Noelle tried to push on it. She fell down three steps into a five-gallon bucket that held about four inches of rainwater.

Luckily, the bucket tipped over as Noelle landed, and she fell out. She was merely dunked, and began to cry. "Had she been drowning, we wouldn't have known until it was too late," says Wendy, who lives in Walla Walla, Washington, with her husband, Chuck.

A year later, the family was visiting a friend with a swimming pool. Wendy was just entering the shallow end of the pool. Meanwhile Noelle, who's afraid of bugs, saw one on the ground and started to back away from it. She didn't realize that she was heading straight for the deep end of the pool. Wendy yelled for her daughter not to go any farther, but the girl misunderstood—she thought her mom was telling her to get away from the bug. She fell into the water and promptly went under. Wendy swam over to her and rescued her. "Things can happen in the blink of an eye. I can't imagine what would have happened had I been a few seconds late," Wendy says.

"I can't say it enough. You have to watch out and be constantly aware when your child is near water," Wendy emphasizes. "I'm apprehensive about other people's houses, because if they don't have kids, their homes and pools may not be childproofed."

Wendy's tips to reduce the chances of a drowning accident:

- **Be proactive.** "Don't be lax about water safety—around *any* source of standing water."
- **Teach your child water safety.** "It's helpful to familiarize your child with water and pools, especially as she gets older and begins to understand more." (Note, however, that this is not useful for young toddlers. Lecturing a child who is too young to understand can breed a false sense of security in parents.)
- **Use safety gadgets.** "My dad bought an alarm that floats on the surface of his pool. It goes off when something contacts the water." You can also put floatees (inflatable bands fastened to the arms or back) on your child at all times when near a pool.

Safety around other sources of water.
Store buckets and other open containers upside-down so they can't fill with rainwater. Buckets and low above-ground pools are a particular danger because a child's upper body and head are heavier than her lower body; it's easy for a child to lean into the bucket and fall over, unable to get back on her feet. Eight percent of all toddler drownings occur in the bathtub. Even if your child still uses a bath seat, never leave her unsupervised there.

Traveling by Car
The number-one killer and crippler of children in the United States is motor vehicle crashes. The best way to dramatically reduce this risk is simply to use a car seat properly.

Double trouble: A two-year-old can drown in two minutes in two inches of water.

After her first birthday, if your child weighs twenty pounds, she's ready to graduate to a front-facing car seat. (Both the age and weight requirements should be met before a child rides facing the front.) When you make this switch, be sure that the seat is correctly installed. Some convertible infant seats, designed to be used from five to forty pounds, can simply be turned around and used in a forward-facing position. Depending on the model, however, your child may outgrow an infant seat and need a larger toddler model. Your child should remain in a car seat until she weighs forty pounds or her ears are higher than the top of the seat, around four years of age. Then she will graduate to a booster seat until she's tall enough to be safely secured with a seat belt (when the shoulder harness crosses her shoulder rather than her neck, and the lap belt lies flat across the bottom of her torso).

More car-safety reminders:

Never place a car seat in front of an active airbag.
The safest place for your child's car seat is in the middle of the rear seat. (If you have two children, both should sit in the backseat.) Do not use a safety seat in a vehicle's side- or rear-facing seat, or in a pull-down jump seat. It may be possible to deactivate your airbag; talk to your car dealer.

HOW TO
Properly Install a Car Seat

As many as 50 percent of all car seats are installed or used incorrectly, according to the National Highway Traffic Safety Administration. The most common mistakes: threading seat belts through the wrong slots, not using a locking clip when one is required, and failing to buckle the child in. To avoid these common pitfalls:

1
Check that the car's seat belt is threaded through the correct slots. Always consult the owner's manual of your vehicle for specific information on using a safety seat in it.

2
If the car seat's latch plate slides freely along the belt, you need a locking clip.

3
Slide the clip onto the belt one-half inch from the latch plate and buckle.

4
Check to make sure that the seat is secure and resists both side-to-side and up-and-down motions.

5
Lift up the harness adjustment lever to loosen and tighten straps.

Buckle up your child every time. Take the time to do this whether you're headed just to the corner market or clear across town. Remember that your child watches everything you do. Wear a seat belt yourself every time you get in the car.

Never leave a toddler unattended in a car, even for a moment. Leaving a child in a car is bad practice because of the risk of heat exhaustion in warm weather. There are also too many dangerous temptations within the car should your child manage to get out of his car seat. And, while it's a remote possibility, cars have been stolen with small passengers still inside.

Pull out and park with more care than ever. Develop the habit of checking behind your vehicle before you get in it and pull out. A small child playing at the rear or sides of your car, van, or truck can't always be seen from the driver's seat. Such accidents are an all-too-common cause of injury and death.

Poison Prevention

For kids under age 6, the following substances (in alphabetical order) are responsible for the majority of calls to poison control centers: cleaning products, cold and cough medicines, cosmetics, household plants, pain relievers, pesticides, prescription drugs, topical medicines, vitamin supplements. To reduce your child's odds of unintentionally swallowing a hazardous substance:

Lock all cupboards that contain poisons. This includes those that seem out of reach. Remember that many ordinary household products can be poisonous if sampled by a toddler. (See checklist, page 226.)

Don't trust claims that a container is child-resistant. Left alone even for a few minutes, some 2-year-olds can open any container. The danger rises if an adult has replaced a cap the wrong way.

Dispose of poisons with care. Never throw containers of expired medications, or those that still contain some product, into open trash containers. A toddler could even pick out a used medication patch (such as those for nicotine withdrawal or to control a heart condition) from the wastebasket and

CHECKLIST
10 Hazards You Might Not Suspect

The following objects seem benign enough. Adults use many of them every day. Yet to a toddler, these same items can pose tremendous danger.

✓ *Shopping carts.* Some twenty thousand children a year visit hospital emergency rooms after mishaps involving shopping carts. Usually kids jump out or fall, or the cart tips over. Always use the cart's safety belt; never allow your child to sit in the basket or leave him unattended, even for a moment. If he's too big or active for the seat, it's best not to use it at all.

✓ *Ride-on lawn mowers.* Risks include falling off, being run over, or getting struck by an object (such as a stick or toy) that has been hit by the mower and flung into the air. Never allow your child to ride on a mower. To prevent eye or head injuries, keep your child indoors when a lawn is being trimmed by any type of mower.

✓ *Balloons.* These are the single most dangerous nonfood choking hazard for kids under age 3. Never let a toddler attempt to blow up a balloon, and make sure you immediately clear away all pieces of any that pop. Mylar balloons are safe because they simply deflate rather than explode into small chokable pieces.

✓ *Coins.* Loose change is a particular threat because it's alluringly shiny, it's everywhere, and it's just the right size to get lodged in a small child's windpipe. Keep your purse out of reach and always pick up dropped coins.

✓ *Vitamins.* Iron pills are the most common cause of poisoning death in children under age 6—and fatalities are on the rise. Store all supplements, including your child's, out of sight and reach.

✓ *Bunk beds.* Small children can fall from the top bunk, even if their designated sleeping place is the lower bunk. The space between the guardrail and the mattress is also a strangulation hazard. It's best to postpone bunk-bed use until your child is past toddlerhood.

Call a pediatrician immediately if you suspect your child has swallowed a coin.

✓ *High chairs.* Most injuries are caused by falls. Always use the restraining straps.

✓ *Electrical cords.* Active teethers have chewed right through the cords—causing burns and electrocutions. Tie up or tape down all loose cords.

✓ *Toilets.* A toddler can drown in the bowl or be injured by a heavy lid. Use toilet latches or, better still, secure the bathroom door.

✓ *Smoke detectors.* It's the lack of one (or one that's not functioning properly) that's the problem. The vast majority of children who die in fires were in homes without a working smoke detector.

mouth it. Use a lidded, child-safe pail for refuse in the bathroom, or keep your waste-basket inside a secured cabinet.

Leave medicines, pesticides, and detergents in their original packaging. Never put poisonous products in containers once used for food—toxic liquid can be mistaken for juice.

Never refer to medicine as candy. This includes chewable children's vitamins (never give more than one a day, even if your child begs and pleads). Some parents use the candy comparison to get a reluctant child to take his cough syrup or antibiotic, but this ploy is not worth the risk. Also try not to take your own medicine and vitamins when your child is watching, since toddlers love to imitate.

Keep syrup of ipecac on hand. This substance, available at drugstores, induces vomiting. You should also store activated charcoal, which absorbs poisons, allowing them to be safely excreted. *However, never use either substance until you first consult a poison control center or your physician.* Check expiration dates periodically.

WHAT IF...

We spend a lot of time at my mother's house, but she doesn't believe in childproofing because she says she never did it for me?

First, recognize that you may not be able to childproof Grandma's house with the degree of thoroughness that you do your own. It's her home, after all. Also, many older people find such safety devices as gates and drawer latches difficult to operate. At the same time, you need to try to convince her that her grandchild's safety is paramount.

If you can't get a full-scale commitment, at least focus on a few select areas where your child spends most of his time, such as the kitchen, living room, and bathroom. Safeguard against where and how medications are stored, too.

GOOD ADVICE
Crossing Streets

"I started talking to my kids about crossing the street from the time they could walk. I taught them to freeze when I say the word *car*. I also hold Chase's hand and talk the entire way across."

—*Kristin Sellers, Colorado Springs, Colorado*

"We practice crossing the street by playing the crossing-guard game on our quiet street. Leah, who's 2½, plays the guard and looks both ways and tells me if it's safe to cross the street. Of course, I can always veto her call."

—*Reed Mangels, Amherst, Massachusetts*

True Toddler Tales

"Our Poisoning Scare"

Juvenal Villarreal was getting his son, Justin, almost a year old, ready to visit Justin's grandparents, who live near his South San Francisco, California, home. While his son played with a toy in the living room, Juvenal went to a bedroom to retrieve a jacket. He was gone only a minute. But by the time he came back, the boy had wandered into the kitchen and found a box of new shoes. Juvenal found Justin sucking on a bag of silica gel beads used to keep shoes free of dampness.

Juvenal panicked. "I kept saying, 'Justin, what's in your mouth?' and got the bag out," he recalls. He realized that his sister-in-law, a nurse who was visiting her parents five minutes away along with his wife, Denise, would know what to do. So he grabbed the silica beads, put Justin in the car, and drove there immediately for help.

"I knew something was wrong the instant I saw Juvenal's pale face at my parents' door," recalls Denise. "Then I saw the poison logo on the side of the pouch he was holding, and I panicked for a second." Her sister calmly suggested they call the local poison control center. They looked up the number in the phone book.

The poison control representative asked if Justin had swallowed a bead. Denise checked the bag. Fortunately, it was still intact and no beads had gotten out. She was also asked about symptoms. Justin looked fine and was acting normally. The poison control center representative assured her that there was no harm done. (Silica gel is not poisonous, although the beads are a choking hazard.)

Denise and Juvenal's tips to prevent poisonings:

- **Be vigilant.** "Don't leave a toddler alone if possible. If you must leave the room for a few seconds, be sure that there are no hazards within reach, or place your child in the safe confines of a playpen until you return."
- **Realize that poisons can lurk in common places.** "Even something as innocent as a box of new shoes had a dangerous substance. Check everything that your child might get into."
- **Keep the poison-control number handy.** "You'll save time."
- **Toddler-proof thoroughly.** "We thought our home was childproofed. But if something is left out on a floor or table that a child can get at, or if a child has access to a cabinet with poisonous materials inside, then none of the other things that you've done will matter."

Post the number of your local poison control center near the telephone. Alongside the number, write down your child's weight and any special medical conditions, such as allergies. You'll find the poison control center number listed at the front of your telephone book with the other emergency numbers.

Keeping Healthy

Doctor Visits

The average healthy toddler doesn't need to see his doctor as often as he did in infancy. This may come as a disappointing change if you looked forward to the frequent well-baby checkups as a chance to learn your child's latest vital statistics and ask questions about growth and development. Most pediatricians like to see their young patients at 12 months, 15 months (optional), 18 months, 24 months, 30 months, and 36 months.

At each visit, your doctor will evaluate your child's growth and development. He or she wants to be sure that your child is growing at a normal rate, with a height and weight gain that are proportionate. Your child's doctor will also check your child's language and motor skills and evaluate her for medical, developmental, or behavioral problems. During toddlerhood your child will also continue to receive her full complement of immunizations.

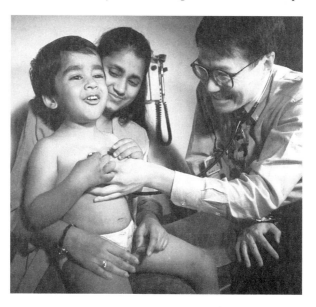

Make the most of your visits with your child's doctor: Come prepared with questions, and take notes on what he says.

WHICH SHOTS WHEN?

This chart will help you keep track of the immunizations your child needs, and when they should be given. Shots that are highlighted in gray indicate the range of acceptable months or years when the vaccine should be administered. Those not highlighted should be given within the indicated month or span of years. (This information is subject to change; always ask your child's doctor for the latest recommendations.)

Vaccine	birth	1 month	2 months	4 months	6 months	12 months	15 months	18 months	4-6 years	11-12 years	4-16 years
Hepatitis B		Hep B-1				Hep B-3				Hep B*	
			Hep B-2								
Diptheria, Tetanus, Pertussis		DTaP or DTP	DTaP or DTP	DTaP or DTP			DTaP or DTP		DTaP or DTP	Td**	
H. influenzae type b			Hib	Hib	Hib	Hib					
Polio			Polio	Polio		Polio			Polio		
Measles, Mumps, Rubella						MMR			MMR or MMR		
Varicella						Var				Var	

*For those who have not completed the full series of three doses   **Tetanus booster

To build a good partnership with your child's doctor and make visits productive:

Write down your concerns. Continue, as you did in infancy, to jot down questions and bring them with you to checkups. It will help you use the doctor's time more efficiently and cover all the ground that you want to during those precious minutes of an appointment. Write down symptoms when your child is ill, too. That way you'll be sure not to leave anything out when you call the office or see the doctor. Be as specific as you can in describing symptoms, providing as many relevant details as possible: "Benjamin has a fever of 103 degrees. He's been sniffling for several days and began to cough yesterday. Now the cough seems very deep and his nasal discharge is green. He hasn't eaten anything all day, and when I put him down for his nap he fussed and cried and didn't sleep well."

Come prepared for waits. The best-paced offices sometimes leave parent and child alone in the waiting room or exam room for long periods of time. This time can pass mighty slowly with a toddler, whether she's sick or well. Even if your pediatrician stocks the waiting room with children's books and toys, bring along a few of your own. A toy doctor kit, with stethoscope and other junior-sized equipment, passes the time while acclimating your child to the exam that will follow. A well-stocked diaper bag should include a snack and your child's favorite blankie or teddy for TLC, too. Appointments at the beginning of a cycle—first thing in the morning or first thing in the afternoon (right after lunch)—tend to be more prompt than those that follow, when late patients or extended checkups can cause the rest of the schedule to back up.

Be honest. Toddlers can put parents in some embarrassing predicaments. What if you can't get your child to swallow his antibiotic, for example? Be honest with your doctor. Withholding the facts can lead to misdiagnosis or

CHECKLIST
When to Call a Doctor

Always alert your child's doctor if your toddler:

✔ Has a fever higher than 103 degrees

✔ Has a fever that's lasted for more than three full days (seventy-two hours)

✔ Has diarrhea more than five times in twenty-four hours (unless it's the side effect of an upset stomach, a dietary change, or a medication)

✔ Is extremely irritable

✔ Is refusing liquids

✔ Has an increased breathing rate

✔ Has a stiff neck

✔ Vomits more than twice in 24 hours

✔ Has ear pain or drainage (or tugs on the ear in tandem with fever)

✔ Has a cold or severe cough that persists more than one week

✔ Reports painful urination or you see blood in the urine

✔ Has a cut that might need stitches

HOW TO

Make the Medicine Go Down

When Mary Poppins sang that "a spoonful of sugar helps the medicine go down in a most delightful way," she didn't mention the age of her young charge. It's a good bet it wasn't a toddler. For one thing, they like to exert their independence and tend to resist being ordered to do anything. Also, many medicines don't taste good, and toddlers are more discriminating than babies. To make the job easier:

1. *Have everything ready.* Avoid prolonging your child's anxiety about the task by making him sit there and watch you hunt for the spoon and measure the prescribed dose.

2. *Be firm.* Say "It's time for your medicine" rather than phrase it as a question ("Are you ready for your medicine?"). If you show signs of wavering, your child will get the message that this is a negotiable task, like picking which clothes to wear or what to eat for snack. It's not.

3. *Mask the taste, if possible.* Ask your doctor or pharmacist if a particular drug can be blended with certain foods. (Citrus or dairy, for example, can render medications less effective.) Try mixing medicine with juice, ice cream, applesauce, flavored yogurt, pudding, maple syrup, or soda—anything that your child loves that also has an easy-to-swallow consistency. Just be careful not to make too large a batch; *your child must eat the entire dose.* Chill liquid medicine to dull its flavor, or give your child an ice pop first, to numb her taste buds. Some pharmacies create special formulations of common childhood medicines that make them taste like chocolate, cherry, and other favored flavors.

4. *Give your child a measure of control.* Older toddlers can usually handle the medicine dispenser themselves. If your child is in charge, he's more likely to accept the medicine than if it's coming at him from you. Consider using spoons in fun shapes (such as animals or airplanes; ask your pharmacist) or a special, easy-to-hold dosing spoon (which features a thick hollow neck into which you pour the medication). Remind your child to go slowly, so he's less likely to sputter or gag.

5. *Bribe rather than threaten.* It's rarely useful to say, "You'll wind up in the hospital if you don't take your medicine!" Even if true, such threats only make an unnerving situation all the more upsetting. Holding out the promise of a reward, however, often works wonders under the circumstances, even if bribes aren't part of your normal parenting repertoire. Make sure the treat is given immediately after the medicine is taken, so it serves as direct positive reinforcement. (Have it ready and waiting so your child sees this desirable goal along with the medicine.) Remember never to refer to medicine as candy to make it more enticing; this makes a powerful substance seem more friendly than it is, and your child may take too much.

6. *Finish with fun.* Praise your child for a job well done. Give him a hug and congratulate him for taking his medicine "like a big boy." Don't offer empathy ("I know that wasn't fun, was it?") or apologize for having had to do it.

7. *Be prepared for the method of last resort.* Ask your doctor how to safely deliver medicine with an oral syringe.

the wrong treatment. Besides, your doctor can make helpful suggestions, such as switching to a more palatable medication. It also helps to inform your child's doctor about special stresses in your child's life, such as a new sibling or a grandparent's death, that may be having an impact on his behavior.

Be clear. Be sure that you understand your doctor's instructions. Don't hesitate to ask for clarification. Even wonderful doctors may use unfamiliar terms or lapse into medical jargon. Well-child visits, in particular, tend to cover a lot of ground. Take notes during the appointment if you find it helpful.

Trust your physician's judgment. Remember that he or she is the expert here. Pushing for antibiotics to cure what ails your child, for example, won't do any good if your child has a viral illness (the most common kind). Nor is it wise to press for tests just because the doctor hasn't arrived at a quick, definitive diagnosis. If the problem persists, however, do feel free to ask for a referral to a specialist or to another doctor for a second opinion.

WHAT IF...

I'm told my child needs tubes for chronic ear infections?

Ear tube surgery (typanostomy) is typically a last resort for the treatment of ear infections (although it's one of the most common pediatric surgeries). It's recommended when a child suffers many repeat attacks of otitis media just weeks apart that don't seem to respond to antibiotics, or if fluid seems to be trapped behind the eardrum long after the initial infection is gone. During the procedure, a surgeon drains the infected fluid from the eardrum via a small incision. A tiny plastic or metal tube is then inserted into the incision for up to a year or two. The tube admits air into the middle ear while allowing fluid to drain out, minimizing the likelihood of infection. The tubes usually fall out on their own when no longer necessary.

Some doctors fear that the surgery is overused. Always get a second opinion, as well as the opinion of an audiologist, who can evaluate your child's current hearing.

Fever

Flushed cheeks, dull eyes, lethargic movements, hot forehead—now that you've got a year or two of parenting under your belt, you can probably tell when your child is spiking a fever even before you get a thermometer's confirmation. Taking your child's temperature, however, is the only way to be certain of a fever. Doing so also enables you to track his progress.

Fever isn't an illness. Nor is it an automatic cause for panic. A fever is usually a healthy response to an infection. When the body is invaded by a virus, bacteria, or fungus, white blood cells and the brain team up to raise the body's thermostat, which helps the immune system fight off the invading microorganisms. Although the fever-producing illness may be of concern, the fever

When deciding whether to consult your doctor, take into account all of your feverish child's symptoms.

itself, unless it's above 105 degrees Fahrenheit, won't cause your child any harm. *Do alert your doctor, however, whenever your toddler's temperature tops 103 degrees or lasts more than three full days.*

It's a myth that the higher the fever, the sicker your child. Every child reacts differently when sick. Some merely grow warm with a serious illness, and others become hot at a slight infection. Behavior is generally a better indicator of the severity of an ailment: A child with a fever of 104 degrees who remains active, continues to drink liquids, isn't having trouble breathing, and is responsive is less worrisome than a child with a fever of 102 degrees who is lethargic and inconsolable.

While most fevers aren't dangerous in and of themselves, they can be very uncomfortable. To help your child weather the heat:

Give her lots of fluids. A feverish body loses fluids through a combination of sweating and rapid breathing. Keep your child from becoming dehydrated by providing plenty of liquids. Offer water, diluted juices, milk, frozen fruit juice pops, Jell-O, and clear soups.

Keep him cool. It's a natural impulse to want to keep your sick child warm and snuggly. But an over-heated room, too much clothing, and heavy blankets will only further raise your child's temperature. Keep rooms about 68 degrees (a slight draft from a fan or open window is okay), dress her in light cotton clothing, and use just a sheet or light blanket for covering.

Give fever-reducing medicine. Acetaminophen and ibuprofen will lower a fever and ease aches and pains. Follow dosage instructions very carefully. Use

---

WHAT IF...

My child can't keep his medicine down?

First, be sure that you're following the pharmacist's instructions properly. Some medicines must be taken on an empty or a full stomach. Sometimes, however, the cause of the vomiting is a stomach virus. Try breaking a dose into two or three parts and administering one every few minutes. It's also possible that a particular medication just may not agree with your child, as is the case with certain antibiotics that can cause nausea. Tell your doctor, who may be able to prescribe a more agreeable match.

the dosing device that comes with the medication, never a kitchen spoon, which is an unreliable measure. Aspirin, which has been linked to Reye's syndrome, a rare but potentially fatal illness, should never be used to treat a fever in a child.

Sponge her down. If you want to, bathe your child in a shallow tub of lukewarm water (or the sink) and rub her body, one area at a time, with a lightly wrung-out washcloth. Let the water evaporate on her skin—this promotes cooling. Don't use alcohol, which can aggravate the fever and harm a child. If you're giving your child acetaminophen or ibuprofen, do so about one hour before beginning a sponge bath.

Colds

Colds are the most common infectious disease among kids and grown-ups alike. But their commonness doesn't necessarily mean they're easy to look after. A toddler with a stuffy nose has a hard time eating or breast-feeding. He may have a sore throat but doesn't have the vocabulary to tell you. His ability to sleep comfortably may be interrupted. And each bout may proceed differently from the last: Because a cold can be caused by one of more than two hundred different viruses, its symptoms can vary in their severity.

Some useful facts about colds:

All kids get them. Individuals do have different levels of resistance. It's also true that children who spend less time in contact with other children (such as at day care) encounter somewhat fewer germs that can lead to a cold—at least in the early years, until they're exposed to more kids in kindergarten. On average, a child gets eight colds during the first year of life. From ages 2 to 5, the total drops to about six a year. Why so many? A toddler's immune system is still developing. He's defenseless against many cold-causing germs that his body will be able to ward off when he's older.

Because cold germs are so prevalent (and most colds are minor affairs), it's

> ### WHAT IF...
>
> #### My child gets constipated?
>
> **C**onstipation tends to cause more anxiety in parents than real problems in children. Realize that not everyone moves their bowels on a predictable schedule. It's neither unusual nor a sign of worry for your child to go a day or two without a bowel movement. Some possible causes for going more than three days without a BM: (1) recently switching to whole milk from formula; (2) not eating enough fiber; (3) anxiety about toilet training. Ask your doctor's advice. Adding more liquids and more fibrous foods such as whole grains, apricots, prunes, and vegetables often solves the problem. If you're toilet training, back off for a few weeks if this seems to be causing your child to purposely withhold BMs. Never give over-the-counter laxatives without a doctor's okay.

HOW TO
Take a Toddler's Temperature

There are four ways to take a temperature: by rectum, mouth, armpit (axilla), and ear canal. A rectal reading provides the truest body temperature. But the other methods, which tend to indicate a temperature one to two degrees lower than by rectum, are also reliable and standard ways to monitor fever. Below age 5, however, oral thermometers aren't recommended because of the need to hold the instrument in the mouth the right way without biting (and possibly breaking). So you'll need to use one of the three other methods. Choose whichever works best for you. By arm or by ear works best for toddlers, who are sometimes too wriggly and strong for the rectal method.

AXILLARY (BY ARM)

Though convenient, taking a child's temperature this way is the least reliable method, usually measuring about one or two degrees below rectal.

1. Use a glass or digital thermometer. With glass, shake the mercury column down to below 96 degrees.

2. Gently place the thermometer well up into the center of the child's armpit (make sure it's dry) and then lower his arm.

3. Keep the thermometer in place by holding your child's elbow against his side for at least four minutes if you're using a glass thermometer, or until it beeps if you're using a digital one.

TYMPANIC (BY EAR)

This method is best used for kids who are 2 or older. Ear temperature tends to be one degree lower than rectal.

1. When taking a child's temperature through the ear, the most important consideration is aim. The ear canal must be straightened to get an accurate reading. To do so, place your child on his side and gently pull the top of his ear up and back.

2. Still pulling, place the thermometer into the ear and press the button—you'll have an accurate reading in seconds. If you're unsure of your aim, take several readings as confirmation.

RECTAL

This is the most accurate method, but toddlers tend to resist staying still long enough to get a proper reading.

1. Use a digital or a glass thermometer (if the latter, shake the mercury column down to below 96 degrees). Coat the end of either kind of thermometer with a lubricant, such as petroleum jelly.

2. Lay your child on his tummy over your lap or on a flat surface with a small pillow under his hips.

3. Slowly insert the thermometer a half inch to one inch into the rectum. Hold the thermometer between your index and middle fingers and use the rest of your hand to cup your child's bottom, which will keep the thermometer from slipping. A glass thermometer needs to be held in place for 2 minutes; a digital one will usually beep or otherwise indicate it's ready to read within 30 seconds.

NOT TO WORRY
Febrile Convulsions

Sometimes a young child's fever spikes suddenly, causing him to turn pale, his eyes to roll back, and his body to stiffen or twitch uncontrollably; he may even lose consciousness. Febrile convulsions—fever-induced seizures—are frightening to witness. But they rarely cause any long-term damage. These seizures are caused by the immature brain's reaction to the abrupt increase in temperature. They're most common between the ages of 6 months and 5 years and usually run in families.

Should your child have a seizure, don't try to restrain him in any way. Lay him down on his side with his head lower than his hips and loosen any tight clothing. Don't put anything in his mouth (he won't swallow his tongue). If something's already in his mouth, such as a pacifier or food, remove it. Then take a few deep breaths and wait. It will seem like forever, but seizures often last only ten to twenty seconds, and rarely more than a minute or two. Should the convulsion continue longer than four minutes, call 911 or take your child to the emergency room.

Call your child's doctor when the seizure is over. Your child will probably fall asleep, but try to lower his temperature by administering acetaminophen or ibuprofen, giving him a sponge bath (not in the tub, because of the risk of hitting his head), keeping him hydrated, and dressing him lightly. And remember: Even though you are anxious and upset, it's unlikely any harm has come to your child. In the event of repeated seizures, your doctor may refer you to a pediatric neurologist to further investigate their source.

an overreaction to isolate your child from playdates with friends or from nursery school in order to protect him. Exception: If your child repeatedly has chronic colds that lead to serious secondary infections, he may have particularly low natural immunity, and your doctor may recommend minimizing his time in a group care situation.

Symptoms can vary. Young toddlers' colds begin with a runny or stuffy nose, sometimes with fever or a cough. A fever may be the first sign of a cold in an older toddler, followed by a sore throat and runny nose. Your child may appear very ill, or the cold may not seem to slow him down at all. Normally a cold lasts from three to seven days. But it can lower the natural resistance of tissues in the nose, throat, and bronchial tubes, allowing bacteria that are normally present (but not usually problematic) in these places to take hold.

As a result, a cold may persist, or a secondary infection, such as an ear infection or bronchitis, may result. If symptoms persist more than a week, or if your child develops a nagging cough, ear pain, or a fever after the initial fever has subsided, contact your pediatrician.

You can't cure a cold. Because antibiotics work only against bacteria, not viruses, they won't clear up a cold. For this reason, it's not always necessary to take your toddler to the doctor if you're sure it's just a cold. Exceptions: See your doctor if a cold persists more than a week; if your child develops other symptoms, such as a persistent cough, or a fever with ear pain; or if your child seems unusually listless and pale, with little appetite. An antibiotic may be prescribed if a secondary infection, such as pneumonia, has developed as a result of the cold.

But you can ease a cold's bothersome symptoms. To ease nasal congestion and help your child breathe more easily, run a humidifier, which emits a cool mist that moisturizes the air. Vaporizers, which release a hot mist,

HOW TO
Prevent a Cold

Young children get so many colds because they touch everything, put their dirty hands in their mouth and eyes, and tend to socialize with lots of friends with similar bad habits. To minimize the odds of a cold—at least for yourself, if not your child—practice the following:

1. Keep your hands clean. Wash your child's hands (and your own) with antibacterial soap when you come in contact with an infected person. Wash hands before snacks and meals, too. Keep a sturdy, child-sized step stool handy in the bathroom to make it easier for your child to reach the sink. Even 12- to 18-month-olds can learn to wash their hands.

2. Use tissues. Because they're disposable, they're more sanitary than a handkerchief. Your child may not be able to blow his nose well, if at all, so wipe it often when it's runny. Take time to teach him how to blow; by age 2 or 3, he should get the hang of it.

3. Use your sleeve. If your child can't get to a tissue in time, teach him to sneeze into his shoulder or sleeve. This prevents virus-carrying droplets from getting into the air or on the hands.

are equally effective, but they pose a scalding risk, making them less than ideal for use in a toddler's room. Saline nasal drops can thin the mucus if congestion is severe; ask your child's doctor. Over-the-counter medications (such as antihistamines and cough suppressants) aren't generally recommended for children's colds, although your doctor may recommend a pediatric formulation for some symptoms.

You don't need to confine your child to bed, unless he's very droopy and is more comfortable there. Keep his activities low-key, though, so his body's resources can go toward fighting off the infection. Let him play around the house or lie on the sofa and watch videos. Keep him warm after the initial fever has passed.

Offer plenty of fluids to keep your child well hydrated. To ensure that your child drinks enough, especially if his appetite lags, present as many options as you can think of: water, juice, ice pops, sodas (even if you don't normally approve of them), and the classic maternal favorite, chicken soup. Milk and chocolate milk are also fine if your child will drink them—a liquid is a liquid, and milk doesn't thicken the mucus, as was once believed. Of course breast-feeding ought to be continued through a cold as well.

You can probably send your child back out into the world sooner than you think. Although the typical cold may last for a week, your child is contagious for only a few days—usually the day or two *before* his symptoms appear. When can you send your child back to day care after a cold? Consult your program's sick-child policy. Most facilities, for example, state that a child must be fever-free for 24 hours before he can return. But a runny nose can persist for weeks—some kids have them because of allergies, not colds, for example—so it's less useful a sign to go by.

The best gauge is often your child's behavior. If she's running circles around the living room, eating

---

WHAT IF...

A neighbor tells me that vaccinations are dangerous? My child already received some as a baby—do I really need to continue now?

It's unwise to forgo or stop immunizations until your child has completed the full recommended course. The risk of a bad reaction from a vaccination is remote—and clearly offset by the threat of the disease itself. This opinion is shared by the American Academy of Family Physicians, the American Academy of Pediatrics, the Centers for Disease Control and Prevention, and the American Medical Association.

Vaccines work by fooling the body into thinking it has contracted a disease. As a result, the vaccine—a weakened, killed, or partial form of the disease-causing organism—prompts the body to produce antibodies. Then, should the person be exposed to the disease later, the vaccine-induced antibodies ward off the infection. It often takes several doses of the vaccine to build up antibodies. Some vaccines require a booster shot years later to maintain immunity.

well, and showing no serious symptoms such as fever, vomiting, or diarrhea, her cold is either mild or waning and she'll probably do fine in a group situation. But if she's especially low-key or clingy, she's better off at home.

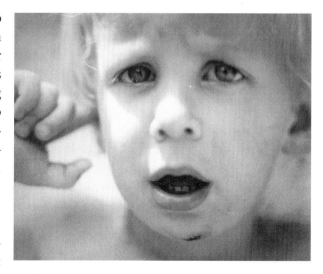

Pulling or rubbing the ear is just one symptom of an ear infecton. Also look for fever, crankiness, and crying during sleep.

Ear Infections

Few children escape toddlerhood without at least one episode of otitis media—more commonly known as an ear infection. It's the second most common illness diagnosed by pediatricians (after the common cold), particularly in children under age 5. Biology is partly the cause. A baby or toddler's eustachian tubes, which connect the middle ear to the back of the nose and throat, are of a size and shape that makes them easily blocked by inflammation (swelling) or by a buildup of the fluid that normally circulates through the middle ear. When bacteria that invade the area infect the fluid, it thickens and accumulates, creating a painful pressure. That's the earache part of an ear infection.

Toddlers are especially vulnerable. As the child's ear grows, however, the likelihood of blockage lessens. Older kids also tend to catch fewer colds, because they've built up a better immunity. Some children, however, are simply more susceptible to blocked ears because of the size or shape of their eustachian tubes; others have weaker immune systems that leave them more vulnerable to infection.

Often you'll have a pretty good idea when your child has an ear infection. Signs include fever, tugging on the ear(s), and persistent crankiness. Complaints can worsen during naps or at night, because ear pressure builds while the child is lying down. It's also possible for your child to have an ear infection with few bothersome symptoms. Some ear infections come on suddenly, while others creep up alongside a cold. They tend to follow upper-respiratory infections because of the way the eustachian tube connects to the respiratory passageways.

Call your doctor anytime you suspect your child might have an ear infection. Prompt treatment is important because, left unchecked, otitis media can cause hearing loss. Other complications include, rarely, infection of the skull bones or, even more rarely, meningitis. A doctor can make a positive diagnosis with an otoscope, the funnel-shaped tool used to look into a child's ear. Home otoscopes are available but not necessary for the average parent, unless your child has very frequent ear infections.

Antibiotics are the usual treatment for ear infections. This is true in spite of mounting concerns that antibiotics are overprescribed and that their misuse is allowing dangerous strains of antibiotic-resistant bacteria to breed. The reason for their popularity is, simply, that they work. Generally a broad-spectrum antibiotic (amoxicillin, Ceclor) is the drug of first choice. If it's found to be ineffective (because the infection doesn't go away) or if the doctor has a good idea exactly what type of bacteria is causing the infection, a different antibiotic will be used. Always be sure your child takes the full course of the antibiotic (typically, though not always, ten days' worth). Don't discontinue treatment once her condition seems improved—even if you'd love to because getting her medicine down the hatch has been a challenge. It's important to finish the whole prescription to ensure that the harmful bacteria are completely wiped out.

TYPES OF EAR INFECTION

If your doctor writes this on your child's chart:	It means this:
Acute otitis media	Bacteria has caused a buildup of inflammation and pressure in the middle ear; requires treatment
Recurrent otitis media	An episode of ear infection that closely follows a previous bout; may require a different antibiotic
Otitis media with effusion	Fluid has accumulated in the ear, although there are no symptoms of infection; just watch and wait
Chronic otitis media	Otitis media with effusion that persists without responding to treatment

COMMON TODDLER AILMENTS

Bronchitis

Cause	Symptoms	Treatment
Virus or bacteria; allergy	Cold symptoms accompanied by a persistent cough, especially during sleep; fatigue; low grade fever	Rest, fluids, humidifier use; doctor may prescribe medication or antibiotic

Conjunctivitis *(pinkeye; inflammation of eye)*

Cause	Symptoms	Treatment
Virus or bacteria; or an allergy	Bloodshot eyes with a yellowish discharge that may crust over during sleep; excessive tearing	Consult doctor; may be treated with antibiotic drops; can apply warm compresses

Fifth disease *(Erythema infectiosum)*

Cause	Symptoms	Treatment
Human parovirus 6 (mild viral infection)	Flaming red cheeks followed by lacy rash on arms and legs, fever	Treat fever; usually clears up on its own without further treatment (but let your doctor know if you are pregnant and are exposed to a child with fifth disease)

Flu

Cause	Symptoms	Treatment
Virus	Low-grade fever, body aches or listlessness, diarrhea, vomiting, symptoms gone in 2–3 days	Treat fever, offer liquids and electrolytes; contact doctor for sure diagnosis to rule out other illnesses

Ringworm

Cause	Symptoms	Treatment
A fungus called tinea spread by people or animals	Pinkish doughnut-shaped rings on scalp or body; may be scaly on edges	Contact pediatrician for antifungal medications; wash all clothing, brushes, and linens used by infected child to prevent its spread

Roseola

Cause	Symptoms	Treatment
Human herpes virus	High fever lasting several days, followed by reddish dots on trunk, face, and neck; child may act well	Provide plenty of fluids (including electrolyte solutions or electrolyte ice pops to prevent dehydration); treat fever

Common Toddler Mishaps

Their curiosity, fearlessness, headstrong independence, and sheer speed make toddlers especially prone to minor accidents such as these:

Bee Stings

Basic first aid: If the stinger is visible, move a credit card or fingernail across the skin's surface to scrape it out. Don't try to pull it with your fingers or tweezers, however, which can release venom into the skin. Apply a cold-water compress on the area to relieve pain and itching. A baking-soda paste (made with just enough water to hold the baking soda together) may also help. An over-the-counter antihistamine spray or cortisone cream may relieve swelling, itching, and pain.

See a doctor if: Your child has serious swelling, hives, itching, light-headedness, or any trouble breathing or swallowing; these are signs of a possible allergic reaction, which may be delayed by up to six hours. Also seek medical help if the child has ten or more bee stings at once.

GOOD ADVICE
Soothing an Injured Child

"Dylan, 20 months, is a daredevil and has taken some hefty falls. I started early by saying, 'Let Mommy kiss it and make it all better.' Now when he falls he says he has an ouchy and asks me to kiss it. He also asks for a Band-Aid."

—*Carrie Schneider, Denver, Colorado*

"Being a toddler is a trying time in general. When Emma, who's now 22 months, started walking, she'd bump into everything. I use the don't-offer-but-don't-refuse method of breast-feeding. It's a quick fix—only a few minutes will work—and it gives her the security to get back to what she was doing. Breast-feeding is a lifesaver when she's sick or injured."

—*Kelly Kilmer, State College, Pennsylvania*

"For something like a simple scraped knee, I put a bandage on Adrienne, who's 2½. It seems to make her feel better and more secure. She also makes her toys trip and fall and then puts bandages on them!"

—*Christine York, Montreal, Quebec*

Bumps and Bruises

Basic first aid: Apply ice (in a hand towel or ice bag, not directly on the skin) or a bag of frozen peas to a bump immediately to help constrict blood vessels and minimize swelling. Most bruises require no special treatment.

See a doctor if: A bump or bruise keeps growing after a day or two, a bump sinks into the skin, the bump is on the head and the child becomes drowsy or loses consciousness, a bruise appears on soft areas such as the cheeks or abdomen, or a bruise interferes with motion.

Burns

Basic first aid: Treat any burn by immediately immersing the area in cool water or running cool water over it for about ten minutes. Cover with a sterile nonadhesive dressing. If the burned area is red, pink, or blistered, it's less severe. Give acetaminophen to ease pain. Never break a blister, which can lead to a bacterial infection. Do not apply grease, butter, or any ointment.

See a doctor if: A burn causes white, yellow, or brown patches; this indicates damage to underlying tissues and requires medical attention. Take your child to the hospital or call 911 for emergency treatment. Also seek medical help if the burn affects a child's hands, face, feet, back, or genitals, or if the burn is from electricity, chemicals, or fire.

WHAT IF...

My toddler keeps sticking objects like beans into his nose and ears?

This is one of those strange-but-true toddler quirks. You'd be surprised how many children's doctors fish pebbles, peas, and other tiny things from their patients' nostrils. Toddlers like to explore everywhere, including the crevices of their bodies. The nose, in particular, is easily accessible for poking or stuffing. Often a parent isn't aware that this has happened until they notice a greenish nasal discharge coming from one nostril only (in a cold or allergy, both sides run). If you can see the object or feel it, provided it's not lodged too far up, you may be able to remove it easily with your fingers or a pair of tweezers. But if you have any difficulty, get medical help. Your doctor will have special instruments to help remove the object.

Even if you keep small beads and dry beans away from your child indoors, he's still liable to find pebbles on the ground outside. Usually one painful episode will discourage a child from doing it again.

CHECKLIST
Medicine Cabinet Must-Haves

Stock these items in a first-aid kit that's always handy:

✔ *A first-aid manual.* If it doesn't fit in your medicine cabinet or first-aid kit, store it someplace you'll always be able to find it, such as with your telephone book or on your cookbook shelf in the kitchen.

✔ *Over-the-counter antibiotic ointment,* to prevent infections in minor cuts and scrapes.

✔ *Bandages,* for minor cuts and scrapes.

✔ *Sterile gauze,* for deeper cuts. Stock pads and rolls.

✔ *Adhesive tape,* to hold gauze in place.

✔ *Children's acetaminophen or ibuprofen,*˙ to reduce fever and body aches.

✔ *Hydrocortisone cream,* for relief from bug bites, stings, minor rashes.

✔ *Cold/cough medications.* Consult your pediatrician about choices and dosage.

✔ *Diaper rash lotion,* to relieve redness, chafing.

✔ *Sunscreen.* Choose a high SPF for toddlers.

✔ *Thermometer*—rectal, oral, or ear.

✔ *Tweezers,* to remove thorns, splinters, and ticks.

✔ *Syrup of ipecac,* for poisoning. Use only under the advice of a doctor or poison control center.

*Never give a child aspirin, which can lead to Reyes syndrome, a rare but fatal illness.

Cuts and Scrapes

Basic first aid: To stop bleeding, apply firm pressure with a piece of sterile gauze (or a clean piece of cloth, if no gauze is available) for five to ten minutes. Try to clean the injury right away with soap and water, then dab on antibiotic ointment. Cover loosely with a bandage; cuts and scrapes actually heal faster when exposed to the air. Minor scrapes may not need a Band-Aid at all.

HOW TO

First Aid for a Choking Child

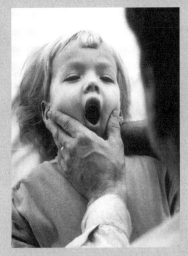

If an object becomes trapped in your child's windpipe, he will probably cough, wheeze, gag, or drool. A complete blockage will make it impossible for him to make sounds. *Don't try to remove the object from his mouth unless you can see it.* You risk inadvertently pushing it back farther into the airway. Nor should you try to slap him on the back or raise his arms over his head. If you suspect your toddler is choking:

1. Call 911 immediately. If you're alone, administer first aid (the Heimlich maneuver described in steps 3 through 5) for one minute, then call 911 and resume treatment.

2. Begin first aid only if your child cannot breathe, cry, or cough.

3. To perform the Heimlich maneuver: Place the child on his back, straddle his thighs, and put the heels of your hands (one atop the other) against his abdomen below the rib cage.

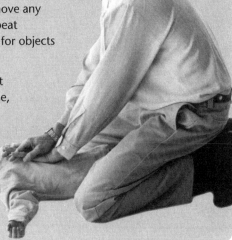

4. Firmly thrust upward, up to five times (gently). Check the mouth and remove any object you can see. If necessary, repeat abdominal thrusts and check again for objects in the mouth.

5. If the child loses consciousness, isn't breathing, or if you can't feel a pulse, begin CPR until help arrives.

(Safety Note: These instructions are for children ages 1 to 3.)

True Toddler Tales

"Our Choking Scare"

It was an ordinary father-daughter day for Scot Bondlow and his 2-year-old daughter, Jenna. For lunch, Scot made ham-and-cheese sandwiches. While they were eating them, Scot happened to look up. Jenna was red in the face and trying to reach into her mouth with her hand.

"It happened in a flash," he says. "I could tell she was struggling to get something out of her mouth. I picked her up and asked her if she was choking." Jenna nodded and began to make gagging sounds.

Quickly Scott did the Heimlich maneuver. He didn't apply much pressure because his daughter was so small and he didn't want to hurt her. When nothing happened, he tried again, pressing harder on her abdomen. On the second try, a strip of ham about three inches long fell out of Jenna's mouth. Seconds later, she caught her breath and began to breathe normally.

Scot's advice to prevent and handle choking:

- *Teach children to chew their food before they swallow.* "I sat both of my children down and told them the importance of chewing their food before they swallow. Because of Jenna's choking incident, they understood right away."
- *Don't let young children eat alone.* "It's hard for anyone, let alone a toddler, to run and find someone to let them know that they're choking."
- *Cut up a toddler's food well.* "I used to cut things into the size that I would eat, but you have to realize that their mouths are a lot smaller than ours."
- *Be prepared before it happens to you.* "I had seen pamphlets and other material about the Heimlich maneuver and made sure that I understood how to do it, just in case. You could also take a class to learn the Heimlich and what to do in an emergency."

See a doctor if: A cut continues to bleed after ten minutes of applying pressure, the child can't move the injured part, a wound is very deep or gaping, you suspect glass or another foreign substance is embedded in the cut, or pain, redness, heat, or pus develops around the injury later.

Nosebleeds

Basic first aid: Pinch the nose just beneath the hard bone of the nose for five minutes to allow a clot to form. Have the child lean forward so that any blood will come out rather than go down the throat and cause choking or an upset stomach. Check to see if bleeding has stopped; if not, repeat pinching for another five to ten minutes. After bleeding stops, put some petroleum jelly on the inner surfaces of the nostrils to help keep bleeding from recurring.

See a doctor if: You can't stop the bleeding after fifteen minutes of pinching, nosebleeds occur frequently, or the child experiences other bleeding, such as from the gums.

Pinched Fingers
Basic first aid: Elevate the finger and apply an ice pack for

---

WHAT IF...

My child won't let me treat a cut?

A child once burned by a stinging alcohol-based solution is bound to be twice shy about first aid. The latest thinking is that cuts and scrapes heal better when cleansed with mild bar soap and water, an over-the-counter saline solution, or no-tears baby shampoo and water. In contrast, the classic medicines for cuts, such as hydrogen peroxide and rubbing alcohol, tend to dry out skin and kill healthy cells, creating a breeding ground for bacteria.

Be as quick and efficient as possible when cleaning a cut. Distract your child by talking about something pleasant—it doesn't help to dwell on the tumble or reprimand your child for not being more careful. Let your child choose the bandage—stock several different kinds in bright colors or festooned with favorite characters.

---

about fifteen minutes to reduce pain and swelling. Usually, pinched fingers cause a surface bruise that will heal on its own.

See a doctor if: You notice deep purple discoloration, pain is continuous or swelling increases, there is bleeding under the nail, a deep cut is present that may require stitches, or the finger appears misshapen (a sign of a fracture or blood vessel damage). Don't move a finger that you suspect may be broken or dislocated.

Illustration Credits (by page number)

Thanks to the following companies for contributing products for use in the photos:

Avent America, Inc.
Babies Best, Inc.
Braun
Century
Evenflo Company, Inc.
Hoohobbers International, Inc.

House of Hatten, Inc.
Infantino
Kapoochi
Lamby Nursery Collection
Munchkin
Primo

Regal Lager, Inc.
Remond for Babies
Safety 1st, Inc.
The Company Store

Index